Built to Brew

Built to Brew

The history and heritage of the brewery

Lynn Pearson

ENGLISH HERITAGE

Published by English Heritage, The Engine House, Fire Fly Avenue, Swindon SN2 2EH
www.english-heritage.org.uk
English Heritage is the Government's lead body for the historic environment.

The views expressed in this book are those of the author and not necessarily those of English Heritage.

First published 2014

ISBN 978-1-84802-238-6

Product code 51779

British Library Cataloguing in Publication data
A CIP catalogue record for this book is available from the British Library.

The right of Lynn Pearson to be identified as author of this work has been asserted by her in accordance with the Copyright, Designs and Patents Act 1988.

For more information about images from the English Heritage Archive, contact the Archives Services Team, The Engine House, Fire Fly Avenue, Swindon SN2 2EH; telephone (01793) 414600.

Brought to publication by Rachel Howard, Publishing, English Heritage.

Typeset in 9 on 11 point Charter

Edited by Susan Kelleher
Page layout by Francis & Partners
Printed in the UK by Butler Tanner and Dennis Ltd.

Front cover
Arkell's Kingsdown Steam Brewery at Upper Stratton, Swindon (see Fig 6.19).

Frontispiece
The mash tun room at Shipstone's Star Brewery, Nottingham, around 1900 (see Fig 5.1).

Back cover
Steam wagons getting under way at John Smith's Brewery in Tadcaster around 1918. Although robust, the steam wagons were fairly slow and more cumbersome than horse drays, but they could carry greater loads.

Contents

Preface

Brewing is an ancient occupation, transformed into an industry from Georgian times onward. Its buildings, often ornate Victorian piles, could be found in every English town and city. The 20th century was not kind to brewery buildings; the rationalisation of brewing companies and consequent demolitions left a diminishing number surviving from the late Victorian boom years. The Brewery History Society (BHS) was well aware of these losses, and at the start of the 21st century began to cooperate with other interested bodies to assess the ongoing threat to the historic fabric of the English brewing industry.

With English Heritage (EH) and the Association for Industrial Archaeology (AIA) we jointly organised the conference 'From Grain to Glass' at Swindon on 13 June 2003. We were delighted at the interest shown and the depth of knowledge of all participants, and followed it up with a joint BHS and Victorian Society study day 'From Hop to Hostelry: the brewing and licensed trades 1837–1914' staged at Young's Ram Brewery in Wandsworth on 25 February 2006.

We were then encouraged by Keith Falconer, at that time EH Head of Industrial Archaeology, to apply for EH funding to undertake an in-depth study of the brewing industry. EH agreed to support this BHS project, which was coordinated by Lynn Pearson and carried out by BHS members between 2007 and 2009. Its aims were to provide up-to-date information on all traditional operating breweries, to produce a database of historic brewery buildings, to consider the future of the industry's archives, and to make a national assessment of the industry (a Strategy for the Historic Industrial Environment report). The results were presented at a conference entitled 'The Last Drop' in Burton upon Trent on 12 March 2011, and are available online at www.english-heritage.org.uk/professional/research/buildings/historic-breweries/

Fortunately, English Heritage's involvement with breweries was far from complete at that point. We strongly welcomed a proposal from John Hudson, Head of EH Publishing, to produce a broader volume on the brewing industry, complete with a wide range of illustrations; this enabled us to make full use of the unrivalled EH archives. We think *Built to Brew* throws new light on beer's social, architectural and cultural roots in England, and hope you will enjoy it right down to the very last drop.

Lynn Pearson and the Brewery History Society

Acknowledgements

I t is always good to be able to thank publicly those who have helped a book along its way to publication, and in this case there are many. Firstly, I was deeply grateful to Andrew Davison for his generous help with medieval brewing matters, and to Amber Patrick who kindly advised me on maltings. I benefited greatly from correspondence with Andrew Cunningham on medals, tokens and the wider brewing world.

I was lucky to receive ideas, amendments, encouragement, illustrations and occasionally beer (you know who you are!) from the following: Liz Allison, Jaclyn Bateman, Claire Blakey, Anne and John Bundock, John Cloake, Georgina Cottee, Peter Cracknell, Lesley Durbin, Richard Greatorex, Friederike Hammer, Linda Wilke Heil, Tony Herbert, Tracy M Hill (Optima Cambridge Ltd), Peter Hoare, Sue Hudson, Simon Inglis, Malcolm C James, Daphne Kemp, Jack Kemp, David Kerr, Geoffrey Lane, Sue Lodwick, David O'Connor, Margaret Perry, Michael Pritchard, Larry J Schaaf, Adam Slater, Joseph Spooner, Jackie Spreckley, Alan Swale, Nick Tomlinson, Tony Waterfield (London & North Western Railway Society) and Vanessa Winstone (Collections Officer, National Brewery Centre). Thank you all.

Many institutions have gone well out of their way to help, and I am pleased to thank Brighton Museum and Art Gallery, East Sussex Record Office, Friends of Playden Church, Guinness Archive, Ipswich Record Office, Northumberland Archives, Richmond Local History Society, UK National Inventory of War Memorials, and the Vauxhall Society.

Without the Brewery History Society, the book would not have been possible, and I should particularly like to thank its Chair, Jeff Sechiari, for his constructive comments and consistently positive attitude to this and earlier projects. I am enormously grateful to the BHS President, Ray Anderson, for his help with technical brewing matters; without his help I might have confused my mash tun with my hop back and got into a vat of trouble. My other BHS colleagues Tim Holt, Chris J Marchbanks, Ian P Peaty, Stephen Peck and Paul Travis have been extremely helpful in many and various ways. In addition, I am delighted to acknowledge the earlier research of Norman Barber, former BHS Archivist, on whose work we all build.

At English Heritage, Keith Falconer (former Head of Industrial Archaeology) has been crucial in supporting the continuing study of the brewing industry, and he has my grateful thanks. So also does Ian Leith, Acquisitions Officer; I have benefited greatly from his astounding knowledge of the EH Archive, and the outcome can be seen in the book's breadth of illustrations. Finally, my thanks to Rachel Howard, John Hudson, Robin Taylor, Sue Kelleher and the publishing team for making it all possible.

The Prologue: Beer

B eer. It could be mild, bitter, brown ale, India Pale Ale, stout, porter, golden ale, barley wine, old ale, wheat beer, not forgetting lager. Or to be more definitive, how about a dark ruby-red malty bitter, or a robust dark-brown stout, or a refreshing pale-golden beer? Or indeed one of the well over 5,000 different beers produced by British breweries in 2013, ranging alphabetically from Abbey Stout to Zingiber, brewed in Northamptonshire and Kent respectively.[1] And that's not counting all the seasonal and occasional beers, brewed to mark dates such as St Valentine's Day, St George's Day and Christmas, and one-off events like the Queen's Diamond Jubilee in 2012, which was commemorated by dozens of Jubilee ales. These special brews continue a tradition originating in the medieval era with drinks brewed for fund-raising festivals known as parish ales. Until the mid-1960s, the brewing and malting processes as described here remained essentially unchanged.

Water and malt

So, if beer lies at the heart of British life and culture, what exactly is it that allows a simple mixture of its two major raw materials, barley and water, to turn – as if by magic – into a drink with such a wide variety of tastes, colours and textures? Let's begin with beer's principal ingredient, water, which is known by brewers as liquor whilst undergoing the brewing process. In the past, and still at some breweries today – for instance Harveys of Lewes in East Sussex (*see* Fig 4.54) – it was often obtained from the brewery's own well. Its particular chemical composition went a long way towards determining the specific flavour range of a brewery's beer, although almost any water can now be chemically modified to replicate a desired

Fig 1.2 (right)
To the rear of the Golden Lion in
Southwick, near Portsmouth, is
England's sole surviving complete
Victorian pub brewhouse. From this
room (with a boiler and steam engine
on the floor below) came beer supplies
for the pub and a small off-licence trade.
It was worked by a single brewer with an
occasional assistant.

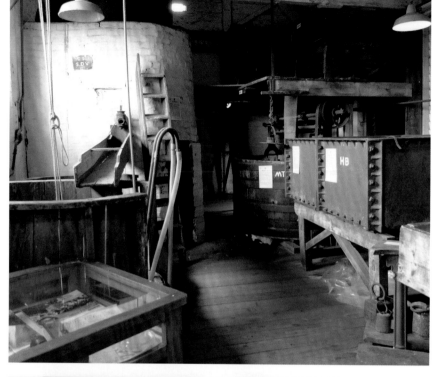

Fig 1.3 (above)
The Southwick Brewhouse inn sign
shows master brewer Dick Olding at
work inside the brewhouse, cleaning out
the mash tun. It is the work of artist
Peter John Oldreive from Bognor Regis,
who has painted well over 2,000 signs
during a lifetime as a traditional pub
sign artist.

Fig. 1.4 (right)
The exterior of Southwick Brewhouse.
Brewing took place on the well-
ventilated upper floor but ceased in the
mid-1950s; the building was almost
derelict before restoration from 1982 to
1985, and is now a museum combined
with a beer and cider store.

source. Most famously the water in Burton upon Trent, with its high calcium sulphate level, enabled the town's brewers to produce the bright, pale ales that became so fashionable in the 1830s and 1840s. Brewers elsewhere later attempted to copy the beer by adjusting the salt content of their water, a process which became known as Burtonisation.

The reason Burton's water was so good for brewing lies in its interaction with beer's other main raw material, barley. Before the barley can be used by the brewer it is turned into malt, a process that begins with screening to remove impurities. At a traditional floor maltings, of which a few still remain in England, the hard grains are then steeped (soaked) in water for up to 70 hours.[2] Water enters each grain by a tiny hole at its embryo end and begins to soften the barley, allowing germination to begin; its appearance changes as the grains produce rootlets. Next the moist grains are spread on a malting floor to a depth of around 150mm and turned occasionally, usually about twice a day (Fig 1.5) – originally by hand using a wooden malt shovel or an iron malt rake – to maintain an even temperature and stop the shoots knitting together as germination continues.

After 8 to 15 days, depending on the type of malt required and the ambient temperature, the process is halted by heating. The grains are dried in a kiln for three to four days, initially at around 50°C to remove the water content and then at a slightly higher temperature, varying with the malt desired, to develop colour and complex flavours (Fig 1.6). The darkest malts, kilned at the highest temperatures, are used to produce dark beers like stouts and brown ales.

Maltings could be large, stand-alone structures completely separate from breweries, but many 19th-century breweries were integrated sites including their own, albeit often smaller, maltings. In either case, once the malt has been kilned it is sent to the brewery for milling, that is crushing and grinding the grain to produce slightly smaller particles or grist (see Fig 2.3). The milled grist is stored in a grist case awaiting the next stage of the brewing process, where it meets and combines with warm water, releasing the malt's starch to produce fermentable sugars. Mixing (mashing) happens in a large, cylindrical mash tun or in a mashing machine giving out into the tun (Fig 1.7). The sugary, porridge-like mash mixture then stands for a little over an hour at a controlled temperature before the sweet liquid – wort – is separated from the spent grains by running it off through the tun's slotted floor. The spent grains left behind in the tun are sprayed or 'sparged' with hot water by a revolving device mounted inside the tun to flush out any remaining sugars.

Fig 1.6

A sack of Hampshire-grown malted barley, ready for milling. Malt can range in colour from pale-yellow to black, and in taste from sweet through nutty to nearly burnt. The barley variety Maris Otter, first bred in 1966, is popular with traditional English brewers as it provides a strongly malty flavour even in relatively low-strength beers.

Fig 1.7 (above)
Steaming mash pours into the mash tun
from a mechanical mixer at McMullen's
Brewery, Hertford. The shot was taken,
probably during the 1960s, by Eileen
'Dusty' Deste, a professional
photographer with a particular interest
in recording old-fashioned industrial
processes and derelict sites before they
were cleared. Her work provides an
excellent record of brewing at the time.

Fig 1.8 (right)
Another shot taken by Deste at
McMullen's captures the hard, hot work
involved in removing the spent grains
from a mash tun. Deste (1908–86),
born Eileen Olive Leach in Croydon,
worked in New Zealand during the
1930s and early 1940s, and was official
photographer to the country's
Centennial Exhibition, held in
Wellington (1939–40). When she
returned to London she carried out
a series of projects on industrial themes
as well as being commissioned by the
National Trust to record the contents
of its houses.

Hops and yeast

Next, the two other major ingredients of beer are introduced, firstly hops (Fig 1.9).
The common hop (*Humulus lupulus*) is a perennial climbing plant which produces
small flower cones known as hops. Many hop varieties have been bred or propagated
in Kent, including Fuggles and Goldings, and 20 varieties are currently produced
in Britain by 55 growers. The South-East and the West Midlands, especially
Worcestershire and Herefordshire, are the most significant hop-growing areas, but
they are grown elsewhere, including at the Eden Project in Cornwall.[3] After picking,
the hops are dried in hop kilns, known in Kent as oast houses; their conical roofs are
still an iconic sight in the county, although most have now been converted for
residential use. Once dried, the hops are packed into long sacks (pockets),
eventually ending up at the brewery, although most hops used today are in the
compressed form of hop pellets, needing far less storage space.

Fig 1.9 (right)
Hops ready for use at Harveys Brewery in Lewes. After drying, hops in their whole form were packed into jute sacks ('pockets') about 7ft long by 2ft diameter. These bulky objects contained 168lb of hops. Modern brewers often use hops that have been compressed after drying and made into pellets or powder, and hop extracts (available commercially since the 1960s) are now popular.

Fig 1.10 (right below)
A postcard view of hop pickers in Kent around 1905. The autumn harvest season saw a flood of outsiders arriving in the county to find employment, although local people were always the farmers' first choice because they needed no farm accommodation. The pickers usually worked in family-based groups of 8 to 10 people and from the early 20th century lived in 'hopper huts' made of timber or corrugated iron.

Fig 1.11 (opposite)
Oast houses seen in 1990 on Whitbread's Hop Farm at Beltring in Kent. Until his death in 1922, the farm was the home of hop breeder Albert White, who supplied hops to Whitbread's. To maintain supplies, the brewery decided to purchase the farm, which later became a tourist attraction as well as employing around 4,000 Londoners annually during the harvest. It was sold in 1997 and is now the Hop Farm Family Park.

Fig 1.12 (above)
Between the wars the Southern Railway advertised its day excursion trains to Kent using a poster by the artist, metal worker and textile designer F Gregory Brown (1887–1941). His bucolic image of oast houses in the sunshine epitomised Kent. The railway companies also ran 'Hoppers' Specials' every autumn to take pickers to and from the hop gardens.

Fig 1.13 (right)
This page from an *Illustrated London News* supplement of 3 October 1874 shows all the stages in the hop-drying process. Once stripped from the 'bines', as the branches were called, the hops were spread on a kiln drying floor, dried by hot air, shovelled to another floor where they cooled, then packed into pockets (bottom right) with a hop press.

In the next stage of the brewing process the wort or sugar solution is boiled with hops for an hour or two in a large metal vessel called a copper (Fig 1.14). Boiling extracts resins and essential oils from the hops, providing bitterness and aroma, and concentrates the wort. Now we are almost at the fermentation stage, but first the wort passes through a metal vessel with a perforated base – a hop back – to sieve out the spent hops, and is then cooled. Originally large, open shallow tanks were used to cool the wort, sited where good ventilation was available. Later came many improved forms of heat exchanger, and eventually artificial refrigeration, the latter being crucial for lager production as it enabled brewers to store the lager for months while it fermented.

After cooling, the wort is run into fermenting vessels, which may be open or closed wooden rounds (Fig 1.15), copper, stone or slate squares, wooden casks or modern cylindrical tanks. Here the last of beer's four main ingredients, yeast –

Fig 1.14
One of the two coppers at McMullen's in Hertford, photographed by Deste around the 1960s. The steam-heated, domed copper has a capacity of c 140 barrels, and may have been converted from a cast-iron hop back which once stood in its place. The copper house is now a small brewing museum accessed through a Sainsbury's store.

9

Fig 1.15

Fermenting vessels at Hook Norton
Brewery in 2002. The traditional round
wooden fermenters, which taper slightly
towards the top, have been lined with
plastic to prevent leaks; two of these
vessels still remain in regular use.

a living, single-celled fermenting organism – is added or 'pitched'. Yeast produces alcohol when it comes into contact with sugar. Breweries all have their own individual strains of yeast, which are closely guarded as they provide much of the beer's character. The two types of brewing yeast are ale (or top-fermenting) yeasts and the less genetically diverse lager yeasts, which tend to cluster at the bottom of fermenters and are thus known as bottom-fermenting. Ale and lager yeasts are better distinguished by the optimum temperatures at which they ferment; for ale yeasts this is 18–24°C, while lager yeasts prefer 5–14°C. Fermentation's mysterious nature was only explained by advances in brewing science during the late 19th century, and recent progress in the study of DNA has finally led to a fuller understanding of yeast.

In the course of fermentation, within 24 hours most ale yeasts will form a thick foam on the surface of the liquid. This is later skimmed off and some is reused, while the excess is compressed in a yeast press and sold to food processors. The complete traditional beer fermentation process generally takes around five days or more. Lager, on the other hand, can take up to a fortnight to ferment and is then stored (lagered) at a temperature just above freezing point for several months. Fermentation not only produces the requisite alcohol, but also provides a balance of flavours within the beer. When ready, the beer can be run directly from the fermenting vessels into casks, but usually it is transferred to conditioning tanks. Here the remaining yeast is cleared from the beer using filtration or fining agents such as isinglass or gelatin, which encourage any remaining yeast particles to stick together and thus settle out faster. Finally, the beer is either bottled, transferred to wooden or metal casks (racked), or packaged into metal kegs and sent out to the country's pubs and shops, eventually reaching its ultimate destination when dispensed from a beer pump or poured from a bottle into a waiting glass. Cheers!

Our beer styles

It is clear that with so many possible variables throughout the brewing process, no two beers – unless brewed to precisely the same recipe using the same plant – will be exactly alike, although late 20th-century brewery takeovers did enhance expertise in replicating beers, as did growing interest in historic beers. The almost infinite variations in outcome brought about by combinations of differing local water supply, type of malt, hops, yeast, fermentation temperature and time, and the equipment used at each stage (its material, age and size), happily result in those 5,000 or more named beers.

But of course there are some signposts for the beer drinker – the general categories or styles of beer, such as stout and mild, are helpful – and the occasional problem of nomenclature. One particularly relevant for historians is the modern conflation of the words ale and beer, which nowadays are used completely interchangeably. Originally ale was brewed without hops and beer with hops, although as beer became more popular some ale brewers began to lightly hop their product; however it was always far less hoppy than beer. So in this book we shall keep to the modern usage, enjoying India Pale Ale for the hoppy beer that it is, and only employ ale as the technical term for a hopless drink when the historical context makes this clear.

Fig 1.16

The finished product: the landlord of the Trout Inn at Lechlade, seen in 1956 drawing beer from a cask brewed by Simonds of Reading.

As well as using different malt types, an important distinction between lager and other beers is that lager is brewed using lager yeasts, rather than ale yeasts. The less diverse lager yeasts give a more subtle gradation of flavours. The ale yeasts give us anything from a rich, dark, imperial stout (perhaps around 7–8 per cent alcohol by volume or ABV) to a pale, dry bitter (maybe about 3–4 per cent ABV). But dark does not necessarily equate with strong or malty, nor pale with weak or hoppy. Traditionally, a specific brewery would become known for its particular range of beers of differing strengths and flavours produced from local ingredients, using its own yeast, and brewed with its own equipment. This direct link between brewery and beer explains the sense of loss felt at brewery closures, and emphasises the significance of our stock of remaining brewery buildings, especially those still engaged in brewing.

Fig 1.17
Perhaps a family celebration, or maybe simply a picnic, this early 1900s group from Langport in Somerset are all enjoying their beer.

Fig 1.18
Morris dancing is thirsty work. The Westminster Morris Men seen at the Axe & Compasses pub in Arkesden, Essex, during 1954, the year after their morris team was founded.

2 The Emergence of the Brewery

VÉRITABLE EXTRAIT DE VIANDE LIEBIG.

Histoire de la bière — 1.
Préparation de la bière au moyen de pierres
échauffées, à l'époque préhistorique.

Our Neolithic ancestors were brewers. They could produce a mash by heating water with fire-warmed stones (Fig 2.1). We know the basic components of a prehistoric 'brewery' were a fairly flat area for malting, grinding equipment, a container for the mash with a stirring implement, a source of heat and a water supply, often a stream. Along with water, the brew's ingredients were milled and malted grain, yeast and herbs. The hot stones were dropped into the prehistoric equivalent of a mash tun, which could be a wooden trough, a stone bowl, or even a diverted section of a stream, causing the wort to heat. Processing the grain was a wet and sticky business, so good drainage was essential. Modern experimental archaeology has shown this 'hot rock mashing' technique to be so efficient that in one recent demonstration 77 pints of light ale were brewed using a small wooden water trough.[1]

Brewing's simple requirements could be met with a variety of stone and wooden utensils, all of which could be and probably were used in other activities. This has led archaeologists to overlook the ubiquity of brewing and its remains. In addition, most products of the brewing process are ephemeral, leaving little trace. However, constant heating and reheating of the stones eventually causes them to fracture and be discarded. The purpose of the resulting piles of fire-cracked stones, known as burnt mounds, has puzzled archaeologists for years. Typically they are kidney-shaped humps near a watercourse and a hearth, often next to a pit or trough.[2] Their function was generally thought to be related to cooking (although few sites have revealed any food debris) or ritual purification, but recent research, much of it

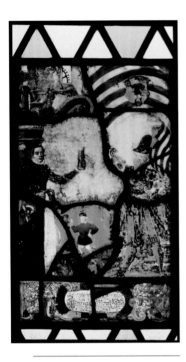

Fig 2.2

A medieval window from the dining room of Turton Tower, near Bolton in Lancashire, showing parts of the brewing process (top left) and its end product, downing a drink. The tower house probably dates from the 15th century and is now a museum.

Fig 2.3

A detail from the Turton Tower window gives us a view of the brewhouse, where power is provided by a water wheel. Malt is being tipped from a sack into the hopper above the grindstones, while the brewster looks on and grist pours out into a grist case. This is a rare depiction on stained glass in England of the brewing process; the glass itself may have originated in Europe, possibly Switzerland or Germany.

experimental archaeology, has strongly suggested that the stone piles could also be evidence of early brewing. Certainly it seems highly likely that brewing was one of several activities performed at burnt mound locations. A local population might have created a series of burnt mounds, with those sites further from the habitation used for the most unpleasant and noxious tasks; dyeing and leatherworking, for instance, might have been carried out at even more distant locations than brewing.[3]

Burnt mounds are found throughout the British Isles, and generally date from the Bronze Age – roughly 2300 BC to 850 BC – but there are earlier (late Neolithic) and later examples. Ireland has over 4,000 burnt mound sites, there are several hundred in Orkney and Shetland, and they are widespread elsewhere, occurring in most areas of England – for instance at the Moseley Bog nature reserve in south Birmingham – although many lowland sites have probably disappeared due to later development. These simple mounds of stones are thus the forebears of Victorian industrial-scale breweries, and also of the ubiquitous modern microbrewery.

During the Iron Age (around 850 BC to AD 100), Celts arriving from France and the Low Countries brought with them the skills of ironworking and woodworking, the two having combined to allow the construction of large stave-built hooped casks – ideal for storage and transport of liquids such as beer – as well as smaller vessels such as tankards and buckets.[4] The invention of the cask was a crucial point in the journey towards industrial-scale brewing. We have few details about brewing during the Iron Age, but the fact that the Roman garrison at Vindolanda in Northern England purchased supplies of beer during AD 110 to 111, probably from a local brewer, suggests that it did indeed continue throughout this thousand-year period. The writing tablets excavated from the fort at Vindolanda also mention one Atrectus the brewer, the first brewer in British history to be named as such.[5]

We may assume that brewing vessels increased somewhat in scale and strength during the Iron Age and into the Roman period. Archaeological evidence implies that brewing, domestic and retail, was widespread in Roman Britain, and the remains of grain dryers or maltings are found in many Roman towns and farms.[6] These buildings date from the 3rd to 4th century AD and have a structure peculiar

to Britain: a covered building, usually in a T-shaped plan, with an underground flue and a drying floor above. Grain was spread on the drying floor and warmed from below. The structures were originally thought to be solely grain dryers, but during the 1970s tests of reconstructed buildings at farm sites in Hertfordshire and Oxfordshire showed they were totally ineffective. However, the temperatures reached were ideal for malting barley, suggesting that by the end of the Roman period, malthouses were commonplace structures.[7] It was to be some time before an equally distinctive brewery building type appeared.

Brewing in medieval Britain

The pervasiveness of brewing in early medieval times is reflected in the number of contemporary regulations, ecclesiastical and secular, relating to ale drinking.[8] But medieval brewing was still a domestic endeavour, an everyday – or almost every day – piece of time-consuming household drudgery, generally carried out by women who bolstered the family income by occasional selling of ale.[9] As an activity, brewing had to be fitted around the demands of family life, and mostly required utensils normally found in the home. Its product could be for household consumption, or increasingly could be sold for profit; women brewers (brewsters) might brew during the whole or part of their adult lives, and be commercial brewers for only part of that time, as family demands came and went. Visually, an alehouse could only be identified as such because an ale-stake – a pole with a garland of leaves or twigs – was hung from its exterior when the ale was available.

Fig 2.4

This window in the north transept of the Cathedral of Notre-Dame, Tournai, by the Flemish glass painter Arnold of Nijmegen celebrates the importance of brewing to the local economy. In the background brewers are carrying out several activities including stirring a mash tun, emptying a copper and filling barrels. The glass dates from about 1490, when Tournai was a French city, although it is now in Belgium; the window was restored c 1845.

The market for beer was substantial, and regulation of this proto-industry began around 1196 to 1197 with the enforcement of standard weights and measures through a wide-ranging royal proclamation known as the Assize of Measures. Brewers were specifically targeted by the mid-1190s Assize of Bread and Ale and later similar statutes, laying down rules on ale quality and measures. By the mid-14th century the Assize of Ale had in effect become a means of licensing brewers, some of whom were now professionals making use of an increasing amount of equipment.[10] This specialisation was partly a consequence of urbanisation, with many residents lacking the necessary space for brewing; another factor was the capital cost of large-scale brewing kit and premises.[11]

The move from kitchen to brewhouse had begun even earlier in the monasteries, where large-scale brewing was the norm, although generally for consumption by the monks and not as a commercial enterprise. A possible exception may have been the Cluniac priory of Castle Acre in Norfolk, where building began about 1090 and we can still see the excavated remains of what could have been a rare commercial brewery at an English monastic site. The brewhouse-cum-maltings building measured 75ft by 45ft and included two malt kilns, an upper malting floor, a mash tun and three lead coppers. There is evidence that three kinds of brew were produced, but no corroboration of sales outside the priory.[12] Curiously, despite widespread and substantial monastic brewing operations in England, there seems little resulting connection with the world of the commercial brewer.[13]

The Black Death reached England in 1349, causing huge depopulation and labour shortages. The effect of the plague years on the domestic brewing industry was also massive, although slow to be fully felt. The corollary of greater employment opportunities was that fewer women needed to supplement the family income by brewing, and a divide grew between the remaining low-profit, small-scale domestic brewsters and those who expanded their operations, becoming brewhouse-based. The latter professional brewers were increasingly male. Compounding this change was the introduction of the hop from the end of the 14th century; the slow shift from ale to beer brought an increase in the scale, complexity and cost of brewing.

The 15th- and 16th-century brewhouse

We can discover what equipment the professional brewer of the 1400s would have used through probate records, which occasionally include inventories of brewing vessels and associated kit. As listed in 1486, the contents of a London brewhouse included a copper brewing kettle, a mash tun with a loose (possibly false) bottom, a lead tap trough, a wort vat, 2 wort coolers, 3 wooden gutters, 3 brass hand kettles, 2 lead cisterns for holding water, 20 little yeast tubs, a little mash tub, a water tub, a lead steeping cistern, 24 kilderkins, a malt mill and a four-wheeled beer dray.[14] The tap trough would have been used to direct liquids flowing between brewing vessels, and the wooden 'gutters' were probably related to drainage. Although we cannot be certain, as the kilderkin was not standardised at 18 gallons until the end of the 17th century, it appears that the brew size could have been up to 12 barrels, where a barrel is a cask containing 36 gallons or 288 pints. (Details of standard cask sizes are given in the glossary.)

As to the brewhouse itself, evidence regarding its structure and appearance is limited, and comes mainly from archaeological investigation, such as the summer 2011 work at Pembroke College in Oxford, which uncovered what may be a 12th- or 13th-century brewhouse near today's Brewer Street. In general terms a brewhouse

Fig 2.5
German medieval brewing as portrayed in Schopper's *Book of Trades* published in Frankfurt in 1568, one of its 133 woodcuts by Jost Amman (1539–91), known for the accuracy of his depictions of costume and technical details. In the foreground barrels are being filled, just to the rear are two large vessels, perhaps mash tuns, and in the background we see what is probably a copper above an open fire.

Fig 2.6
A pair of casks and crossed mashing rakes mark the grave of a Flemish brewer at Playden Church in East Sussex. The stone commemorates refugee Cornelis Zoetmans, who died around 1530. The traditional mashing rake is often used as a symbol of brewing; the patron saint of Belgian brewers, St Arnold of Soissons, is normally pictured holding one.

might still be domestic in scale but with attention paid to good ventilation and drainage, and location near to a pure and constant water supply. A London fire prevention regulation of 1189 forced alehouses to be licensed unless they were stone built, perhaps favouring the larger-scale brewing concern; it also required brewhouses to be whitewashed inside and out.[15]

Beer brewing, as opposed to ale production, was well established in London by 1500 and eventually spread slowly throughout the country. Although beer kept

Fig 2.7
In the centre is the Black Lion Brewery in Brighton, said to date from the mid-16th century, although the buildings we see in this late 1960s view are probably early 18th century. Door openings on first and second floors allowed brewing materials to be hoisted up and into the brewery. It was once owned by Flemish refugee Deryk Carver, who was burnt at the stake in Lewes in 1555 for refusing to recant his Protestantism; he was put in a barrel before his execution, in order to mock the brewing profession. The Black Lion was rebuilt as a facsimile in 1974, but the cellars beneath, which may be 16th century, are probably still extant.

better than ale, and therefore was more economic to brew in large quantities, it had several disadvantages for small-scale brewers. Not only was the brewing process longer and more complicated, thus burning extra fuel, but it required expensive, specialised equipment. On top of that, the hops were an additional cost. By the end of the 16th century domestic brewing was in severe decline and the era of the 'common brewer' had begun. These were large-scale, mainly urban operations; as early as 1603, John Stow's *Survey of London* mentions 'great bere-houses' clustered on the Thames at St Katherine's, near the Tower of London.[16] They brewed preponderantly for wholesale rather than retail sale, and were the precursors of the great breweries of the 18th and 19th centuries, as we shall see in the next chapter.

The country house brewhouse

But in specific settings, including the new country houses and institutions such as Oxford and Cambridge colleges, domestic brewing thrived, in some cases right up until the early 20th century. At Queen's College, Oxford, ale and beer were brewed from the inception of the college in 1340 to the start of the Second World War, when the brewhouse – probably remodelled during the 16th or 17th century – was converted for other uses; it still stands, complete with much louvre ventilation (Fig 2.9).[17] A good number of rural monastic brewhouses survived the dissolution of religious houses during the late 1530s, because their monasteries were converted to palatial country houses and the service buildings were just as useful to the new occupants as they had been to the previous inhabitants. The Cistercian brewhouse at Buckland Abbey, Devon, survived to supply the new owners until around 1770, while the medieval brewhouse at Nostell Priory in West Yorkshire is still extant.[18] The priority in these private brewhouses was not profit but the production of a consistent supply of good quality ale or beer. Private brewers and their employers resisted the adoption of new technology in the brewhouse, preferring to stick with tried and tested methods and kit, unlike the commercial brewers.

The dedicated country house brewhouse was commonplace by the 16th century.[19] It was generally a small, well-ventilated structure either standing alone or most often attached to a cottage, farm or other offices. Inside was a set of basic equipment: a pot surrounded by brick or stone and heated from beneath, along with assorted tubs and coolers (Fig 2.10). By the 18th century substantial, purpose-built brewhouses could be found on larger country estates, usually sited well away from the house itself due to the steamy, smelly nature of the process. It was often close to the bakehouse and laundry, which shared these drawbacks.

A brewhouse would ideally be a good two storeys high, with large, unglazed louvred windows and a ventilation lantern on the roof ridge (Fig 2.11). The height also allowed the brewer to take advantage of gravity, to help out inadequate or even non-existent pumps. Inside was a specialised brewing copper with a convex bottom, drained through a tap; by the 18th century many brewhouses had two coppers, the second for boiling the wort. Other equipment included coolers and a barrel-like mash tun; the fermenting vessels, similar to mash tuns but smaller and covered, were either in the brewhouse or

Fig 2.8

This alleyway through a Georgian town house in Kendal led to the Highgate Brewery owned by Whitwell, Mark & Co, founded in 1757 by John Whitwell. Its painted stone sign, an unusual survivor, is a reminder of earlier times when a brewery was simply an outbuilding at the rear of the owner's house. The passage now gives access to the Brewery Arts Centre.

Fig 2.9
Men tending a copper at Queen's College brewhouse in Oxford during the 1930s. The brick-built copper tower, reinforced with metal bands, has a fuel storage section below and the firebox above, reached via steps and substantial staging. The grade II listed brewhouse, possibly dating from the 16th or 17th centuries, was largely remodelled in the 18th century and there were later alterations; it now functions as the college carpenters' shop.

the cellars. Local builders, coopers and coppersmiths normally built or supplied all the equipment.

On occasion, fashionable architects might stoop to brewhouse design, generally when asked to provide a grand plan for an estate or new mansion, although the brewhouse detailing would normally be drawn up by an employee in the architect's office. Surviving and publicly accessible country houses brewhouses include those at Knole (Kent), Charlecote Park (Warwickshire) and Lacock Abbey (Wiltshire) (Figs 2.12 and 2.13), and two where brewing still takes place, Shugborough (Staffordshire) and Traquair House (Scottish Borders).

Fig 2.10
Country house brewing equipment
designed by architects Robert Smythson
(c 1535–1614) and his son John around
1600. On the left is the copper, heated
by a fire beneath. It discharged into
a mash tun (centre), via a tapered vessel
which broke up the stream of water.
Next, a hand pump raised the wort from
the underback to the copper for boiling,
and it then passed along a moveable
pipe to the long, flat cooler (right);
underneath is the fermentation tun.

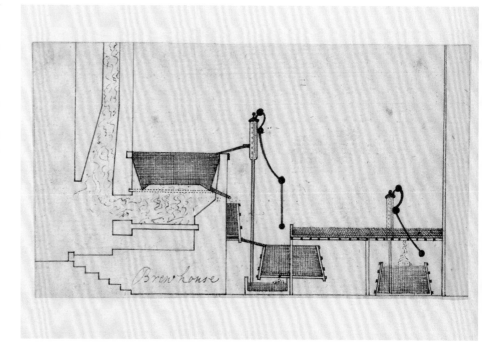

Fig 2.11
A hand-coloured engraving of a small
brewhouse, published in the *Universal
Magazine* (January 1747/8). On the left is
the tall copper housing, with a hand
pump beside it and the mash tun below,
being stirred by three men using
mashing rakes. On the right, at roughly
head height, is the flat cooler and inset
above is a view of the brewhouse
exterior, lavishly equipped with
louvre vents.

Fig 2.12 (right)
Lacock Abbey brewhouse, Wiltshire
(16th century with later alterations),
showing the steps leading to the copper,
from which a trough discharges into the
lead-lined cooler on the right, above the
fermenting vessel. The firebox is in the
adjacent room, beyond the wall to
the left.

Fig 2.13 (below)
Workers outside Lacock Abbey
brewhouse during the middle to late
19th century; note the louvre ventilation
to the right. Brewing was essentially a
two-person operation, so these workers
were probably general estate workers,
and perhaps a few coopers, assembled
for a photograph. We do not know who
took the picture; it was probably not the
photographic pioneer William Henry
Fox Talbot (1800–77), although the
abbey was his home.

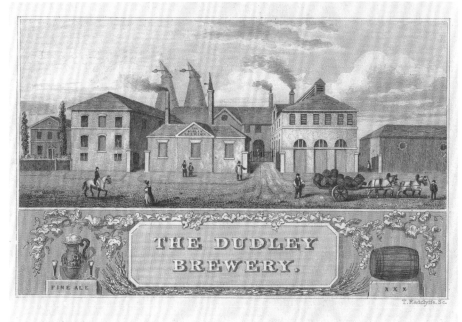

Fig 2.14 (right)
An advertisement for the Dudley
Brewery, published in 1838. A small
industrial brewery, it retains the ample
ventilation apparent in earlier
brewhouses but on a larger scale.
Two malt kilns stand to the rear of the
brewery, the stables occupy the low
block to the right and on the far left is
probably the brewer's house.

Fig 2.15

The industrial brewery: looking towards
the west end of Whitbread's Chiswell
Street Brewery at the start of the 1790s,
the decade in which it became the
largest beer producer in the world.
This mezzotint, by engraver William
Ward (1766–1826) after a painting by
George Garrard (1760–1826), shows the
massive scale of the brewhouse
buildings and their ample ventilation.

Even though the country house brewery is something of a byway on the road to
the industrial-scale brewhouse, it gives us a significant visual clue as to how the
massive new 18th-century breweries eventually appeared. A typical country house
brewhouse combined the essential functional attributes necessary for beer
production – ventilation and height in particular – with a nod towards the easy
elegance of the Palladian style, a muted neoclassicism. The Georgian industrial
brewhouses pushed these architectural elements to a new and distinctive scale.

3 The Development of the Brewery

During the 17th century, the number of commercial brewers – generally known as common brewers – in London had risen from 26 to 194. Many of the older and larger concerns were based in Southwark, home of the nascent brewing industry, with premises on a substantial scale, but none yet dominated the trade in terms of individual production. It is notable that a handful of these breweries were to continue in business on the same sites, often as family concerns, for 200 to 300 years. In 1699 the average annual output of a London common brewer was around 5,000 barrels, while in total the city's common brewers produced 962,440 barrels of strong beer and ale; the publican-brewers, with only 6,000 barrels in all – not a great deal more than a single common brewer – were insignificant players in an expanding trade.[1] This growth in number of common brewers was eventually mirrored outside London, although on a smaller scale. In 1701 there were 574 common brewers outside the capital, each typically with production about one-sixth that of a London brewery.[2]

The situation was then much the same in Scotland, where industrial-scale breweries existed only in Edinburgh. During the 1630s Sir William Brereton, an English writer and politician, visited the 'common brew-house' established in the early 17th century by the city's Society of Brewers. He was stunned by its scale, commenting that it had 'the greatest, vastest leads [cauldrons], boiling keeves [vats], cisterns and combs [tubs]' he had ever seen; the leads 'were as large as the whole house'.[3] Likewise, in London, the common brewers' tuns were described as 'extraordinary large' at the end of the 17th century, but there are few comments on the external appearance of these new brewhouses. We have to make do with an intriguing guidebook reference to the Red Lion Brewery at St Katherine's, just east of the Tower of London, dating from the early 1710s. It describes the brewhouse and storehouses as being 'not unworthy of a Strangers View', adding that one vessel in the store contained 155 barrels of beer – nearly 45,000 pints, assuming a 36-gallon barrel.[4]

The interests of London's brewers were looked after by the Brewers' Company, a body dating back to at least 1292, when the first written reference to such a group appears.[5] By the early 15th century they were one of the first guilds to acquire a hall of their own (on the site of the present hall) in which to conduct business and social events; the latter included the organisation, in the early 1440s, of football matches played by brewers' apprentices on fields at the city's edge.[6] However, the small livery company lacked political influence, and after the 1666 Great Fire of London destroyed the hall – along with 16 brewhouses – many brewers refused to join. The hall was rebuilt between 1670 and 1673, destroyed by bombing in 1940, and rebuilt again on Aldermanbury Square from 1958 to 1960 (architect Sir Hubert Worthington).

Much of the brewers' unease was due to the unending and expensive flow of brewing-related legislation. The 17th century saw the introduction of the first tax specifically concerned with beer: a levy of 4d per quarter (a volume measure of 8 bushels or 64 gallons) was imposed on malt around 1614. The legislative framework continued to grow, shaping the evolving industry. In 1643 beer costing over 6s a barrel was hit with a levy of 2s per barrel duty, then in 1657 and 1660 revenue officers were given wide powers of inspection. The measurement or 'gauging' of

Fig 3.2

One of a set of six advertising trade cards depicting the history of brewing produced around the late 19th century by Liebig's Extract of Meat Company. This one shows brewing in the 18th century, with large mash tuns being stirred mechanically via line shafting, although it is not clear whether the power comes from a horse wheel or a steam engine.

Fig 3.3

An 1807 bird's-eye view into the yard of the Genuine Beer Brewery in Golden Lane, just north of Whitbread's Brewery. It was established in 1804 on subscription principles to challenge London's highly capitalised porter brewers, and although initially successful, a series of court cases followed by rising raw material prices resulted in the plant being sold off in 1826 and the brewery pulled down.

vessels to determine their precise capacity was crucial. Once this systematic organisation of collection was in place, future changes – generally increases – to malt and beer duty became simpler to enforce.[7] The larger brewers responded by seeking to influence Parliament through personal contacts, lobbying and, in time, representing business interests and constituents by becoming brewer-MPs.

Legislation also indirectly affected brewhouse design, as revenue officers were required to inspect premises prior to a brewer setting up in trade. All vessels and pipes had to be declared or 'public'; no private plant was allowed. The revenue might object to utensils being sunk into the floor (as is often seen in Europe), or being too close to a wall and thus hiding illegal pipes. Experimentation and alteration was inhibited by the need to gain permission from the officers beforehand.[8] In addition, every moment – or so it must have seemed – of every brew had to be recorded in gauge books. Amidst this flood of regulation, it is curious that the business of making casks, and more significantly certifying their capacity, remained the prerogative of the Coopers' Company in London until the end of the 18th century. Although a standard barrel capacity of 36 gallons was introduced at the end of the 17th century, allegations of fraud through passing off ale barrels (32 gallons) as beer barrels continued throughout the 18th century.[9]

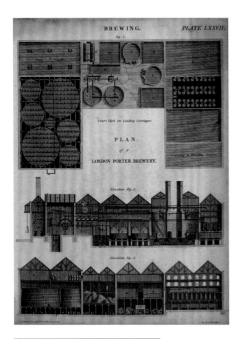

Fig 3.4 (above)

The Golden Lane Brewery, drawn by the polymath John Farey junior (1791–1851), engineer and artist, for the *Edinburgh Encyclopaedia*, and published between 1808 and 1830. This is a general representation, rather than a scale drawing; the storage vats on the left of the plan, for instance, occupied a far greater space than is shown. Also, the elevations depict the relative levels of the vessels rather than their actual positions. There were several layers of coolers in the wing to the right of the courtyard.

Fig 3.5 (right)

Williams's Porter Brewery on the quayside in Bath, shown on a trade card or letterhead dating from the late 18th century. At seven storeys in height and at least 10 bays by 9 bays, it is an imposing structure, but one likely to have been exaggerated in size by the artist to impress potential customers. The brewery burnt down around 1800.

The rise of porter

Around 1720 a London alehouse would have offered its customers a choice of about 30 brews including recently brewed brown beer known as 'mild', matured 'mild' ('stale'), amber beer, strong stout and several less hoppy ales. The various beers and ales were often mixed by drinkers. Their habits were soon to change, as the fad for the new beer, porter, took over. Over the first two decades of the 18th century London's brewers had slowly improved their production of strong brown beer, making it more hoppy, thus enabling it to be stored longer. By the 1720s it was a much more consistent product and found popularity with the city's thirsty street porters, earning it the name porter. It was a brew made from a complete set of mashes of the same malt, known technically as 'entire', and was then matured in huge casks called butts. In strength it was probably around 5–6 per cent ABV.

The brewing season for London porter ran from the start of September to early or mid-June, depending on the outside temperature. Porter was a robust brew and could withstand more heat than ale before deteriorating, allowing porter brewers a longer season than ale producers. Porter demanded a great financial commitment from brewers, but also promised rich rewards. It is significant as the first mass-produced beer, allowing economies of scale in the brewery but requiring substantial capital for raw materials and for the enormous vats in which the brown liquid matured. Brewers also had to keep sufficient capital to allow for a deferred return on their investment, while maturing took place. The vats took up large areas of the brewery; brewhouses and stores expanded to cope with the impact of porter brewing, and land had to be acquired. Porter had a real impact on the architecture and design of the great brewhouses (Fig 3.5).

The great common brewhouse

By the end of the 18th century, four-fifths of London's beer was brewed in six giant porter breweries.[10] Even though brewhouses in the later 1600s had been viewed by observers as astonishingly large – perhaps not surprisingly, given their relatively massive scale amongst low-rise, working neighbourhoods – the porter breweries were something new, 'a magnificence unspeakable' as Thomas Pennant described Meux's Griffin Brewery in 1790 (*see* Figs 3.7 and 3.8).[11] It stood in Clerkenwell's happily named Liquorpond Street (lost after the construction of Clerkenwell Road), was one of London's 10 largest breweries, and was still expanding.

Although the first-known illustrations of porter breweries date from towards the end of the 18th century, we have descriptions of ideal brewhouses written by brewers, and in some cases dimensions of actual brewhouses as built. William Ellis, who worked as a London common brewer in the early 18th century, published his views on planning in his *The London and Country Brewer*, emphasising the crucial part played by gravitation in moving the ingredients around an efficiently designed brewhouse.[12] George Watkins, who began work as a brewer in the 1730s, agreed with Ellis, suggesting in his *The Complete English Brewer* that a brewhouse would ideally be a two-storey structure standing apart from other buildings. The lower floor would have solid walls on all four sides, but the upper floor would have only a single solid wall with three of 'lattice work' (louvres) to let in air. The brewhouse would be angled to keep the sun out, by siting the solid wall at the south-west; the copper was to stand against this wall, about 11ft above the ground.[13] The positioning of the copper determined the location of all other vessels, placed for maximum labour saving.

Fig 3.6

An etching published in 1820 showing Calvert's Hour Glass Brewery (later City of London Brewery) beside the Thames; the original drawing was by the topographical artist Robert Bremmel Schnebbelie (1803–49). The buildings date from the last quarter of the 18th century, when the brewery was mostly reconstructed. It was destroyed by bombing in 1941.

Schnebbelie del.t   Howlett fec.t

VIEW of the BREWERY & DWELLING HOUSE belonging to MESS.rs CALVERT & C.o
Erected on the Seite of Cold Harbour.

London. Published. 27.th September 1820.   by Robert Wilkinson 125 Fenchurch Street.

Fig 3.7

This watercolour shows Meux's Griffin Brewery in Liquorpond Street around 1800. By this time we see London's industrial-scale breweries becoming more imposing, rising to at least four or five storeys in height, with rows of tall, semicircular-headed openings, some for ventilation, others providing access for incoming supplies and outgoing casks.

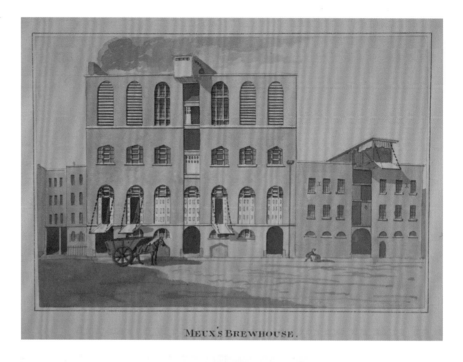

MEUX'S BREWHOUSE.

PLAN of the BREWHOUSE in LIQUOR-POND STREET.

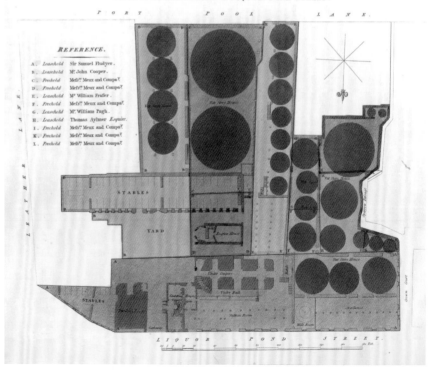

Fig 3.8

The largest of the 26 vats shown in this 1796 plan of Meux's Griffin Brewery measures 100ft across its base. A steam engine designed by Hornblower & Maberley was installed at the brewery in April 1797; the engine house shown in the centre of the plan probably accommodated the new machine.

However, efficiency in brewing was only one side of the problem. The other was storage. The huge vats, in which porter aged, took up a significant amount of space. For the central London brewers this was a particular difficulty as they were often constrained by narrow sites, and had to expand by taking in adjacent properties or building upwards. Calvert's Hour Glass Brewery in Upper Thames Street (Fig 3.6), for instance, had a four-storey malt store and a six-storey warehouse by 1766. In contrast, out in what was then almost countryside at Pimlico, William Greene's Stag Brewery, built around 1720, included a great brewhouse measuring 111ft by 83ft, bigger than any in the country at the time. These huge brewhouses were as much a part of the industrial revolution as the first multi-storey spinning mills built during the early 18th century in the silk-producing areas of Derby and east Cheshire.

Production plant too was on the heroic scale. By the 1760s, yet another brewer-cum-author, Michael Combrune, concluded that brewhouse utensils 'seem to admit of very little farther improvement'.[14] Size truly did matter, and continued to do so throughout the 19th and 20th centuries, as brewers continued to boast – doubtless mainly for publicity purposes – of the increasing dimensions of their brewing kit (or, occasionally, chimney stacks).

Samuel Whitbread (1720–96)

Samuel Whitbread was something of an exception to the general run of London porter brewers, as he had no direct family connections in the trade and worked his way up from apprentice to common brewer. He set up in business in 1742 at a couple of small brewhouses, then in 1750 bought the derelict King's Head Brewery on Chiswell Street in order to brew porter, at which he became spectacularly successful (*see* Fig 2.15).

He dramatically expanded the site and buildings, but the real key to his future prosperity was innovation, notably in porter storage. Initially, many brewers managed with cellars and tun rooms full of casks, but the large vat was a more economic solution and was commonplace after 1760. Whitbread went a stage further. Beneath his Great Storehouse (1774) were vaults, which he realised could be completely filled with huge tanks (cisterns) rather than a series of vats. The idea took nearly 10 years and quite some ingenuity to put into practice, due to leaking walls. He consulted some of the great names of the day – the architect Robert Mylne, the engineers John Smeaton and Matthew Boulton, and the potter Josiah Wedgwood – but it was his persistence and experimentation that finally solved the problem. By 1787, the year of a visit by King George III to the brewery, Whitbread proudly calculated that his seven cisterns held a total of 12,350 barrels; vats in the same space would have held only 1,000 barrels (Fig 3.9).[15]

Whitbread was also an innovator with respect to the introduction of steam power. He was the second brewer in London (although only by a few months) to order a steam engine, which powered the malt mill and enabled the brewery to dispense with 24 horses. Whitbread's final building was a massive new vat warehouse, built in 1796, the year of his death. At that time the brewery's annual production had reached 202,000 barrels, over 58 million pints; easily the greatest in Britain, and indeed the largest in the world at that time.

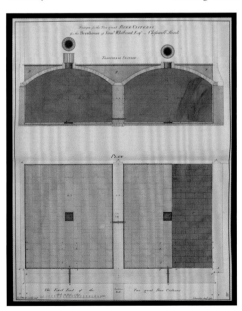

Fig 3.9
John Smeaton's design for two beer cisterns at Whitbread's Brewery. The section and plan, dated 1782, also refers to Samuel Whitbread as being the inventor of the cisterns. Each one measured 30ft wide by 36ft long, and 19ft to the highest point of the domed top.

Steam power

When Samuel Whitbread moved to Chiswell Street in 1750, his brewery was powered by labourers and horses. The horses, often blind, spent their time connected to a horse mill or engine, trudging around in a circle to provide the rotary power required for milling and pumping. Larger breweries might have one or more four-horse mills. Although the mill horses did not constitute a great capital cost, being cheaper than the breweries' flagship dray horses, they still had to be fed and housed. In contrast, steam engines represented a larger capital outlay but could be worked for longer with lower running costs. The firm of Boulton and Watt, based at the Soho works near Birmingham, initially produced steam-pumping engines aimed at the Cornish mines, but soon realised that rotary engines would be ideal for milling. Their first such engine was completed in 1782. News spread fast to the London brewers, and the Barclay, Perkins Anchor Brewery of Southwark was first to enquire about installing a steam engine, in August 1782 (*see* Figs 6.13 and 6.14).[16]

It took two more years before a steam engine actually began to power a London brewery. The pioneer, in 1784, was Henry Goodwyn's Red Lion Brewery at St Katherine's with a four-horsepower engine. Samuel Whitbread immediately went to inspect the machine at work and ordered a larger model for his own brewery. It began to power the Chiswell Street brewery in 1785 and continued to do so for over a century, before being retired in 1887. Most of the larger London brewers and some in the provinces – Bristol, Faversham, Nottingham, Liverpool – soon followed the example of Goodwyn and Whitbread, and by 1800 almost all operations inside major breweries had been mechanised. Aside from pumping and milling there were mashing machines, Archimedean screws, Jacob's ladders and other forms of elevator, and cask-raising mechanisms. These engineering innovations were matched by advances in the science of brewing.

From art to science

Prior to the mid-18th century brewing was more an art or craft than a science. The chemistry of the brewing process was not understood, and brewers worked from custom and practice handed down by their forbears. As the common brewers expanded and amounts of ingredients increased, this previously satisfactory empirical method was seen to be flawed and incapable of resulting in a product of uniform quality. A mistake in the mashing temperature, for instance, was insignificant on a small scale but costly when industrial quantities were involved.

Early 18th-century brewers judged the mashing liquor to be at the correct temperature using tried and trusted but splendidly vague methods such as putting an elbow into the liquid (it was too hot if the heat could not be tolerated) or waiting for the liquid surface to become mirror-like after the steam cleared. Even after the invention of the thermometer in 1714, and the endorsement it received in Michael Combrune's 1758 *Essay on Brewing*, the industry was slow to take up this cheap and accurate invention. It was the mid-1780s to 1790s before it was widely accepted, and brewers were careful to keep their trade secrets to themselves by using thermometers without numbered scales, instead marked with signs or letters at appropriate mashing and fermenting temperatures.[17]

Just as significant was the introduction of the saccharometer (Fig 3.10), a hydrometer calibrated for measuring the specific gravity of beer, and thus its fermentable sugar content. The device is a long glass stem with a weighted bulb at its bottom end. The wort to be tested is poured into a tall, thin container into which

Fig 3.10

A display of saccharometers from the 1907 catalogue of instrument makers W R Loftus of Tottenham Court Road. The firm, which was established in the 1850s, also made beer engines, and bottling and corking machines, as well as being suppliers of general brewing and bar equipment to the drink trade.

W. R. LOFTUS Ltd., 18, Tottenham Court Road, London, W.   3

TO HIS MAJESTY'S INLAND REVENUE.
TO HIS MAJESTY'S STATIONERY OFFICE.
TO HIS MAJESTY'S COLONIAL GOVERNMENTS.
TO HIS MAJESTY'S FORCES.

THE REVENUE SACCHAROMETER.

As adapted by H.M. Board of Inland Revenue, and supplied to Revenue Officers for testing Specific Gravity of Beer, as required under the Beer Act, 1880.

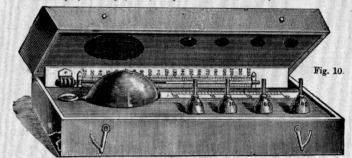

Fig. 10.

Fig. 10.—BATES' REVENUE SACCHAROMETER, extra and best double gilt, with four Poises, Thermometer, and Book of Tables, ...   £ *s. d.*   4 4 0

Ditto   ditto   with extra Poise for Syrups, &c.   4 10 0

(NOTE.—*For Bates' Patent Distillery Saccharometer, see page 37.*)

IMPROVED SPECIFIC GRAVITY SACCHAROMETER.

For showing Specific Gravity of Worts, in accordance with the New Beer Duty Act. The most simple and durable Instrument made, and only manufactured by W. R. LOFTUS, Ltd.

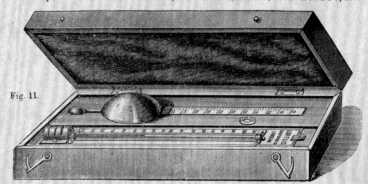

Fig. 11.

Fig. 11.—IMPROVED BREWING SACCHAROMETER, showing degrees of Specific Gravity, extra and best double gilt, with Thermometer and Book of Tables, complete   ... ...   £ *s. d.*   3 3 0

Ditto   ditto   ditto   Brass 2 10 0

LOFTUS'S NEW GLUCOMETER, for ascertaining the extract per 2-cwt. in Glucose and all kinds of Sugars used in Brewing. This Instrument will be found very useful to Brewers, as by merely dissolving a small portion of the Glucose, &c., the true extract is obtained. Extra double gilt, in Mahogany Case, with Thermometer, Graduated Glass and Instructions, complete £3 3 0

W. R. LOFTUS Ltd., 18, Tottenham Court Road, London, W.

B 2

Saccharometers repaired and adjusted to Government Standard—reliable accuracy guaranteed.

is lowered the saccharometer; buoyancy causes it to float and the specific gravity may be read off a scale on the stem. Its potential for use in brewing was widely publicised in 1760, but it only began to be generally adopted by the industry in the final 15 years of the 18th century.

The third innovation in the brewing process was a method of controlling temperature during fermentation; in part, its importance was that it would allow brewing to take place throughout the summer. The new gadget, first proposed in 1791 and in everyday use by the start of the 19th century, was an attemperator, a coil of copper piping inserted into the fermentation tun through which cooling water could flow. Along with the thermometer and the saccharometer, it gave much greater control over the still poorly understood brewing process.

Brewhouses in the townscape

These mechanical and scientific advances allowed the London porter breweries to continue increasing production. The brewhouses themselves grew upwards and – where land ownership made it possible – outwards. Gravity was a less important factor in brewery design after the introduction of the steam engine, and the great brewhouses were often half a dozen or more storeys in height by the end of the 18th century. Their blank walls and louvres were a substantial presence in the London townscape; it was not only their towering height but the vast floor areas of the new beer factories that impressed: 'The immensity of the Brewery astonished me' as an awestruck observer said of Southwark's Anchor Brewery in 1773.[18]

The top five London porter breweries were huge structures, all producing well over 100,000 barrels by 1799; indeed, the Whitbread Brewery's output was over 200,000 barrels. The core of the Chiswell Street brewery – which covered six acres by the end of the 19th century – remains immediately north-east of the Barbican estate, including the 160ft-long Porter Tun Room, built as the Great Storehouse in 1774. Second to Whitbread's in output came Meux's (by then Meux Reid's) Griffin Brewery, which stood at what is now the western end of Clerkenwell Road, near

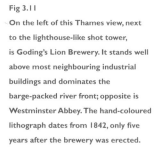

Fig 3.11
On the left of this Thames view, next to the lighthouse-like shot tower, is Goding's Lion Brewery. It stands well above most neighbouring industrial buildings and dominates the barge-packed river front; opposite is Westminster Abbey. The hand-coloured lithograph dates from 1842, only five years after the brewery was erected.

Fig 3.12
The massive vats 'in which you would have to drag carefully for the body of an elephant' at the 'Town of Malt and Hops', otherwise the Barclay, Perkins Anchor Brewery, Southwark. They were the subject of one of 180 engravings by the French artist Paul Gustave Doré (1832–83) carried out between 1869 and 1872 for inclusion in *London: A Pilgrimage* (1872), a classic piece of social comment written by journalist and playwright Blanchard Jerrold.

Gray's Inn. The completely decoration-free seven-bay main building faced north and included a row of double-height louvre openings in its six storeys, topped by a hoist serving the central bay. Inside were huge vats installed by Richard Meux, not only to age the porter but to emphasise the ever-growing success of his undertaking. In 1790 200 people celebrated Meux's new 60ft-diameter vat by dining within it; at nearly 3,000sq ft in area, this seems reasonable, although the brewery also claimed that another 200 souls squeezed inside to drink to its future. Five years later Meux unveiled his final flourish, a vat double the size with a capacity of 20,000 barrels.[19]

Nothing remains either of the Griffin Brewery or the third largest porter brewer, Barclay, Perkins, whose Anchor Brewery was located east of Southwark Bridge on a long, relatively narrow site stretching south from what is now Park Street. Although 100 people are said to have dined in a vat at the Anchor around 1773, Barclay, Perkins competed on overall volume rather than individual vat size, and owned 52 vats totalling 47,400 barrels capacity by 1784 (Fig 3.12). This was a more flexible approach, allowing for different aging times and giving a constant flow of mature porter. In contrast to the loss of these two sites, there are substantial buildings of varying ages remaining at the fourth and fifth largest porter brewers of 1799, Combe's Wood Yard Brewery (*see* Figs 3.35, 3.36 and 5.37)(on what is now Shelton Street in Covent Garden), and Truman's Black Eagle Brewery (*see* Fig 4.42) on Brick Lane in Spitalfields.

A greater deterrent to the vat size war was the disastrous beer flood of 17 October 1814 at the Horse Shoe Brewery (Fig 3.13, *see also* Fig 3.1), its site off Tottenham Court Road, just north of Centre Point, now taken up by the Dominion Theatre. Richard Meux's son Henry Meux moved to the Horse Shoe in 1809 and immediately expanded the premises, raising porter production significantly. It was on the tourist trail by 1812 when the Scottish novelist Mary Brunton (1778–1818) visited; she noted a vat 70ft in diameter containing 18,000 barrels of porter, one of over 70 in the store. The iron hoops restraining the cask weighed 80tons.[20] It was the failure of one such iron hoop that caused the beer flood, which emanated not from

Fig 3.13
A postcard view of Meux's Horse Shoe Brewery; the card was posted in 1910, just over a decade before the brewery closed. Note the ornate ironwork marking the gateway, and the contrast between the smart shopping streets of central London and the curiously antiquated structures overlooking the cramped brewery yard.

New Oxford Street, London.

the Horse Shoe's largest vat, but a 22ft-high vat filled with 3,555 barrels. Well over a million pints of dark liquid surged out, crashing through the brewery's back wall and flooding nearby streets and cellars. Eight people died, drowned by the black wave, and the earthquake-like devastation drew crowds of onlookers.[21] The brewery itself eventually continued in production, closing only in 1921 and being demolished the following year, when *The Daily Telegraph* described the 'dirty brick buildings' as 'frankly hideous'.[22]

By the early 19th century the brewhouses had become one of the great sights of the capital, a must-see item particularly for the well-connected foreign tourist. They were generally surprised at the silence, even solitude of the brewhouse itself, in contrast with the bustle of men and dray horses in the yard. The steam engines ran fairly quietly, and needed little attention. In addition, as *The Illustrated London News* reported in 1847, a visitor to Barclay, Perkins would hardly fail to be impressed by 'the potentiality of growing rich beyond the dream of avarice'.[23] Indeed the possibility of cashing in on the porter boom may have been responsible for the construction of the gargantuan but fairly short-lived Thorne's Westminster Brewery (Fig 3.14) on Horseferry Road in 1831, just at the point when the popularity of porter began to decline.

The first brewers' architects

Of course, breweries were also beginning to make their mark on the townscape away from the capital. The buildings themselves were smaller than their London counterparts, but their long-term occupation of central locations was to have a lasting impact on the development of Britain's towns and cities.[24] Provincial firms began to brew porter from around 1780 and large commercial breweries began to appear from the 1790s as the population density increased enough to make a mass market viable. Some of these new or enlarged breweries were designed with the involvement of architects, but as in London, many more were erected to the plans of the brewers themselves, their engineers and surveyors, and local builders. Southwark's Anchor appears to have been first brewery to employ a surveyor, Richard Summersell, from around the 1750s; he was succeeded, probably during the 1770s, by George Gwilt (1746–1807).

Fig 3.15

This shot of Collins's Brewery, beside the Thames in Richmond, was taken by the artist Calvert Richard Jones (1802–77) around 1844 and is the earliest known photographic image of an English industrial brewery. Collins's Brewery had been rebuilt about 1835, and most of its buildings (now listed grade II) survive as the Slug & Lettuce pub on Water Lane.

Fig 3.16
The yard at Cox & White's Hockley
Brewery seen on a trade card dating
from around 1840; the black clouds
emanating from the tall chimney
probably indicate that it was steam
powered. Hockley Brewery was taken
over by Showell's Brewery in 1890.

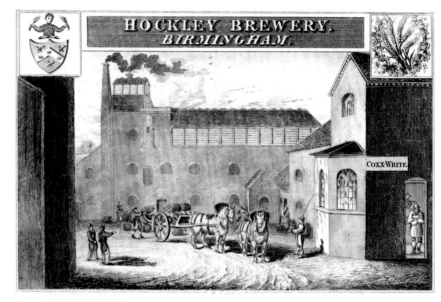

Fig 3.17 (right)
Johnson's Tunstall Brewery in
Stoke-on-Trent shown on an
earthenware jug manufactured by the
local Clayhills Pottery of Elsmore &
Forster during the mid-19th century.
The jug is unusual for a brewery
advertising piece in that it shows the
brewery in great detail; normally
brewers were rather more coy about
their premises.

Fig 3.18 (below)
A view into the yard of Morrell's Lion
Brewery in Oxford, taken around 1900
by the well known local professional
photographer Henry Taunt (1842–1922).
He was particularly interested in
recording industrial processes, and took
a series of photographs at Morrell's.

Both in London and away from the capital, architects were involved with brewery design from the late 18th century. The only surviving provincial Georgian common brewhouse, indeed a particularly elegant example (and still brewing), is the North Brink Brewery in Wisbech, Cambridgeshire, on the River Nene. Merchant and alehouse owner Denis Herbert and a partner bought the Wisbech quayside site in 1786. A few years earlier Herbert had built a fine mansion house further south in Bedfordshire at Biggleswade; it stood on one of the town's wharfs but was lost in the great fire of 1783.[25] Herbert converted the existing Wisbech premises to a brewhouse – the present brewery – before selling it on as a going concern in late 1795. Thus it appears, like many brewers-cum-businessmen of the time, he had an interest in architecture, but his involvement in the design of what is now Elgood's Brewery is unknown.

Other turn-of-the-century brewhouse architects include John Soane, who designed the brewhouse built for W B Simonds of Reading in 1789 (*see* Fig 6.7); George Saunders, who rebuilt the Stag Brewery in Pimlico from 1796 to 1807; and William Teanby, who designed Cobb's Brewery in Margate between 1807 and 1808 (Fig 3.20). The early 19th century was the era of the first specialist industrial

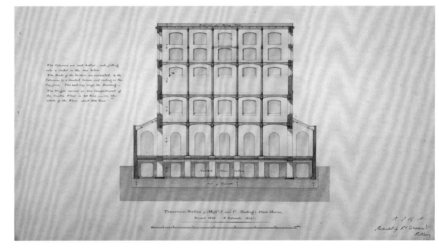

Fig 3.19
Francis Edwards's 1836 design for part of Goding's Lion Brewery in London shows a framework made up of hollow, cast-iron columns, which fit into one another, and the connecting girders, which slot into grooves on the columns. At 18ft 3in, the top floor was the tallest of the four.

Fig 3.20
A view of Cobb's Brewery in Margate taken by architectural photographer Eric de Maré in 1956. The unusual circular structure, often described as a brewhouse, is more likely to have been a horse-wheel house; the original brewhouse was a rectangular block with a higher wing to either side. Although listed, Cobb's was demolished in 1971 as part of the local corporation's development plan.

architects, notably Francis Edwards (1784–1857), whose best-known work is Goding's Lion Brewery in Lambeth (1836–7; *see* Fig 3.11), topped by a Coade stone lion regally surveying the Thames (*see* Figs 9.7 and 9.8); it was demolished in 1949 to make way for the Festival Hall.

Brewing in the Royal Navy

The Royal Navy's brewhouses remained amongst the largest provincial breweries until towards the end of the 18th century, and several well-known architects became involved in their design. A naval brewhouse had been built in London at the East Smithfield yard, east of the Tower of London, by 1683. Its success then encouraged the Victualling Office to administer other breweries directly, rather than relying on contract brewers, and the new brewery erected at the Deptford yard in 1792 is likely to have been one of the biggest breweries in the capital.[26]

Away from London, Henry Player's Weevil Brewery (Fig 3.21) at Gosport in Hampshire supplied beer to the Navy from the late 17th century. By 1716 the brewery complex comprised 10 separate buildings, including the 128ft-long brewhouse, a cooperage, stables and beer store. In 1751 the Admiralty bought the Weevil estate and the brewery came under the control of the Victualling Board, which built a new brewhouse in 1757. Production from the pair of brewhouses was soon found to be inadequate for the Navy's needs, and another new brewhouse, an impressive state-of-the-art design by the architect Samuel Wyatt, was put up between 1782 and 1783. Equipment inside the colonnaded building, which measured 214ft by 80ft, included two coppers and a 60-quarter mash tun; water was supplied from a horse engine pumphouse (*see* Figs 6.9 and 6.10) designed by the

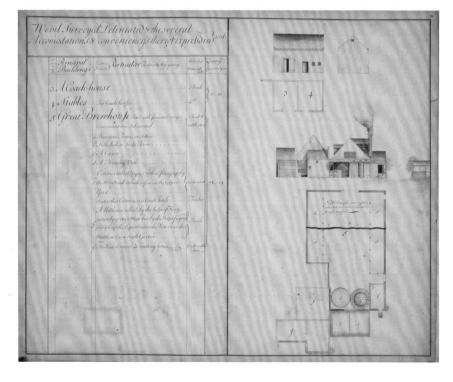

Fig 3.21
The Weevil Brewhouse at Gosport, shown on a 1716 plan and elevation. The brick and rubble stone brewhouse was 128ft long and, as detailed in the list on the left-hand page, was 'fitted with furniture very convenient and substantial', including a copper and mash tun located side by side. The drawing formed part of the collection of the antiquary and topographer Richard Gough (1735–1809).

engineer John Smeaton in 1788. After these alterations, the Weevil could produce up to 300 barrels a day at its maximum, about the same as a medium-sized porter brewery.

The Weevil, known as the Royal Clarence Yard from 1828, was extensively rebuilt from 1828 to 1832 to the designs of George Ledwell Taylor, Civil Architect to the Navy. Wyatt's brewhouse continued in use until 1831 and stood until bombing destroyed it in the Second World War. However, its foundations, and those of Smeaton's pumphouse, survived and were excavated in 2007 prior to residential development of the site. This archaeological study told us much about the appearance and content of the brewhouses, but fortunately the grandest victualling yard of them all, the monumental Royal William Yard at Stonehouse in Plymouth, is still intact, although redeveloped after its closure in 1992.[27]

The Royal William Yard was a huge food-processing centre, built between 1825 and 1833 and designed by John Rennie junior; it is a unique example of early 19th-century industrial state planning on a vast scale (Fig 3.22). The massive stone-built brewhouse dates from 1830 and 1831, but as the Admiralty discontinued the beer ration in 1831 – before the building was complete – it remained unused for many years. Unlike in part of the bakery, which stands across the basin (now marina), fireproof construction – stone floors with iron columns and beams – was not used for the brewhouse, which is now in commercial usage. Although the naval brewhouses were but another byway in the architectural evolution of the English brewery, the very existence of the beer ration meant profitable business, especially for provincial brewers like Cobb's of Margate, allowing them to build larger breweries than they could have done without naval brewing contracts.

Fig 3.22
Looking north across the grade I listed brewhouse at the Royal William Yard, Plymouth in 1994, two years after its closure. The brewhouse was restored at a cost of £9 million between 2005 and 2006 by Urban Splash with Ferguson Mann Architects; the award-winning conversion includes apartments and mixed commercial uses.

After the 1830 Beer Act

By 1800, Britain's common brewers were producing almost four million barrels of strong ale every year, and their output hovered around that figure throughout the first three decades of the 19th century.[28] The number of domestic brewers continued to decline, and gin once again became popular, although not as crazily fashionable as it had been during the early 18th century. Political dislike of powerful common brewers and their tied estates, combined with a wish to reduce the number of gin shops, resulted in Parliament passing the Beer Act in 1830. It was intended to liberalise the beer trade by allowing any ratepayer to sell beer in exchange for an annual excise fee of two guineas. Beerhouses by the thousand – which could, but need not, brew their own beer – opened almost immediately, and by the end of the year 24,342 new beer sellers had paid their dues.[29]

Curiously, despite the huge number of extra alcohol outlets, the new Act did little to diminish the power of the major brewers. In general, those beerhouses which brewed their own beer offered customers a product markedly inferior to that of the common brewers; often their brewing was unscientific, they had little space for storage, and they could hardly afford the utensils required. Only in the Midlands and the North, where publican-brewers were already more common, did the beerhouses take root.[30] Ultimately of more significance than the Beer Act to the major brewers was the abolition of beer duty in 1830, although the tax on malt and hops remained; the tax on hops was removed completely in 1863.

Finally in 1880 the malt tax was repealed and what came to be known as the 'free mash tun' system brought in, giving brewers much greater scope in their choice of materials used to brew beer, which was then taxed at an initial rate of 6s 3d per standard gravity barrel. This not only encouraged experimentation in the

Fig 3.23
A late 19th-century view of Alfred Eadon's Plant Brewery in Doncaster, where louvre ventilation takes up nearly half the main facade. The brewery was sold to Warwicks & Richardsons of Newark in 1897. The building is extant, but almost unrecognisable now, as windows have replaced the openings.

Fig 3.24
The Godwin Brothers' Belmont
Brewery in Swindon's Old Town, a nice
example of a tower brewery, probably
seen during the early 1920s. It was
bought by Wadworth's in 1938 and later
sold on to Usher's, but although the
archway has been lost, the tower and
its ornate turret are extant and still
clearly recognisable.

brewhouse but emphasised the importance of science in the brewing process, as the saccharometer was crucial to the accurate measurement of beer's fermentable sugar, and hence strength.

Total UK annual beer production topped 30 million standard barrels during the late 1870s, and after a slight dip during the 1880s, continued at well over 30 million barrels until 1914, while annual personal consumption – having peaked at just over 265 pints per head in the late 1870s – rose again to nearly 250 pints per head in the late 1890s.[31] With the smaller brewers in decline, these continued good trading conditions encouraged the growth of larger firms. The number of breweries with an annual production of over 50,000 barrels grew from just over 50 during the early 1870s to top 100 in the late 1890s and reach 142 in 1914.[32] The consequence was a spate of new brewery building, expansion and alteration, reaching a peak in the 1880s, along with advances in production plant. Many of these breweries occupied completely integrated sites, where all the processes took place in an area focused on the brewhouse – often a tower – together with maltings, fermenting rooms, cooperages, stables, offices, laboratory and a brewery tap or pub.

The changing quarter

A quarter was originally a measure of malt volume. Towards the end of the 19th century this was gradually replaced by a weight equivalent, fixed at 336lb malt. A brewery's size was based on its mashing capacity, that is the amount of malt which could be mashed in one day, thus a brewery could be briefly described as a '90-quarter brewery' and suchlike. In the late 19th century it was assumed that one quarter of malt would produce four 36-gallon barrels of beer at standard original gravity (1055); so, as a rough rule of thumb, we can say that one quarter is equivalent to brewing about 150 gallons. Thus a 150-quarter plant could produce 600 barrels or about 20,000 gallons per day. Annual brewing capacity was usually calculated on the basis of five working days per week in a 50-week year; hence each quarter capacity gives an annual production of 1,000 barrels. A common brewer was often defined as one having an annual output of over 1,000 barrels, although capacity of around 10 quarters upward would be a more commercial scale; the massive industrial breweries of the late 19th century were over 150 quarters.

Fig 3.25
Rye Pottery currently occupies what was probably the brewhouse of the former Strand Brewery in Rye, a grade II listed building. Cooling and fermenting would take place in the long, well-ventilated section to the right, which bears datestones 'LM 1802' (referring to Lewis Meryon, from the local brewing family of Huguenot descent) and 'MH 1840', probably connected with the historian William Holloway, who took on the brewery before 1845.

Fig 3.26 (right)
A postcard view showing the splendid tower of Bentley's Old Brewery in Rotherham, which brewed until taken over in 1956; demolition followed in 1965. Only two street names, The Maltings and Maltkiln Street (off Alma Road), remain to remind us of the brewery and its extensive maltings nearby.

Fig 3.27 (below)
Staff outside Wethered's Marlow Brewery during the mid-19th century. They are standing outside the original brewhouse, built during the late 18th century and replaced by the tower (1903–5), which survived the brewery's closure in 1992 and was converted to apartments.

Beer and Burton

Brewing in Burton upon Trent dates back to the 11th century when the Benedictine monks of St Mary and St Modwen's Abbey brewed for their own consumption and that of their guests. Following the dissolution, local licensed victuallers took on production, and by around 1620 'esteemed' Burton beers could be bought in London, brewed from the town's hard water, rich in calcium sulphate.[33] The 18th century saw Burton become an important distribution centre for a wide range of goods; navigation on the Trent was improved and in 1777 the Trent and Mersey Canal opened. This increased market for Burton beers encouraged businessmen to invest in larger brewing premises and equipment, and some of the biggest breweries in Britain's history – Worthington, Allsopp and Bass – originated in this period. At least 40 per cent of their output was exported to the Baltic states, but the collapse of this market in the early 19th century brought hard times to the town; several smaller breweries closed.

Salvation came in the form of India Pale Ale (IPA), which Allsopp's first exported to India in 1823.[34] Burton's water was ideally suited to the production of this pale, hoppy, long-keeping beer, which became popular at home after the 1830 Beer Act resulted in a huge increase in the number of beer retailers. The arrival of the railway in Burton in 1839 also provided a significant boost to sales. The town's breweries expanded and were joined by new arrivals, from London and the regions, during a period of massive growth in the four decades following 1840. By 1888 – when the Prince of Wales visited Burton – the town was home to 32 brewers, and the annual output of their breweries topped three million barrels.

At this point the town had been completely overtaken by the brewing industry (Fig 3.28). Its breweries, maltings and stores could be found throughout the town,

Fig 3.28

A pre-First World War postcard view of Burton upon Trent, looking west over Stapenhill Cemetery and the river to the town. Breweries and their smoking chimneys dominate the scene. On the far right is the Trent Bridge, completed in 1864, and to the far left the Bass Old Brewery water tower (1866).

and were connected by a system of railways that ran through the streets. Over 8,000 people, almost one in five of the population, worked in the industry. Burton was the ultimate brewing town of the Victorian age.[35] Its prosperity, however, peaked around the turn of the 19th century, and the industry's buildings, which we shall look at in detail later (*see* chapter 7), have since suffered many losses.

Other prominent, although rather smaller, brewing towns known for their hard water and pale ales were Alton in Hampshire, where two breweries occupied the same street (*see* Figs 4.50 and 4.51); Tadcaster in North Yorkshire, where (albeit only from 1884 to 1899) there were four breweries, and three still remain (Fig 3.29); Wrexham, 'the Burton of Wales'; and the tiny village of Duddingston (Fig 3.30) in the Craigmillar area of Edinburgh, where seven breweries opened between 1887 and 1901. In contrast, Great Yarmouth's water was ideal for producing mild, the sweet, salty Yarmouth Ale that became popular in London from the 1830s; Lacon's was the town's best known brewery (*see* Fig 4.17).[36] However, as brewers adopted a more scientific approach in the late 19th century, they learnt how to treat their local water to provide the desired mineral content. So, to produce pale ale, the water could be 'Burtonised'. Although scientific brewing had many benefits, this placeless replication of local conditions was a forebear of 20th-century brewery mergers, the loss of beer's intimate connection with the landscape or *terroir*.

Fig 3.29

Tadcaster from the air, photographed in June 1926. Looking north-eastward, in the centre we see John Smith's Brewery with its two tall stacks; directly behind is the smaller chimney of Samuel Smith's Old Brewery. Out of view are the Tower Brewery, about a quarter mile north-west, and the site of the short-lived Victoria Brewery, just north of John Smith's.

The science of brewing

Brewing had become a more exact craft over the years following the coming of
industrial-scale breweries in the 18th century. The thermometer and saccharometer
gave brewers the ability to measure rather than estimate, but the brewing process
itself was still not fully understood in the 1870s, although this did not prevent
Britain's brewers making perfectly decent beers. The first qualified chemist to be
employed by a British brewery was almost certainly Robert Warington (1807–67),
who worked for Truman, Hanbury, Buxton & Co from 1831 to 1839, and two of the
Burton brewers employed chemists as early as the mid-1840s, partly to refute
suggestions of adulterating their products. It was the French chemist and
microbiologist Louis Pasteur who finally explained the fermentation process in
terms of the lifecycle of yeast, publishing his work – some of which had been carried
out in London during 1871 – as *Études sur la Bière* in 1876; it was translated into
English three years later. Combined with E C Hansen's experiments on yeast species
at Carlsberg's brewery in Copenhagen (although not available in English until 1896),
this new knowledge led to a slow and rather variable revolution in British brewing.

Most receptive to incorporating microscopes, chemists and laboratories into the
brewery were the Burton firms, but by the late 1880s most large breweries had a
laboratory, usually within the brewhouse. An acquaintance with science eventually
became almost the norm; a brewer advertising in search of a situation in 1890 felt it
desirable to mention that he 'understands the microscope'.[37] The Laboratory Club,
formed in 1886, provided the opportunity for professional brewers and scientists to
meet and exchange views, and – after the formation of various regional groups –
led to the foundation of the Institute of Brewing (now Brewing & Distilling) in 1904.
Earlier proposals for brewing schools had been thwarted, but eventually training

courses were set up at various academic establishments, firstly in 1900 at Mason University College (later the University of Birmingham).[38]

Some brewers, however, took no part in these initiatives and simply carried on their good practice as before, producing fine beers without knowing the detailed science, but keeping up with their peers by reading the brewing trade journals and occasionally modernising their plant.[39] Part of this disdain for scientific brewing originated in the incorrect perception that scientific findings applied largely to foreign bottom-fermented lagers rather than English top-fermented ales, although lager was first produced in Britain before Queen Victoria ascended to the throne.

Britain and lager

Lager was first brewed in Britain in 1835. It was produced, albeit briefly, by the Edinburgh brewer John Muir, using a strain of yeast sent to him as a gift by a German brewer. Although lager proved successful in the city, Muir was unable to keep the yeast strain pure and soon ceased to brew. As lager rose in popularity in Europe, the name 'Bavarian' became attached to several breweries beyond Germany, which hoped to capitalise on the fashion for the new, bright beer. It was 1868 before lager – 'Vienna beer' – went on sale in London, and imported lager continued to be enjoyed by a growing audience over the next decade or so. Although contemporary commentators suggested lager would begin to threaten the dominance of traditional ales, it was to be almost a century before this transpired.

The first British brewery to incorporate the word 'Bavarian' into its name as a sales ploy was the Anglo-Bavarian Brewery (Fig 3.31) of Shepton Mallet in Somerset, which was founded in 1870 and the following year took over the splendid premises built in 1864 for the Shepton Mallet Pale Ale Brewery. Although the Anglo-Bavarian brewed using an unusual process, one designed to replicate German-style beers without the need for extended storage, it produced only the standard range of English ales; it never brewed lager. The first English brewers of

Fig 3.31
The Anglo-Bavarian Brewery in Shepton Mallet around the turn of the century, photographed for the Francis Frith & Co studio. The grade II* listed brewery was the first in Somerset to be lit by electricity, in 1889. The building has been used as a warehouse since the Second World War; redevelopment plans have been discussed but nothing had transpired at time of writing.

lager, in 1877, were Joseph Spink & Sons of Bradford's Brownroyd Brewery, but it was a short-lived experiment. Only slightly more successful was William Younger at the Holyrood Brewery, Edinburgh, in 1879, who persisted with lager for a few years before giving up, possibly defeated by the increasing popularity of the imported product.

Britain's first lager-only brewer appears to have been the Bayerische Lager Beer Brewery, formed in 1881 and based at the former Eltham Brewery (rebuilt in 1872 by the architect Arthur Kinder) near Greenwich. Their intention was to exploit the London market, but it is not certain they ever brewed any lager, and by the late 1880s the venture had failed. Other brewers, including the St Anne's Well Brewery, Exeter in 1881, tried their hands, but the first to erect a brewery specifically to brew lager was the Austro-Bavarian Lager Beer Brewery (Fig 3.32), located just off Tottenham High Road in north London. The impressive-looking brewery (at least in its advertising material) opened in 1881 and produced at least four beers, including Tottenham Lager, but after reforming as the Tottenham Lager Beer Brewery in 1886, the company was liquidated in 1895.[40]

The second purpose-built lager brewery was in Wrexham, put up between 1882 and 1883 for the Wrexham Lager Beer Company, which was relaunched during the 1890s; it continued brewing, under several changes of ownership, until closing in 2000. Austrian engineers designed the brewery, basing it on one of their previous

Fig 3.32

The Austro-Bavarian Lager Beer Brewery, shown in one of its advertising leaflets dating from 1884. Note the ice factory to the left of the boilerhouse and chimney. An imperial pint bottle of their Tottenham Lager would cost 3s 6d delivered to your door in London.

Fig 3.33
Massive lager vats under construction at Allsopp's in Burton around 1905. The company started to brew lager at their Old Brewery in 1899, using American plant that could produce up to 60,000 barrels annually. However, sales were never more than 40,000 barrels a year, and in 1921 the plant was moved to Arrol's Alloa Brewery.

plans, and the works were overseen by the general manager, Stanislav Fenzl. Novel features included the lager cellars containing 200 huge casks, each capable of holding 1,446 gallons, and the associated ice machine.[41] Also purpose-built, by architects Charles Johnson & Sons in 1891, was the English Lager Beer Brewery in the Bath suburb of Batheaston, but it only lasted two years. J & R Tennent's Wellpark Brewery in Glasgow produced lager from 1885, and built two completely separate lager breweries, the first opening in 1891 and brewing until 1906, when the second took its place. Back in England, Allsopp's of Burton installed a 60,000-barrel lager plant (Fig 3.33) in part of their disused premises during 1897, around the time their neighbours Ind Coope began brewing 'Burgomaster' lager.[42]

Overall, lager fared better in Scotland and Wales than in England (Fig 3.34).
A handful of English brewers made sporadic attempts to brew and sell lager up to
the Second World War, but there was little impact on the buildings of the industry,
as most lager brewing was carried out in older premises with new plant. Such a case
was the Moss Side Brewery in Manchester, which produced its Red Tower Lager
from the 1920s onward. When German-built equipment was installed in 1933 it
became known as the Red Tower Lager Brewery, and – as the Royal Brewery, much
redeveloped from the 1960s onward – still brews Heineken lager. Indeed the 1960s
saw the start of a dramatic rise in the popularity of lager throughout Britain,
resulting in the construction of several giant lager breweries, the most architecturally
interesting being the Carlsberg Brewery (1971–3) in Northampton (*see* Fig 4.67).

The late 19th-century building boom

While brewing science progressed during the latter part of the 19th century, the
growing population, many living in towns and cities, provided a ready and profitable
market. Annual per capita consumption of beer in England and Wales, having hit
over 40 gallons (less than a pint a day) in the late 1870s, remained at over
33 gallons for the remainder of the century, while production peaked in the early
1900s.[43] We can see from the brewing licence returns, which record brewers and
their annual beer production, that the number of significant commercial brewers
(producing over 10,000 barrels annually) rose from 360 in 1869 to a maximum of
627 in 1899, before declining to 530 by 1911. But the real story here concerns the
major brewing firms, those producing over 50,000 barrels per annum, who came
to dominate the industry at the expense of the dwindling number of low-output
common brewers and publican brewers. In the early 1870s an average of 57 major
brewers were licensed per year; by the early 1890s the number was 93, and it
reached 135 in the period from 1910 to 1914.[44] So around the turn of the century,
in terms of buildings, these figures suggest there were over 100 major brewing
sites and more than 500 lesser but still large-scale breweries. Apart from their
sheer number, their often central urban location has made them of additional
townscape significance.

For more detail on the construction of these new and expanded breweries,
we can turn to contemporary sources such as brewing trade journals and the *Noted*

Breweries of Great Britain and Ireland, a four-volume record of journalist Alfred Barnard's odyssey around 118 breweries throughout the British Isles during 1889 to 1891.[45] This evidence indicates a gentle rise in the amount of brewery building work taking place during the 1870s, followed by a construction boom during the 1880s, when an average of over 20 major works were completed annually, and peaking in 1885 with 34 completions. Activity dipped in the early 1890s but rose again around the turn of the century. These works were generally carried out on the premises of the medium to large industrial brewers, often to plans drawn up by one of the 25 or

Fig 3.35
Looking north along Langley Street, in the midst of Combe's Wood Yard Brewery in Covent Garden; the photograph was taken by Alfred Bool (1844–1926) and John Bool (1850–1933), probably during the 1870s or 1880s. Apart from the bridge connecting the brewhouse with the vat rooms, most of the buildings shown are still extant.

more specialist brewers' architects and engineering practices which sprang up to meet this demand towards the end of the 19th century.[46]

The new buildings tended to be more opulent than their starkly functional predecessors, incorporating lavish ironwork, rich decoration and corporate symbolism. By the late 1880s they were being referred to as 'ornamental breweries' and Barnard, during his legendary brewery tours, was surprised to find one (Armstrong's Star Brewery, Cambridge) to which the label could not be applied, 'destitute as it is of that ornate style which distinguishes the modern brewery'.[47] The appearance of the brewery was fast becoming an integral part of the brewer's brand.

Fig 3.36 (right)
Combe's Wood Yard Brewery on a Goad Fire Insurance Plan of 1888. It extended over four blocks, the northernmost containing the stables and ice house, linked by a bridge to the cooling and fermenting rooms immediately south; the brewhouse and vat rooms were on either side of Langley Street. The plan is so detailed that individual coppers are shown in the brewhouse.

Fig 3.37 (below)
Coopers at work in the depths of a London brewery about 1900. The shot was taken by keen amateur photographer Edgar Tarry Adams (1852–1926), owner of the Halstead Brewery in Essex.

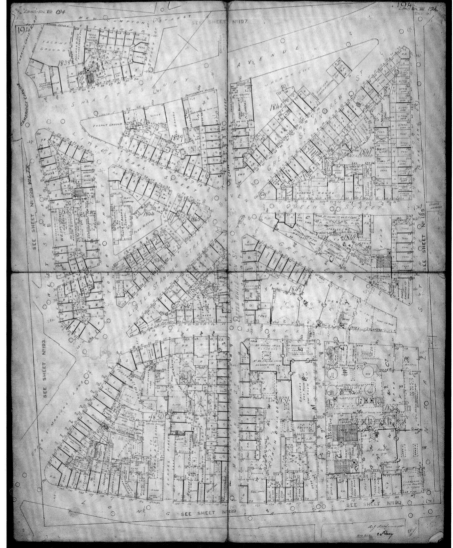

Fig 3.38 (above)
Ind Coope's Star Brewery in Romford,
seen in 1908 by photographers from
Francis Frith & Co. Note the extensive
railway sidings, which connected to the
main line via a tunnel, and the malt
tower and elevators to the right,
between the chimneys.

Fig 3.39 (right)
From 1912 to 1913 Allsopp's bought up
two breweries in Aberdare, the Rock
Brewery and the Black Lion Brewery,
the combination becoming known
as Aberdare Valley Breweries.
The photograph, probably taken around
1913, shows all the firm's drays (some
are marked Black Lion) in front of the
Rock (renamed Town) Brewery.

Fig 3.40 (above)
Workers pose outside (and on the hoist platforms of) a classic small tower brewery, Attlee's Tooting Brewery, in a shot taken soon after 1900. Attlee's bought their hops from Southwark hop merchants Arthur Morris & Co, sending their own drays to collect supplies from Borough.

Fig 3.41 (above right)
The vaulted cellars at Barclay, Perkins Anchor Brewery, Southwark photographed for the brewery in 1898 by Adolphe Boucher (1868–1937), principal assistant at Bedford Lemere & Co. In the mid-19th century Barclay, Perkins had a stock of 60,000–70,000 casks.

Fig 3.42 (right)
Barley, barrels and hops decorate the vehicle archway leading from Hampstead High Street to the former Hampstead Brewery (now flats) at the rear. Although converted, the unlisted four-to-five storey, yellow stock-brick brewery building retains its industrial feel, enhanced by the presence of an ornamental well head in the yard.

Fig 3.43
Behind the gateway on the north side of London's Whitechapel Road lay Mann, Crossman & Paulin's Albion Brewery. After closure in 1979 much of the site was cleared for a supermarket, but the head brewer's house (left), stores and fermenting rooms were converted to offices and flats between 1993 and 1994. Most intriguing is the 1860s fermenting house at the rear, remodelled in the early years of the 20th century when the massive carved pediment was added; the sculptor is unknown.

Brewers' Exhibitions

Robert Dale, a serial organiser of trade fairs, seized upon the opportunity presented by the burgeoning market in brewing equipment to instigate the annual Brewers' Exhibitions, the first of which took place in October 1879 and drew around 105,000 visitors to the Agricultural Hall in Islington. The following year there were about 300 exhibitors, including not only brewers and manufacturers of brewing kit but makers of a huge variety of items used by maltsters, distillers, wine merchants and licensed victuallers. There were bottle stoppers and barrel tilters, malt roasters and brewing maize, and much, much more, all detailed in a special supplement to the *Brewers' Journal*. Drinks of all kinds were freely on offer, and 'this circumstance alone will not render the exhibition less generally popular' as *The Globe* pointed out. Reviewing the 1881 event, possibly after a tipple or two, *The Daily Telegraph* gushed 'The art and mystery of brewing has reached its highest point of perfection in Great Britain.'[48] During the 1880s the exhibitions were well supported by the brewers – it was reported that two-thirds of the UK's brewers turned out for the 1882 show – although there was persistent grumbling about the unprofitable sightseeing public who were only there for the beer (and the wine, spirits and liqueurs).[49]

Perhaps to placate the brewers, the 1885 programme included a Brewers' Congress, intended as a day of learned papers concerning the brewing trade. It was ill organised and poorly attended, but the initiative was repeated, with no great success, at several more exhibitions during the late 1880s. Rather better received was a competitive display of beers, first held in 1886 and then annually from 1888 until 1914, for which medals were awarded in various classes (Figs 3.44 and 3.45).[50]

By 1890 feeling in much of the trade had taken against the annual show, with its large number of visitors and exhibitors not directly relevant to brewers. A less frequent exhibition was proposed, but the organisers were uncooperative, and in 1895 about 30 firms – some brewers' engineers amongst them – who had supported the exhibition for many years declined to participate. Instead they attempted to organise their own show with the backing of the Brewers' Company and the Country Brewers' Society, which acted for provincial brewers.[51] The outcome was a series of smaller exhibitions held from the mid-1890s onward in cities including Leeds (Fig 3.46), Birmingham, Manchester and Newcastle upon Tyne. The *Brewers' Journal*, clearly worried by temperance crusaders, damned the London exhibition of 1896 as 'little better than a trade carnival' which would 'bring discredit and ridicule on the trade'.[52] This seems rather a harsh verdict; although the shows always involved imbibing the product, they must have done much to educate the drinking public.

Fig 3.44 (right)
Gillman and Spencer of Rotherhithe, suppliers of brewers' requisites, sponsored the early beer competitions at the Brewers' Exhibition. This medal, undated on its obverse, was awarded at the 1888 show.

Fig 3.45 (far right)
Reverse of the medal awarded to Drybrough's of Edinburgh in the beer competition at the 1888 Brewers' Exhibition; Drybrough's won a gold medal when the competition was first staged in 1886.

Fig 3.46 (right)
Obverse of a medal prepared for the beer competition at one of the smaller brewers' shows at the Coliseum Theatre, Leeds in 1896. The local press delighted in mocking the quantity of free drink available.

Fig 3.47 (far right)
Brewers also displayed their wares at major international exhibitions, such as the Paris Exposition of 1878, where Ballingall & Son of Dundee's Park Brewery were awarded this medal (reverse shown).

Fig 3.48
A ceramic version of the gold medal
won by Henry Mitchell & Co of
Smethwick at the 1889 Paris Exposition
on display at the Queens Arms in
Birmingham. The right-hand figure on
the obverse (left) is seated atop the
Eiffel Tower, built specially for the
exhibition. The brewery had become
Mitchells & Butlers by the time the pub
was renovated in 1901.

Southwark's hop trade buildings

Some hop merchants took part in the annual brewers' shows, which coincided with the end of the hop harvest. By the late 19th century much of the hop business was carried out in London, although Worcester continued to be an important centre. Its Hopmarket, which incorporated a hotel, market and warehouses (rebuilt between 1899 and 1903, now shops and flats) remains, as do the former premises (1874) of hop merchant Sidney Myers, the pediment bearing a carved stone panel by local sculptor William Forsyth (1834–1915) showing a wonderfully detailed hop-picking scene.[53]

London's hop trading was focused on Borough High Street in Southwark, where the numerous offices, showrooms and warehouses of two groups of middlemen, hop factors and hop merchants, could be found. The hop factors acted as consultants to the growers and arranged the purchase of crops from many small producers, while hop merchants bought from the factors and sold on to brewers, or occasionally to further middlemen. Before the Second World War there were 37 hop warehouses in Southwark, but only a dozen survived, and all those remaining, for instance in Maidstone Buildings, have been converted to other uses.[54]

Curiously the grandest remnant of the trade, the Hop Exchange (1866–8; Figs 3.49 and 3.50) on Southwark Street, was one of the least commercially successful. It was the result of an ambitious scheme specifically designed to bring growers and brewers into more direct commercial association. Its backers were the Hop and Malt Exchange and Warehouse Company, whose in-house architect R H Moore was responsible for the design, an open trading hall surrounded by galleries of showrooms and offices on four levels. The balconies, balustrades and outer gates drip with hop-related decoration, and the pediment above the entrance encloses a farm scene depicting hops and barley. However, few takers were found for the offices, and the proposed hop market collapsed after less than two years; all parties involved in the hop business preferred the traditional way of trading.[55] The building itself was badly damaged by fire in 1920, losing its original iron and glass roof as well as its two top storeys.

Fig 3.49

The pediment above the main entrance to the Hop Exchange in Southwark. Men, women and children strip hops from the bines (centre), while hops are loaded into pockets (left) and a farmer surveys his barley (right).

Almost across the road from the Hop Exchange, but actually on Borough High Street, the former premises of hop factors W H & H Le May are distinguished by a large, high-level relief of hop pickers in Classical costume (Fig 3.51). One of the Le May family, who died in the First World War, is amongst those commemorated on the London Hop Trade War Memorial, a bronze plaque by the silversmith Omar Ramsden (1873–1939) sited on an outer wall of a nearby pub (formerly a bank).

Fig 3.50
A stereocard of Southwark's Hop Exchange towards the end of the 19th century, showing the original iron and glass roof of the exchange hall. It was produced by London photographic publishers York & Son, best known for their lantern slides.

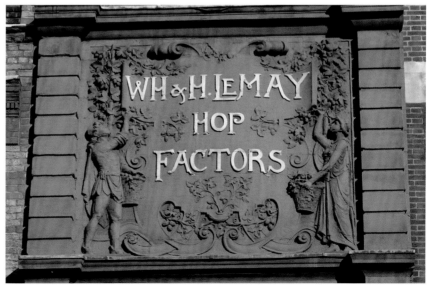

Fig 3.51
The arcadian medieval hop-picking scene on the facade of hop factors Le May's late 19th-century offices in Southwark's Borough High Street was carried out in stucco, coloured to resemble old red sandstone. The relief measures almost 10ft square.

Brewery wars

By 1890, when a Liverpool journalist wrote 'A great Brewery is come to be considered as something more profitable even than a good gold mine', industrial-scale breweries could be found in almost all UK towns and cities, and popular perception was of a trade in good health.[56] But even as breweries were constructed apace in the 1880s, brewers were facing greater difficulty in selling their beer. The 1872 Licensing Act allowed magistrates to reduce public house numbers by refusing licenses, or to insist the premises were improved before a license was granted, while temperance organisations continued their crusade against the drink trade. Brewers wanted to expand their tied estates (pubs committed to serving their own beer) to ensure sufficient outlets, but were faced with a costly rising market in licensed property. The result, particularly in London where the tied trade was strongest, was a massive scramble to buy pubs. Once secured, they were often lavishly and expensively rebuilt, to encourage custom.

The brewers rapidly became short of capital. It seemed that Dublin brewer Arthur Guinness had found the answer in 1886, when the company floated on the stock market, raising £6 million. It was not the first brewer to take this action but it was certainly the biggest and best known, and its action set off a hectic round of flotations; by the mid-1890s all the major breweries were publicly owned. Between 1886 and 1900, around 260 brewing firms went public, generally retaining the same management, although some – especially outside London – had to amalgamate to provide a reasonable basis for a share issue. When the funds flowed in, the brewers then had the capital required to modernise their breweries and of course expand and improve their tied estates.[57]

However, the speculative licensed property bubble burst in 1899 in London and a little later elsewhere, while the early years of the new century brought economic depression and declining beer consumption. As the market continued to deteriorate, there was a trend towards greater concentration in the industry; larger brewers grew at the expense of their smaller competitors with a series of amalgamations, takeovers and brewery closures.

The Great War

The First World War brought severely truncated pub opening hours, imposed by magistrates using the powers of the Intoxicating Liquor (Temporary Restrictions) Act, passed on 31 August 1914. The government considered nationalising the entire drinks industry, but instead opted for regulation, and on 10 June 1915 the Central Control Board (Liquor Traffic) was set up by Order in Council under the Defence of the Realm Act No 3 to manage the wartime drink trade. Not only did the Central Control Board (CCB) enable restrictions to be placed on the sale of alcohol, but it also tried to provide alternatives, including industrial canteens and improved pubs.[58]

In the area surrounding Carlisle (Cumbria) the CCB also tried its hand at running breweries, taking 207 pubs, 27 off-licences and 4 breweries into state control during 1916. By 1920 three of the city's breweries had been closed, leaving only the Carlisle Old Brewery (founded in 1756) in production. The CCB was abolished in 1921, and responsibility for the Carlisle and District State Management Scheme passed to the Home Office under section 16 of the 1921 Licensing Act. Although the much improved and architecturally attractive pubs resulting from the 'Carlisle Experiment' were generally popular, rationalisation and state control had

Fig 3.52

Between 1908 and 1914 the artist Frank Brangwyn (1857–1956) painted a series of mural panels, featuring porters in the London docks, for the committee luncheon room of Lloyd's Register of Shipping in Fenchurch Street; the panels were removed in the late 1960s and subsequently lost. One panel depicted beer porters, as shown in this Brangwyn cartoon.

done little for beer production; in 1922 defects were found throughout the State Management Brewery's brewing process.[59] Eventually the Carlisle Scheme was ended by the Licensing (Abolition of State Management) Act 1971, and the city's brewery was sold to the North Yorkshire firm T & R Theakston of Masham. It closed in 1987 and was converted to residential use.

Most brewers lost considerable manpower to the war effort (some were replaced by women workers, *see* Figs 4.9 and 7.25) and had to deal with shortages of raw materials; overall beer production dropped and its average strength decreased. There was a reduction of 22 per cent in the number of licences issued to brewers over the war years, as some went out of business, amalgamated or sold up. However, the survivors, most of whom had made reasonable profits during the war, were no longer worried by the prospect of nationalisation; the main problem turned out to be declining consumption.[60]

Into the 1950s

In 1914 there had still been 1,111 brewers producing over 1,000 barrels annually in the UK, along with 2,536 smaller concerns, mostly publican-brewers. By 1939 a total of only 840 brewers remained, the publican-brewers having almost completely

Fig 3.53

A lift in the foyer of Tetley's Brewery former offices (1931) in Leeds. The brewery closed in 2011 and much has been demolished, but the small art deco block was converted to a contemporary arts centre, The Tetley, which opened in late 2013.

disappeared.[61] Brewery construction was generally restricted to modernisation at existing sites, although this involved the building of some quite substantial brewhouses, for instance between 1925 and 1929 at Frederic Robinson's Unicorn Brewery in Stockport (*see* Fig 9.25), between 1936 and 1939 at Greene King's Westgate Brewery (Fig 3.54) in Bury St Edmunds, Suffolk, and most spectacularly on the Park Royal industrial estate in west London, where the Guinness Brewery (Fig 3.56) was erected during the period 1933 to 1935 by engineers Sir Alexander Gibb & Partners.

Fig 3.54
On the right is a rare example of an
inter-war brewhouse, at Greene King's
Westgate Brewery in Bury St Edmunds.
The £80,000 neo-Georgian building
(1936–9) was designed by the company's
head brewer, Colonel B E Oliver, and
consultant engineer Mark Jennings in
conjunction with plant suppliers Adlam's
of Bristol and Briggs of Burton.
The latter firm made the copper
(foreground) stationed outside the
brewery's visitor centre and museum.

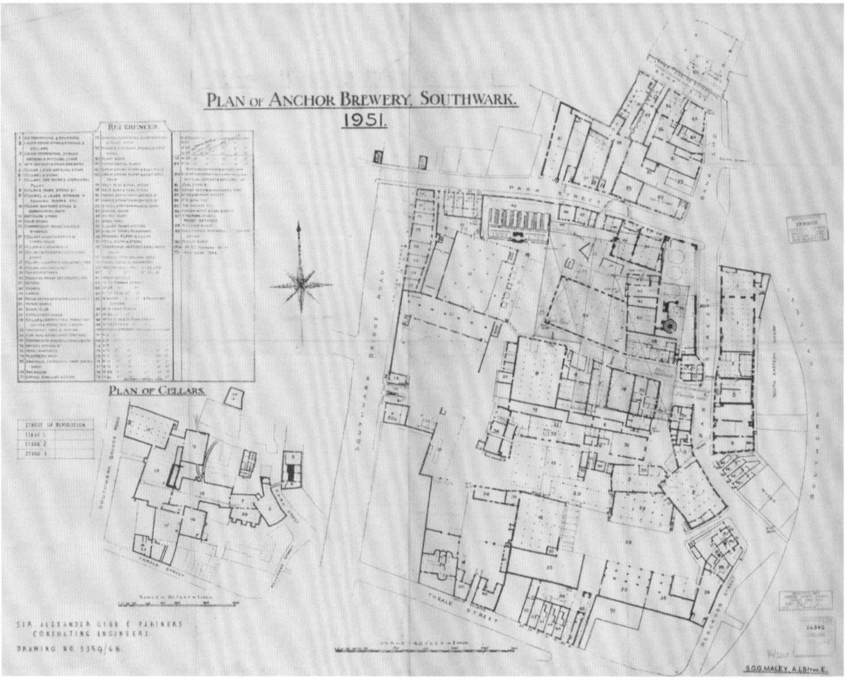

Fig 3.55
Proposed alterations to Barclay, Perkins
Anchor Brewery in Southwark by civil
engineers Sir Alexander Gibb &
Partners during the early 1950s.
The plan is valuable as it shows the
layout of the brewery buildings and even
some plant in great detail. The brewery
had its own jetty (top right), next to the
railway bridge and opposite the grade II
listed Anchor pub.

Sir Giles Gilbert Scott joined the team early in the construction process and advised on modelling the five massive blocks as well as designing their elegant brick facades.[62] Although its plant was traditional, in appearance Park Royal was certainly the most modern brewery of the interwar years, and a fine piece of 20th-century industrial architecture. This did not, however, save it from demolition in 2005 to 2006.

Further destruction of the industry's buildings occurred during the Second World War, including the loss of most of Long's Southsea Brewery – its chimney stack aside – in 1941 and Morgan's Old Brewery in Norwich the following year. By 1952, only 524 working breweries still existed, but it was during the latter part of this decade that interest in old industrial buildings began to increase as their numbers dwindled dramatically. The *Architectural Review* led the way with its 'Functional Tradition' issue of July 1957, which included a large section on breweries, maltings and oast houses, all beautifully recorded by one of the century's finest architectural photographers, Eric de Maré (1910–2002).[63] The conservation movement that grew from these small beginnings eventually ensured the survival and conversion of many redundant breweries and maltings which would otherwise have been reduced to rubble.

Another late 1950s development was the increasing popularity of 'keg', a filtered, pasteurised and carbonated long-life draught beer which mirrored the reliable taste and quality of the increasingly popular bottled beers. Keg-style beer had been pioneered by Butler's Springfield Brewery of Wolverhampton, amongst others, in the decade before the First World War. It was taken up by Watney's in the 1930s, although the first beer to be promoted as such (with keg-shaped beer mats) was Flowers Keg, produced from 1954 at the Phoenix Brewery in Luton. However, keg sales really took off from the late 1950s when Watney's began to advertise its now-notorious Red Barrel, which was then seen as a premium product.[64] The rise of keg, and with it draught beer sales, offered brewers economies of scale if production could be centralised, as transport costs were relatively cheap.

Fig 3.56
Guinness Park Royal Brewery during its demolition in 2006. The brewhouse (centre) is flanked by the fermentation house (left), and the hop and malt store, part of which has already been pulled down. Two smaller blocks contained the offices and vat house.

The rise and fall of the Big Six

Concentration within the brewing industry, by acquisition of or merger with competing firms, was fierce during the 1960s when the Big Six companies came to dominate production. Static beer consumption, the need to expand market share by acquiring new outlets, and the significance of economies of scale drove these amalgamations, the resulting groups being Allied Breweries, Bass Charrington, Courage, Scottish & Newcastle Breweries, Watney Mann and Whitbread. By the mid-1970s the major British companies accounted for 70 per cent of beer production and owned over half the country's pubs.[65] But not long after these mergers took place came talk of brewers ceasing to brew, in order to pursue profits elsewhere, through retailing and property ownership.

The withdrawal of brewers from production was accelerated by the Department of Trade and Industry's 1989 Beer Orders, intended to weaken the tie between large brewers and their public houses, and today only four big brewers remain, all subsidiaries of foreign giants: AB InBev UK, Carlsberg UK, Heineken UK and Molson Coors UK. They operate 10 major breweries, 29 fewer than the Big Six ran in 1989.[66] Some closures were of recently built breweries, such as the Courage Brewery in

Fig 3.57
Charrington's Anchor Brewery in the Mile End Road was still brewing in 1970 when this dray passed by. Note several occurrences of the brewery's Toby jug symbol, and the war memorial, visible inside the gates. The brewery closed in 1975 and only the grade II listed office building on the far right now remains.

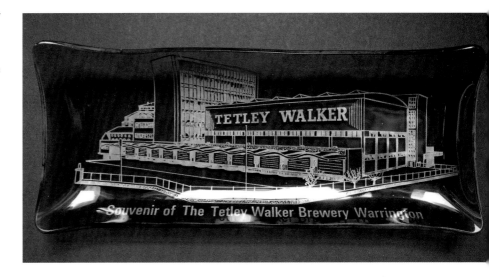

Fig 3.58

Tetley Walker's in Warrington were so proud of their fab new brewery and offices built in 1967 on Dallam Lane that they commissioned this piece of souvenir glassware. The slab block (offices) and what was probably the bottling and canning hall are in the foreground, while almost hidden at the rear is part of the original Walker's Brewery. The brewery closed in 1996 and the site was cleared.

Reading, with its glass curtain walls and striking concrete colonnade; it opened in 1979, closed in 2010 and was torn down in 2011. The 117 old-established working breweries that existed in 1986 have now been reduced to fewer than 40, many of them major regional companies, but while the big breweries declined, microbreweries or 'micros' were on the rise.

Micro revolution

From the 1970s, microbreweries – small-scale breweries initially producing a limited amount of beer – increased in number, many housed in modern premises but several in buildings of architectural interest including former industrial breweries. They took brewing back to its ancient roots as a cottage industry, generally brewing 'real ale' (cask-conditioned beer) in contrast to the keg and lager offered by the national firms. One pioneering micro was Selby Brewery in North Yorkshire, established in 1972 and the first independent brewery to be launched in Britain in half a century.[67] Litchborough Brewery in south Northamptonshire was another significant early micro; it opened in 1974 and was run by Bill Urquhart, former head brewer at Phipps of Northampton, who later took on apprentices and thus spread his knowledge of brewing through the growing micro world.[68] The Campaign for Real Ale (CAMRA), founded in 1971 to campaign for the survival of this traditional beer, was able to include five micros in its 1976 *Good Beer Guide*. The 2013 version lists a total of 1,025 breweries, the vast majority of them micros (often referred to as craft brewers) or in some cases former micros that have grown into rather larger concerns.

Around 20 micros occupy former brewing industry premises, including Phoenix Brewery in Heywood, Greater Manchester, working from 1991 in the fine Victorian buildings of the old Phoenix Brewery (which went bankrupt in 1939); Exmoor Ales, founded in 1980 at the old Hancock's Brewery (closed 1959) in Wiveliscombe, Somerset; and Lymestone Brewery, opened in 2008 at the former Bent's Brewery (closed by Bass Charrington in 1968) in Stone, Staffordshire. Other micros can currently be found in the whole range of the industry's buildings, including a water tower (Fig 3.59), stables and maltings.

Fig 3.59

Inside the Tower Brewery, a microbrewery established in 2001 and housed in the converted water tower built in the 1870s for Thomas Salt's Walsitch Maltings at Burton. The height of the tower allows gravity to assist with parts of the brewing process, as in a traditional Victorian tower brewery.

Old breweries, new uses

Although large-scale brewing has gradually disappeared from many urban centres, fortunately its buildings have not. Since the 1960s conversion to other uses has become the presumption, rather than demolition. One of the earliest conversions saw the derelict Freshford Brewery in Somerset become an architect's office in 1964; on a larger scale, Sich's Lamb Brewery (architect William Bradford, 1901) in Chiswick was successfully turned into offices during the 1970s. Most significant, because of its stunning site and the publicity it received, was the conversion to luxury flats of Courage's Anchor Brewery, beside Tower Bridge and overlooking the Tower of London; work on the Anchor Brewhouse (Fig 3.60) was completed in 1990.

More problematic are larger sites retaining smaller buildings such as the cooperage and stables. Wolverhampton's Springfield Brewery (Figs 3.61 and 3.62)

Fig 3.61 (right)

One of a series of photographs taken by Bedford Lemere & Co of William Butler's Springfield Brewery (1881–3) in Wolverhampton. They were commissioned by its architect Robert C Sinclair (1825–93), who showed them at the 1883 Brewers' Exhibition to publicise his practice. Judging by the positive reaction, this may have been the first such use of photography by a brewers' architect.

Fig 3.62 (below)

The grade II listed early 1880s gateway to Wolverhampton's Springfield Brewery. The 'M&B' section of the lettering, if not the whole of it, dates from after 1960 when Mitchells & Butlers of Smethwick acquired the brewery. The distinctive falcon and hop crest, however, belongs to the original incumbents, William Butler & Co.

closed in 1991, but despite several attempts at redevelopment, little has transpired and a fire caused serious damage in 2004. Much more positive is the transformation of Truman's Black Eagle Brewery in east London, where brewing ceased in 1989, into what is now known as the Old Truman Brewery. Completed in 1998, with a mix of creative businesses, offices, shops and event spaces, the area is seemingly always packed with crowds enjoying the atmosphere.
In Newark-on-Trent (Nottinghamshire), at the Castle (*see* Fig 4.41) and Northgate Breweries (*see* Fig 9.16), where brewing ceased in 1983 and 1966 respectively, well over a decade passed before any redevelopment activity, but the Castle was completed in 2001 and Northgate in 2011.

Although parts of the Northgate site were finished and in use well before 2011, there was a staggering gap of almost half a century between the end of brewing and the opening of the final part of the development. Working with former brewing industry buildings – potential heritage assets – can (but need not) be a lengthy process. The buildings and structures of the brewing industry, whether in use for brewing or otherwise, constitute a significant part of Britain's architectural and industrial history. A report on the industry's remaining assets, commissioned by English Heritage from the Brewery History Society and published online in 2011, located nearly 900 extant sites, a huge heritage resource to be enjoyed and protected.[69] If all aspects of the heritage of beer are 'at risk', then the more we understand about our breweries, the better we can ensure their future.

4 Designing and Planning the Brewery

Whether brewing in medieval or modern times, brewsters and brewers faced the same major problem in the brewhouse, that of moving, mixing and storing substantial quantities of liquids and solids while maintaining appropriate temperatures throughout the process. Industrial-scale brewing required a complex layout of large vessels connected by a network of pipework and elevators, along with heating, cooling and pumping equipment. The many solutions to this problem, devised initially by brewers, and later their engineers and architects, resulted in a wide range of designs; no two large-scale breweries are completely alike.

The brewhouse lay at the heart of the brewery. Arranged alongside it, often around a courtyard, were other diverse buildings including the stables, malthouse and cooperage, which we shall explore later. Ideally there was easy road, rail or water access. Integrated brewery complexes, where the brewhouse and one or more associated structures survive, are often idiosyncratic in design and picturesque in appearance; they are the most significant sites remaining from the high point of brewery construction at the turn of the century. We can look in more detail at their design and planning, beginning at the start of the brewing process with malting.

Fig 4.2 (right)
A late 19th-century impression of
Charrington's Anchor Brewery in
London's Mile End Road. Particularly
notable are the number of chimneys,
malt towers and elevators; the tallest
malt tower was 160ft high.

Fig 4.3 (below)
Stansfeld's Swan Brewery (1881–2) in
Fulham, photographed in 1928; it was
the first large brewery to be designed by
the architect William Bradford. The City
of London Brewery acquired the Swan
Brewery in 1914.

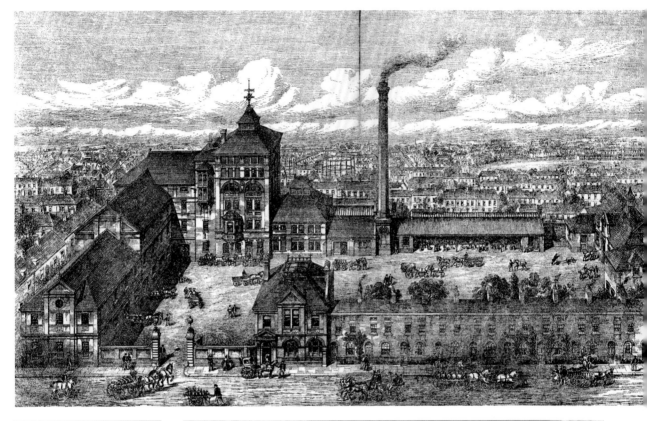

Fig 4.4 (above)
In 1889 William Bradford published his
ideal design for a 60-quarter brewery,
then built it for the New London
Brewery in Vauxhall; the Oval cricket
ground is visible to the right.
The brewhouse tower and a small office
building survive, although altered, as
part of Westminster Business Square.

Fig 4.5 (right)
A typical brewery yard shown on this
early 20th-century advertisement for
Melbourn Brothers All Saints Brewery
in Stamford. It was rebuilt as a steam
brewery in 1876 then operated until
1974; after restoration in the 1990s it
now brews fruit beers.

Fig 4.6
Fig 4.6

An early 20th-century postcard view of
Rayment's Pelham Brewery in Furneux
Pelham, Hertfordshire, with the brewery
tap on the left. The brewery was built in
the early 1860s, unusually with the wort
cooler located on the first floor of the
brewhouse. The grade II listed brewery
complex has been converted to
residential use.

Growth of the malting industry

Although the earliest malt production was relatively domestic in scale, from around
1500 purpose-built malthouses were commonplace; they were known as floor
maltings, as the germinating grains were spread on the floor to grow. Initially the
malting industry was run by specialist maltsters and by the 18th century almost
every sizeable town had its own floor maltings. As the brewing industry expanded in
the 19th century, brewers began to demand more control over one of their prime
ingredients. A brewery might then have its malthouse on-site, own malthouses
elsewhere, or have a single-brewer contract with a maltster; however, some
independent maltsters remained, selling their products on the open market.[1]
The major malting firms included Paul's of Ipswich, Taylor's of Sawbridgeworth
(Hertfordshire) and Simpson's of Alnwick (Northumberland); when the Newark
business Gilstrap & Sons amalgamated with its neighbour Harvey & Earp in 1880,
the resulting partnership – Gilstrap, Earp & Co – became the largest malt producer
in Britain with an annual output of around 100,000 quarters.[2] Towards the end of
the century, as in the brewing industry, many maltsters moved to corporate status
in order to raise funds for construction, in this case to build maltings and grain
elevators.[3]

Fig 4.7

Meux's Maltings on the quayside at
Ipswich, seen in this 1950 photograph,
is a fine example of a stand-alone
maltings. It was one of several large
maltings on the Ipswich waterfront,
some of which have been restored and
converted to new uses.

In the 17th and 18th centuries malthouses were often built on farms, and as the canal network expanded, alongside canals; by the late 19th century rail access was a critical factor, due to the volume of malt being transported. The largest remaining set of floor maltings, the Bass Maltings (1892–1905) at Sleaford in Lincolnshire (*see* Fig 7.28), stands beside a railway line in barley-producing country. In contrast the huge maltings at Mistley, Essex (*see* Fig 4.14) and Ipswich (Fig 4.7), on the Rivers Stour and Orwell respectively, were built where imported Californian barley was unloaded. Other massive maltings were erected in brewing towns, especially Burton, but generally maltings at integrated brewing sites were a little smaller than stand-alone maltings. An exception is the truncated but still immense eight-to-nine storey maltings (*c* 1902) at London's Stag Brewery, overlooking the Thames in Mortlake.

The maltings

Inside the maltings was a barley storage area, recognisable externally by the presence of hoist canopies (lucams) well above ground level, sheltering the doors through which barley was taken into the building. It was then dried and cleaned, using a screening machine which removed grit and broken corns. Next came steeping in water, normally in a rectangular stone or brick trough with a flat bottom, so revenue officers could gauge (measure) the amount of malt. From the late 19th century cast-iron steeps were introduced, with – following repeal of the malt tax in October 1880 – hopper-bottoms to allow emptying by gravity; previously the malt had to be dug out by hand and shovel. The barley was then spread on the growing floor, a broad, open area with low headroom and ranks of cast-iron or wooden columns. The malt was turned, originally by hand, to prevent it matting together and ensure even growth. Finally the partly germinated barley went to the kiln, where it was laid on the drying floor, which was often made of perforated ceramic tiles, and dried until it could be stored safely, ready for grinding into grist at the brewery.

Fig 4.8
Mitchells & Butlers Cape Hill Brewery maltsters show off the tools of their trade, an assortment of shovels, forks, ploughs and rakes used for turning and moving the grains in a floor maltings.

Fig 4.9

Women maltsters turning the partly
germinated grains at Mitchells & Butlers
Cape Hill Brewery maltings in
Smethwick during the First World War.

Fig 4.9
Women maltsters turning the partly germinated grains at Mitchells & Butlers Cape Hill Brewery maltings in Smethwick during the First World War.

The requirements of the malting process produced an easily recognisable building type: a typical floor maltings has a long, low profile, compressed floor heights and (where these remain) distinctive, often conical or pyramidal, kiln roofs. Externally the repetitive fenestration or louvre ventilation is very characteristic. However, floor malting was not the only way to produce malt; as early as 1842 Patrick Stead (1788–1869) patented what was known as the pneumatic method, in which air temperature and humidity were controlled after steeping. Stead, whose main maltings complex was in Halesworth (Suffolk), supplied 'steam malt' to London brewers Truman, Hanbury, Buxton on a commercial basis for four years before his equipment failed.[4]

Maltings design

The pneumatic method was not taken up elsewhere until the 1870s, and the first British maltings to try out Galland's Patent System of Pneumatic Malting, a new French invention, opened in Beeston (Nottinghamshire) in 1880. In Galland's system the germinating grains were laid more thickly than normal, allowing the area taken up by malting to be smaller, although turning was still done manually. Beeston Brewery, designed by the Frome engineers Wilson & Co, was an integrated site with both brewing and malting functions. Although much altered, the building remained in use as a maltings until December 2000, but was demolished in September 2012. As they developed towards the end of the century, the Galland drum system and its rival the Saladin Box (invented by French engineer Charles Saladin) came to include mechanical turning of the grains, thus reducing labour costs, although initial building expenses could be high.[5] Pneumatic and mechanical malting was never as popular as floor malting in the Victorian period, but it eventually resulted in the huge, silo-like industrialised maltings built from the 1950s onward.

There were innovators amongst Britain's maltsters too, notably Henry Stopes (1852–1902), born into a Colchester brewing family but better known to the non-brewing world as an antiquarian and anthropologist. After a fact-finding tour of European breweries in 1879 Stopes set up his own brewers' engineering firm, H Stopes & Co, based in Southwark (later at the Hop Exchange), issuing a catalogue of brewers' machinery and plant in December 1880. He then built a new gravity-based Eagle Brewery (1882) in Colchester for the family firm, C Stopes & Sons, on the principle 'that no greater mistake can be made in a brewery than to have it inadequate to the required work'.[6] Although he did design other breweries, including Barrett's Vauxhall

Fig 4.10 (above)
Langley Maltings (1898) stand beside the Titford Canal on the southern edge of Oldbury. The grade II listed maltings, originally owned by the nearby Showell's Brewery, were photographed in 1956 by Eric de Maré; they are extant but much diminished due to a fire in 2009.

Fig 4.11 (right)
The massive Melbourne Street Maltings (1892) in Newcastle upon Tyne. The photograph was taken in 1894 for the local firm W B Wilkinson & Co, pioneer patentees of reinforced concrete. They probably supplied the concrete for the malting floors, although in this case it was unreinforced concrete. The maltings was acquired in 1918 by Newcastle Breweries and was in use until the early 1970s; it was demolished in the late 1970s.

Fig 4.12

A 130-quarter maltings designed by
Henry Stopes's company, illustrated in
The Engineer of 7 July 1882. All three
malting floors were 81ft long with a roof
height of 8ft.

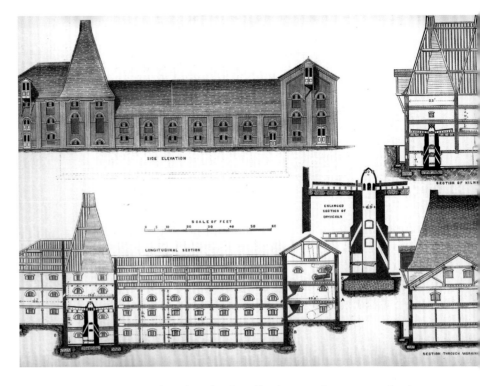

Fig 4.12

A 130-quarter maltings designed by Henry Stopes's company, illustrated in *The Engineer* of 7 July 1882. All three malting floors were 81ft long with a roof height of 8ft.

Brewery (1885; Fig 4.13) – thought to be the tallest brewery in Europe at the time and topped by a huge, illuminated revolving bottle advertising Barrett's Stout – he concentrated on maltings and improvements to the malting process.

Stopes advocated hopper-bottomed steeps and offered an improved pneumatic process along with his own design of double-floored malt kiln. His 662-page tome *Malt and Malting*, published in 1885, became something of a maltster's bible, and by the following year Stopes & Co were working on more than 20 breweries and malthouses in Britain, and others abroad.[7] Henry Stopes was a frequent and lengthy speaker on the problems of the malt industry; in the 1890s he gave evidence on the malt trade to several government committees. His Eagle Brewery in Colchester still stands, although converted for office and residential use.

Another proponent of labour-saving self-emptying steeps was the Essex maltster Robert Free, who was in partnership with ironfounder William Rodwell from the 1850s. The firm Free, Rodwell & Co was incorporated in 1893 and the business erected a series of monumental maltings (1896–1904; Fig 4.14), up to eight storeys in height, on and near the quayside at Mistley. Some were designed by Free and all incorporated his innovations in kiln technology, the cast-ironwork being carried out by Lawford Ironworks of nearby Manningtree. Robert Free, whose improved steeping tank design was patented in March 1882, died in 1902, before the last of the Mistley maltings was complete. Free, Rodwell was acquired by Ind Coope in 1956; several of the malthouses remain, and although altered significantly, are still an impressive reminder of the peak years of malting.

Amongst other maltster-cum-designers was Newson Garrett (1812–93), one of the Garrett family of agricultural engineers from Leiston in Suffolk. He designed

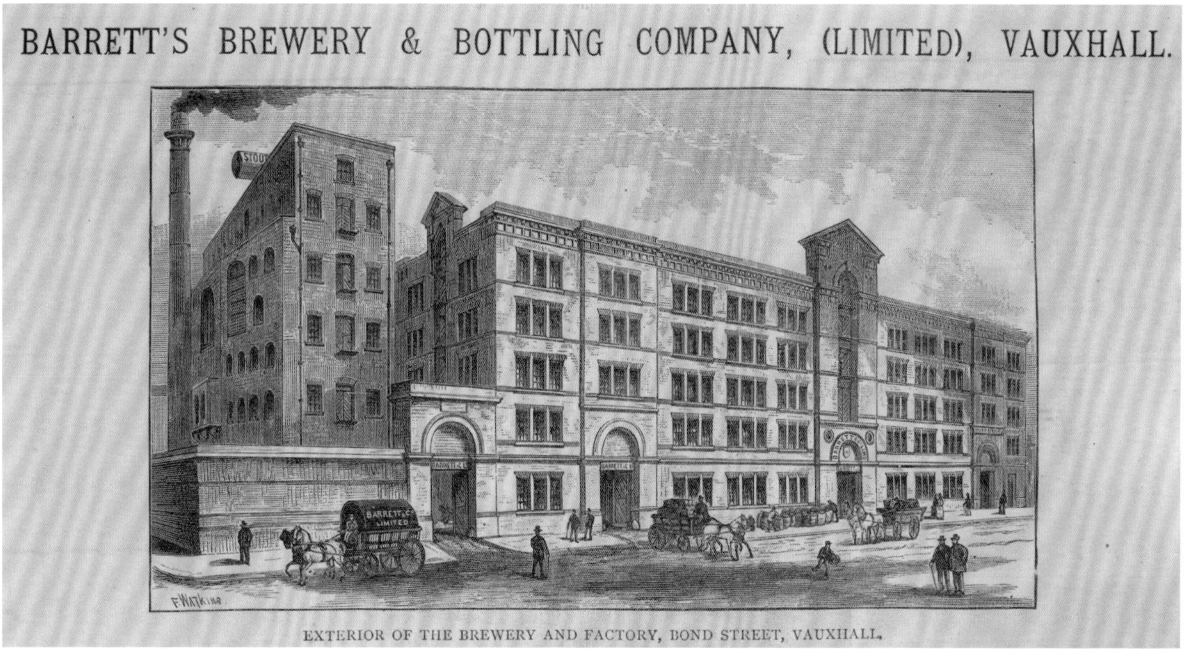

BARRETT'S BREWERY & BOTTLING COMPANY, (LIMITED), VAUXHALL.

EXTERIOR OF THE BREWERY AND FACTORY, BOND STREET, VAUXHALL.

Fig 4.13 (above)
Barrett's Vauxhall Brewery (1885),
designed by Henry Stopes, was so
unusual that it featured in *The Pictorial
World* of 4 March 1886. The revolving
advertising bottle of Barrett's Stout
('for invalids') can just be seen mounted
above the tall, gravity-worked
brewhouse on the left. The top of the
150ft-high chimney shaft took the form
of a beer bottle screw-stopper, which
Barrett's pioneered in the 1880s.

Fig 4.14 (right)
Part of the extensive Free, Rodwell &
Co maltings at Mistley Quay in Essex,
built around 1896 and photographed in
1956 by Eric de Maré.

Fig 4.15

William Bradford's design for a
100-quarter maltings, from his book
published in 1889. The kiln was topped
by his patent cowl, which had no moving
parts and used the vacuum created by
cooling the rising hot air from the kiln
(by mixing with cold external air)
to create an upward draught.

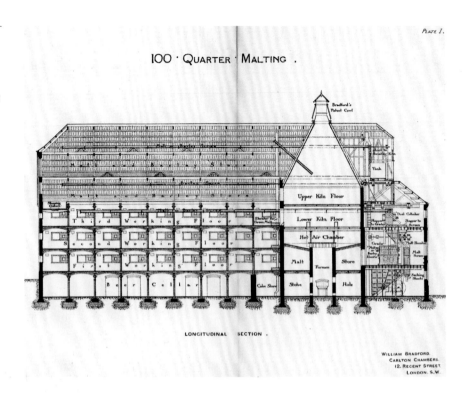

The brewhouse – tower or pumped?

At the brewery, steam-producing machines and processes – boiler, engine, pumps, wort copper and hop back – were normally located in a smaller building adjoining the brewhouse. The fermenting vessels and racking room were usually housed in a third building, often longer and lower than the brewhouse. This typical tripartite layout (Fig 4.16) was complemented by assorted towers and stacks. Malt was moved

and built the maltings at Snape Bridge in 1854, doubling their capacity in 1859.[8] A single malthouse on the extensive but remote Snape site was converted between 1966 and 1967 to house a concert hall. After a disastrous fire in 1969 the concert hall was rebuilt and the entire maltings restored from 1969 to 1970, all the work in both phases being carried out by Arup Associates.

Most of the larger maltings, particularly the stand-alone structures, were designed by specialist brewers' architects and engineers (*see* p 94), some of whom made their own innovations in malting methods. As to the buildings themselves, Henry Stopes remarked upon the 'almost infinite diversity of arrangement of building and modes of construction' and put the emphasis on the skill of the maltster in getting the best out of his equipment.[9] He would probably have agreed with the brewers' architect William Bradford (although there is no record of these eminent gentlemen ever having met) that 'any kind of malthouse, however well constructed in itself, without the constant care and applied skill of the maltster, may produce bad malt – just as bad beer may be, and frequently is – made from the best of malt; but properly made malt, properly brewed, must always produce that beverage so dear to the heart and the palate of the Englishman'.[10]

Fig 4.16 (right)
Henry Lovibond's Cannon Brewery (1867) in Fulham, seen in a photograph dating from around 1885, is a good example of the three-part structure of a typical small Victorian brewery. On the left is the copper house, boiler and stack; the tall section is the brewhouse, with high-level water tank; and on the right is the long fermenting house.

Fig 4.17 (below)
Lacon's Falcon Brewery (built 1895) in Great Yarmouth photographed by Eileen 'Dusty' Deste during the 1960s or 1970s. Note the malt tower and elevator in the background. The brewery closed in 1968 and was later demolished; the brewery stores survived until 1997 before being pulled down to make way for a supermarket.

A View of the Malt Tower, The Brewery, Chiswell Street. E.C.

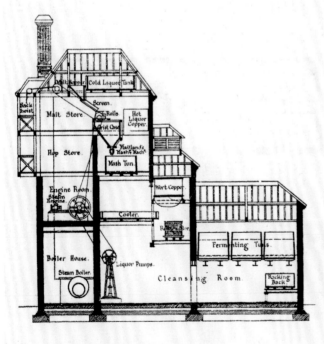

Longitudinal Section.

around by a system of Jacob's ladders (elevators or conveyor belts with hinged flaps) and larger breweries might have several tall malt towers linked by elevators. In addition to the malt towers and a boiler chimney, there was often a water tower.

The basic form of the brewhouse itself was determined by the processes within. Industrial brewers of the Georgian era were quick to adopt steam power for their huge beer factories, but brewers on a smaller scale found it economical to make as much use as possible of gravity, a free power source. By the 1870s this resulted in the iconic tower-shaped brewhouse where liquids and solids – once pumped or hauled to the top of the tower – simply flowed or dropped between vessels. However, this gravity-based system only made sense up to a point, due to the large areas required for cooling and fermentation, and the weight of the biggest vessels. The alternative involved a combination of extra lifting and pumping, for instance pumping hot wort between copper and coolers, while other processes were gravity assisted. There was much debate in 1880s trade journals about the merits of 'tower' versus 'pumping', but most architects concluded that the

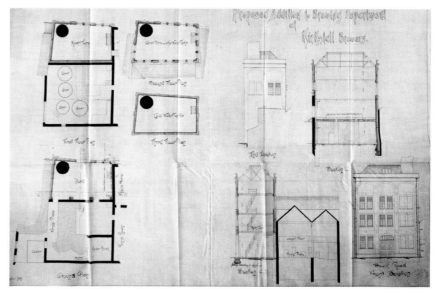

Fig 4.20 (above)

Men of the Romsey Fire Brigade pose with their extending ladder at Strong's Horsefair Brewery in Romsey, soon after the 50-quarter tower was erected in 1890. It was designed by brewers' engineer Charles Johnson, who until the previous year had worked for the Bristol firm Llewellins & James. Brewing ceased at Romsey in 1981, although the brewhouse tower survives as office accommodation, having been completely rebuilt internally.

Fig 4.21 (above right)

Plans and elevations of the small tower brewery designed by Leeds architect Thomas Winn (1818–1908) in the early 1870s for the Kirkstall Brewery Company. Although the brewery closed in 1983, the four-storey tower, with its unusual balustraded parapet, still survives along with most of the associated buildings (all grade II listed) after an award-winning conversion to student housing in the late 1990s.

tower or gravitation system was only suitable for smaller breweries, or extensions on existing sites. Although a brewery constructed on the pumping system resulted in a greater footprint, it was more flexible than a tower, easier to extend if greater capacity was required and more convenient for the brewer overseeing operations.[11]

Inside the brewhouse

What exactly goes on inside a brewhouse? At first glance, all we can see is a confusing mass of pipework and gleaming utensils, stairs and conveyors, mills and hoists, all on interconnecting floors. So let's start at the beginning of the brewing process with water and malt. In a traditional brewery there were hot and cold water tanks on or near the top floor of the building. Nearby was a malt hopper, awaiting the arrival of sacks of malt, which were hoisted up from below. Once tipped into the hopper, the malt was allowed to drop through a screen to a malt mill. Originally the milling process was carried out with grindstones, but these were superseded by roller mills, with varying numbers and sizes of rollers depending on how fine or coarse a grist was required.

Gravity or an elevator, depending on the exact layout, carried the grist to a grist case sited above the mash tuns. The grist either dropped directly into the mash tun and mixed with hot water, or was first sent through a masher, which combined grist and water before spewing the mixture out into the tun. After a time the mix – known as wort – was run off to a holding tank (underback) and eventually drained or pumped into a copper to be boiled with hops. The next step was passage through the hop back, to sieve out spent hops, then cooling. This used to take place in large, open copper tanks; like the coppers themselves, they could be very attractive pieces of industrial metalware. However, the coming of various methods of heat exchange and refrigeration towards the end of the 19th century saw open coolers phased out, and along with them the need for the brewhouse to be more-than-usually well ventilated; previously, extensive louvre windows and one or more roof ventilators were the norm.

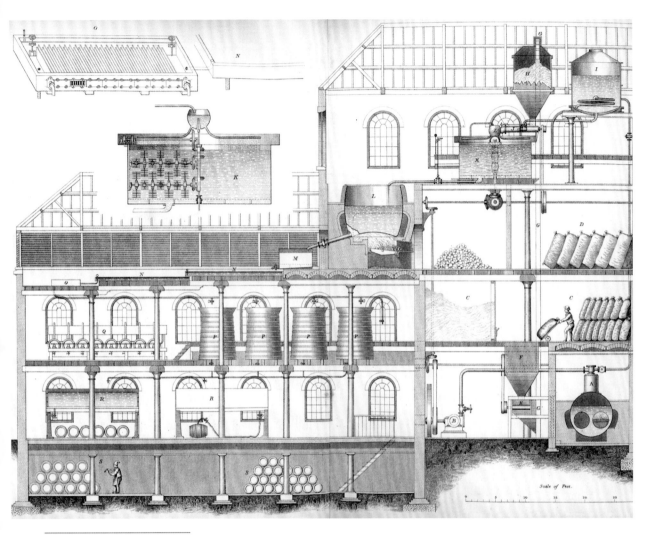

Fig 4.22

The interior of a brewery, as shown in the 1882 edition of the *Popular Encyclopaedia or Conversations Lexicon* published by Blackie & Son. Brewing begins with malt milling (bottom right), then the grist is raised in an elevator (G) to the grist case (top right) and the process continues diagonally to the bottom left. An enlargement of the mash tun (K) shows the internal mashing machine. The drawing is unusually detailed in that it includes most of the pipework and elevators, which were often omitted for clarity.

After cooling, the wort was sent to fermenting tuns, where yeast was added and fermentation completed. The final stage of the process involved conditioning then bottling or transfer to casks (racking). Altogether, from water tanks and malt mill through to fermenting tuns, even a small brewery with only one example of each piece of equipment would have a dozen items of kit, along with all the intermediate pipeware and pumps. In a more substantial brewery, the individual vessels would be larger, and there would be many more of them. The fermenting tuns would be sited in a dedicated fermenting house. As we shall see in the next chapter, the manufacture and supply of brewing equipment became a significant industry from the mid-19th century. Arranging these many and varied elements within the brewhouse, along with the brewer's office and the laboratory, was challenging for brewers and their engineers; there was no single correct solution in any given situation, and there were almost as many different brewhouse layouts as there were brewers.

Cooperage and stables

Beyond the brewhouse and fermenting house lay a number of low-rise buildings requiring significant space, notably the cooperage and stables. By the late 19th century coopers were using steam-powered machinery, although several machines were needed to make a single wooden cask. Mending casks had to be carried out by hand, and as a beer cask could be in use from 30 to 50 years, typically 90 per cent of a brewery cooper's time would be taken up by repairs.[12] Simply storing the casks took up a large area (Fig 4.24); in 1877 Bass had over 170,000 casks in storage around Burton, and the massive pyramidal piles became one of the wonders of the age.[13] Barnard, visiting Bass in 1887, noted an 11-high stack of up to 13,000 empty casks and spent an entire day touring their cooperage department, where 400 men and boys were employed. The steam cooperage (Fig 4.25), the most advanced cask factory in Britain, was 'crammed with machinery' and a sight 'not easily forgotten'.[14] At that time Bass were using a total of 518,121 casks in their business, and it took 35 clerks in the cask office to keep track of their movements. Each cask was individually numbered; Barnard witnessed the branding of cask 929766 when at the Guinness cask factory in Dublin, the only one on a similar scale.

Fig 4.23

A cooper's initiation ceremony at Mitchells & Butlers Cape Hill Brewery between the wars. After serving his apprenticeship, a newly qualified cooper has to be 'trussed in' by his workmates. They put him in a barrel, which he made himself, pour stale beer and wood shavings over his head, then roll him around the yard. After this he is presented with his indentures.

Fig 4.24

An eight-high stack of barrels at Bass in Burton, seen on a postcard dating from around the 1920s. The pyramids could go at least five layers of barrels higher. Although Bass kept some of their cask stock in the Middle Yard, this view is one of their other cask stores, either Shobnall Maltings (west of the town) or more likely the Dixie sidings, north of the centre.

STACK OF BARRELS AT BASS AND CO'S, BURTON-ON-TRENT.

Fig 4.25 (above)
A postcard view of the famous Bass
steam cooperage in Burton, which
measured 197ft by 87ft. Two
70-horsepower engines operated all
the band saws, circular saws, rotary
cutters and other machinery; note those
at the rear of the cooperage being
driven by a single line shaft. About one
hundred men and boys are visible
in the photograph.

Fig 4.26 (right)
Part of the cask sheds at Shipstone's
Star Brewery in Nottingham,
photographed about 1900. In the
foreground casks are being checked and
mended, while at the rear is the
cask-washing area.

Fig 4.27
In the early 1870s unreinforced mass concrete was used to build a four-storey wine, spirits and beer store at Simonds' Brewery in Reading; even in the 1880s the store's construction was still said to be unique. The designer was Blackall Simonds junior (1839–1905), a partner in the firm and an engineer by profession.

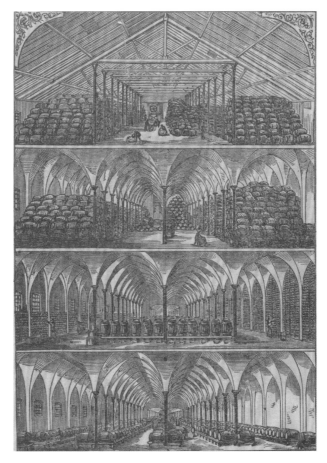

Fig 4.28
A postcard of Burton dating from around 1902 showing the extensive Bass Middle Yard cooperage, located north of Horninglow Street and the Middle Brewery itself.

Bass and Guinness, with their huge export trade, had unusually high cooperage requirements, as did Liverpool brewers during the 1870s for their bottled beer, which was exported in 'dry' (non-watertight) casks. The pint bottles were packed in straw, 95 to a cask; five local cooperages supplied up to 300 casks daily.[15] More typical was an arrangement like the cooperage and cask-washing sheds at Eadie's Cross Street Brewery in Burton, a near neighbour of Bass; it had just been rebuilt when Barnard visited in 1888. Cask cleaning and management were important to the brewery, as casks were expensive and a clean cask was a vital part of the process of turning out good beer. Cask washing was normally carried out using steam and assorted patent cleaning machines. The cask-washing sheds at Eadie's were 150ft long, and stood next to the steam boiler. Nearby were the coopers' shops, where a dozen men worked on cask repairs, the coopers' stores, and another coopers' shop where new casks were made. Beside these buildings was the cask bank, an area of at least an acre occupied by piles of empty casks. Thus even a small brewery like Eadie's needed significant cask storage space, although employing far fewer coopers than Bass or Guinness.

Brewery architects and engineers had little to say about cooperage arrangements, other than emphasising the importance of a convenient layout for ease of unloading empty casks and conveying clean casks to the racking room; 'there should not be any unnecessary labour in rolling (casks) about'.[16] And they had almost nothing to say on the matter of stables, which is curious as brewery stables could be immense. Originally the horses were used for power, to drive horse wheels, but by the 1830s in London, and perhaps a little later elsewhere, horse engines had been replaced by steam engines. However, the numbers of draught horses – shire horses that pulled delivery drays – continued to increase towards the end of the 19th century. Ind Coope of Romford (see Fig 3.38) (with 78 country depots) had by far the largest horse population, with 543 in 1899, but the numbers went into the hundreds at several London breweries.[17] Further afield, brewers made more use of the railways for shipments, so stable blocks were smaller.

The pick of the London brewery stables, thought to be the best laid out in the city, were those at Mann, Crossman & Paulin's Albion Brewery on Mile End Road. They were put up in 1885 and accommodated 105 horses, mostly in a large two-storey stable designed by the brewery's own architect-engineer, Mr Spence (about whom we know nothing). Inside was a dado of red and blue brick, with white glazed brick above, and 84 stalls; food and water was delivered to the horses by a semi-automatic system. The upper floor, supported on iron columns, was used for feed storage. This space was 145ft long, enough to 'make a capital ballroom' as Barnard put it.[18]

Often the larger stables extended over two floors, with a connecting ramp (sometimes surprisingly steep) between the two, and perhaps an additional storey for the forage store. The stables at Whitbread's Chiswell Street Brewery, rebuilt during the 1860s, could accommodate nearly 300 horses on the lower two of its three storeys. Watney's Stag Brewery in Pimlico also housed its horses in a double-decker arrangement, as did Boddington's Strangeways Brewery of Manchester. Horses reached the top floor of the late 1880s stables at Combe's Wood Yard Brewery in Covent Garden by ascending a semicircular ramp under cover of a glazed roof. The ramp divided halfway up, like a grand staircase, branching off to two sets of stalls. Internally this was an impressive structure but externally, like most English stables, it was plain and functional. North American brewers of the time were far keener to add ornament to their stables.

Fig 4.29
Moving casks around the brewery was made easier by the development of various types of cask lift. This early 20th-century photograph shows a lift worked by pulleys and chains, but engine-driven lifts were also available; Hook Norton's cask lift, powered by line shafting from the steam engine, was installed in 1900.

Fig 4.30
Whitbread's Garrett Street stables, built in 1897 just north of the brewery, could accommodate 100 dray horses over three floors of stalls. Two ramped walkways ('rides') allowed the horses to move between the floors. The stables were in use until 1992, and the grade II listed building now houses a builder's merchant. The ramps are extant, but covered by steps.

Fig 4.31
Draymen returning empty to Mitchells & Butlers Cape Hill Brewery, Smethwick, in 1949. The casks were loaded sideways-on, and in some designs of dray tilted towards the middle of the wagon. The driver's seat was mounted above cask level, while the trouncer (drayman's mate) guided the team by walking beside the lead horse.

Fig 4.32
Motor drays, being readied for morning deliveries, packed into the Cape Hill Brewery yard between the wars. Note the dray numbers; 53 is the highest visible, but the brewery garage could house about a hundred motor lorries.

Fig 4.33 (above)
More than 150 people were employed in Mitchells & Butlers Cape Hill Brewery bottling stores by the end of the 1920s. Here, women workers supply the electrically powered machines which fill and cap the beer bottles.

Fig 4.34 (right)
The Camden Brewery's bottling store (1900–1) was designed by William Bradford and sported several elephantine decorative features, referring to the company's trademark Elephant Pale Ale. Brewing ceased at the site in 1925 and the grade II listed building, now the Elephant House, has been converted to offices.

By the late 1890s brewers were beginning to try out motorised transport, initially steam wagons or traction engines which pulled trailers. In May 1897 the *Brewers' Journal* reported that Nimmo's Castle Eden Brewery in County Durham had just adopted 'mechanical traction' in place of drays; it added 'will other brewers be disposed to try this experiment?'[19] By 1905 London's brewers were using nearly 100 motor wagons, Mann, Crossman & Paulin (who had been one of the first to try them out from 1902 to 1903) being in the lead with 12 vehicles.[20] Wethered's of Marlow (Buckinghamshire) bought their first traction engine in 1905 and their first petrol-driven truck in 1911. By 1930 their open dray sheds and stables had been transformed into steam-heated garages for the motor fleet.[21] Charrington's Anchor Brewery of London's Mile End Road, which owned 160 shire horses in 1887, converted one of its stables to a bottling store in 1929. At Benskin's Cannon Brewery in Watford, where motor transport was brought in from 1905 to 1906, the maintenance department had grown to the point in 1921 where it was made a separate subsidiary company.[22] Trucks were seen to cause more congestion in the brewery yard than drays when loading and unloading. The various building alterations that accompanied the move from horse to motor also typically served, where possible, to increase the size of the yard.

The brewery office

One area of the brewery where appearance certainly concerned the owner was the office. Visitors to the Bass general offices in Burton, built over a period of nearly four years during the mid-1880s, found themselves in a magnificent stone-built, double-height entrance hall. To reach the boardroom and directors' office they ascended an imperial staircase, the flights dividing at a half-landing; this too was stone built and equipped with marble handrails. The open arcade at the summit was lit by a large stained-glass window.[23] This was unusually lavish, perhaps reflecting the style of the owners' country mansions, but early brewery offices were indeed inside private houses. A brewhouse or malthouse might have been built to the rear of the house, then as the business expanded, a counting house or other office would be added, and eventually also houses specifically for a partner and other significant staff, such as the head brewer or chief engineer.

Late 19th-century offices on integrated brewery sites were normally part of the street frontage, sometimes along with the brewery tap, which was often sited on a street corner. The offices and brewery tap generally followed the architectural style of the brewery, but rather more flamboyantly. There were also stand-alone brewery offices, which could be quite ornate and might be situated well away from the brewery, as in the case of the Liverpool office (1876) of Warrington brewer Peter Walker. It resembled a small Venetian palazzo, with a warehouse to the rear, and was designed by the Liverpool architect John Elliott Reeve; it was eventually illustrated in *The Architect*.[24]

Internally, the best rooms in office buildings would typically be wood panelled with stained glass, as in the boardroom of the Newcastle Breweries' office (1900) in Newcastle upon Tyne designed by Joseph Oswald, who worked on many pubs for the company. The Breweries' Haymarket office, close to the stables but not part of an integrated site, has an imposing exterior of red brick and sandstone on a granite plinth; shaped gables and a corner turret ensure the building attracts notice in the busy street. Its interior is exceptional for a brewery office, with brown, green and buff ceramic tiling and glazed terracotta throughout the ground floor, including an

Fig 4.35 (above)

Like their Vauxhall Brewery, Barrett's offices were a showcase for their products, in this case the beer bottle screw-stopper. Their advertising postcard shows two outsize bottles, with stoppers mounted aloft, topping the gateposts at the entrance to their Wandsworth Road premises.

Fig 4.36 (right)

This house on London's Mile End Road was built around 1905 for the chief engineer at Mann, Crossman & Paulin's Albion Brewery, which stands a little way to the west. The house stood in front of the brewery's 1880s cart sheds, stabling and yard, which were accessed through the grand carriage archway. The building lost its roof to a bomb in 1941, and much of the present attic storey was added in 1984.

Fig 4.37 (right)
The Crown Inn on Birmingham's Broad Street was the brewery tap for William Butler's Crown Brewery, which towers behind the pub. The brewery and pub originated in the 1870s with a small pub brewhouse, which Butler expanded as his beers became successful. Eventually, in 1898, he combined with Henry Mitchell of Smethwick's Cape Hill Brewery and brewing ceased on Broad Street.

Fig 4.38 (above)
The oldest surviving building at the former Cannon Brewery in Islington is the brewery yard office (1874–5), built by Thomas Elkington of Golden Lane. Carved barley and hops decorate its doorcase, while inside is a tile and mosaic floor featuring detailed images of hops.

Fig 4.39 (right)
Mansfield Brewery, designed by William Bradford & Sons, seen here in 1929 with the single-storey, curved facade of the offices in the forefront. After the brewery closed in 2001, the brewhouse tower was converted to the Making it! education centre.

Fig 4.40
The Newcastle Breweries' logo seen in a ceramic fire surround at their Haymarket office in Newcastle upon Tyne.

open arcade and two chimney pieces, and continuing along the corridors on the first floor. The Breweries' name and logo features in the tilework, which was made by the Leeds Fireclay Company (Fig 4.40). These 'ceramic rooms' were popular around the turn of the century (there were others in Newcastle), particularly for banks and utility companies; this is almost certainly the sole such brewery office.

A tale of two offices

The construction of lavish offices for two Newark-on-Trent (Nottinghamshire) firms had very different outcomes.[25] Caparn, Hankey moved to the Castle Brewery's present site in 1879, putting up a brewhouse that Barnard described as 'in no way remarkable'. This 'extensive pile of red brick buildings' was joined in 1881 to 1882 by a magnificent £10,000 office block (Fig 4.41) in French Renaissance style, complete with a 100-seat concert hall on the top floor; its architect is unknown. This piece of brewer's extravagance led to the company going bankrupt in 1885, when local maltster James Hole picked up the brewery at a bargain price from the liquidator.

Fig 4.41
The lavish offices at Newark's Castle Brewery, which caused the downfall of brewers Caparn, Hankey three years after its building was completed in 1882. Brewing at the site continued until 1983, but the complex of buildings, including the offices, survives almost intact after conversion to housing in 2001.

One of Hole's competitors was Richard Warwick, with a brewery in the centre of Newark. In 1863 he purchased a riverside site towards the town's eastern outskirts, on which he initially built a maltings.[26] He put up a brewhouse on the site, known as the Northgate Brewery, in 1871 and by the mid-1870s the Nottingham architect William Bliss Sanders (c 1841–96) was employed to alter and restore pubs in the brewery's tied estate. As the Northgate Brewery continued to expand on its new site a larger brewhouse was called for, which Sanders – an expert on 16th- and 17th-century woodwork and furniture – designed in 1882. Most notable are its delightful 20-bay polychromatic brick arcade, which extends the length of the brewery yard, and the Queen Anne Revival-style slabs of chimney stacks.

Sanders used the same style for the brewery offices, built between 1889 and 1890 to accommodate the firm's 40 clerks and travellers, and decorated its exterior with the town's crest; inside was a Renaissance-style wooden stair and a fine curved mahogany counter. Building was also taking place at the Castle Brewery, where a new brewhouse went up at the same time as Northgate's grand offices. It was designed by William Bradford & Sons and allowed the firm to increase their range of beers from 10 to 15. Hole's survived independently until 1967 while Warwick's, which merged with another local brewer in 1890 to become Warwicks & Richardsons, was taken over in 1962.

Mid-Victorian brewery architecture

The middle of the 19th century was a crucial period for the development of brewery architecture. Earlier progress in plant and design originated with the brewers themselves, when the industry operated on a relatively small scale. With the introduction of steam power around the start of the 19th century came the professional brewery engineers, an inventive and informed group who rapidly came to dominate the field of brewery design and construction; generalist architects were seen by brewers as lacking the requisite specialist knowledge. This happy and profitable relationship between brewers and their engineers was mirrored by a lack of communication with the world of engineering away from the brewery. There was never a specialist professional body for the brewers' engineers, and they initially failed to publicise their own work to other engineering institutions. When the London brewers' engineer Thomas Wilkins did eventually give a paper on brewing equipment to the Society of Engineers in 1871, their president remarked that 'very little really was known to the engineering profession in general respecting machinery used in breweries'.[27]

Up to the end of the 1860s, these engineers relied on architectural precedent for their brewhouse exteriors, producing plain, functional structures with little decoration, for instance repeated blank arcading and round-headed windows. Ornament only appeared occasionally on internal ironwork or external lettering, perhaps giving the building's date, brewer's name or trademark. But these new breweries made a significant impact on the townscape, with their landmark towers and chimneys. Two of the most eminent brewers' engineering practices, both founded in the mid-19th century, were Davison, Inskipp & Mackenzie and Scamell & Colyer.

Robert Davison (1804–86)

Robert Davison was the first of the specialist brewery engineers. He was born in Northumberland but his parents moved to London when he was five, and in 1818 he was apprenticed to Moorman's iron foundry in Old Street. He eventually became foundry manager and remained with the firm until 1831 when he was appointed resident engineer at Truman, Hanbury, Buxton & Co's Black Eagle Brewery in Brick Lane. He 'to a great extent remodelled' the brewery and brought in a variety of new equipment such as the Archimedes screw, used for shifting malt both upward and horizontally.[28] He was the first engineer to apply the Archimedean screw principle to large-scale brewing, and the two such screws introduced by Davison around 1834 – one of which was 250ft long – were reputed to be the first used in London.[29] The stable block (Fig 4.42) designed by Davison and built between 1836 and 1837 still stands, although much modified internally. Topped by an eagle pediment and costing £10,000, it had room for 114 horses in iron-framed stalls; the roof originally combined cast and wrought iron with timber rafters.[30]

Davison stayed at the Black Eagle until 1845, taking out several patents on his designs for brewing plant, including cask-cleaning and cask-lifting machinery, then set up his own civil engineering practice in London. As a brewing specialist he was the first of the new generation of brewery designers who came from within the industry rather than being trained architects. He succeeded in the competition to design Findlater's Mountjoy Brewery in north Dublin, and the substantial, stone-built premises were erected in 1852 beside the Royal Canal. With its maltings, vat houses and cooperage the brewery covered an area of four acres. Although it produced only porter and stout, its export trade was at one point second only to that of Guinness.

Allsopp's New Brewery (1859–60; *see* Fig 7.12) in Burton was designed by the London architects Hunt & Stephenson in conjunction with Davison, who was also responsible for all the internal plant arrangements; when built, it was said to be the biggest ever put up from a single plan, as opposed to being extended. He significantly enlarged the building in 1867, during his six-year partnership with George Scamell (*see* below). When that ceased in 1870 Davison carried on single-handed until 1875, when he took his youngest son – also Robert Davison – into partnership along with John Mackenzie, who had already been working with Davison for about two decades. Davison junior left in 1881, to be replaced by George Inskipp, formerly Davison & Scamell's office manager. At this point the firm was known as Davison, Inskipp & Mackenzie, before Robert Davison himself retired in the early 1880s. Altogether Davison and his successive partners

Fig 4.42

Designed by Robert Davison and built between 1836 and 1837 the stable block at Truman, Hanbury, Buxton & Co's Black Eagle Brewery is seen from Brick Lane. Now part of the Old Truman Brewery complex and known as the Boiler House, it is an all-purpose warehouse venue centred on the base of the Truman chimney.

Fig 4.43
A maltings designed by Davison, Inskipp
& Mackenzie for Robjohns & Co of
Napier, New Zealand. The hand-
coloured illustration from the *Building
News* of 3 August 1883 shows the
weatherboarding, intended to minimise
earthquake damage, and the
corrugated-iron roofs with projecting
eaves, giving shade from the sun.

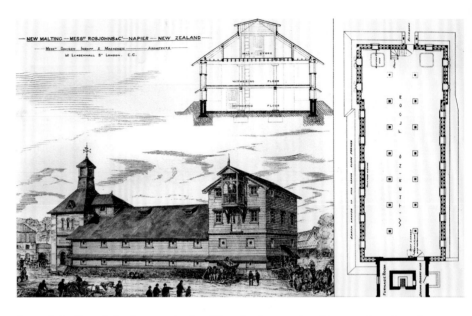

formed the first of the three major late Victorian brewers' architect and engineering
practices, their breweries including several works for Phipps & Co at Northampton
and Towcester, Adnams in Southwold (1897), and additions at two London
breweries: Taylor Walker's Barley Mow Brewery (1889) and Courage's Anchor
Brewery (1895), and both topped with distinctive octagonal turrets.

Scamell & Colyer

The second of the major brewers' design practices, also based in London, was begun
by George Scamell (1840–1927), who we first encounter as an employee in the
engineering department of Truman, Hanbury, Buxton & Co during the 1860s.
He then went into partnership with Robert Davison from 1864 to 1870, after which
he published the textbook *Breweries and Maltings: Their Arrangement, Construction
and Machinery* (1871) and worked as an independent consulting engineer and
architect.[31] His book, which included precise costings and plans for several sizes of
brewery, was reviewed positively and at length by *The Builder*; the journal
recommended it to 'architects to whom the class of work is new', while gently poking
fun at brewers for their inability to agree on 'one consistent system of brewing'.[32]

In 1873 Truman's, then the largest brewery in the world, called on Scamell
again to design their new Burton brewery, in fact a rebuilding of the former Phillips
Brothers Brewery, which they bought to compete with local brewers in producing
clear, sparkling pale ales. As Truman's own history recounts, they 'put in the most
famous brewery engineer and architect of the day to reconstruct it'.[33] Scamell's new
brewery, which Truman's also called the Black Eagle, was built from 1874 to 1876,
along with 18 foremen's cottages. It was a long, red-brick block lying just west of the
main railway line; Scamell designed a conventional Classical facade, 21 bays in
length, to be seen from the train and a more industrial aspect overlooking the
brewery yard, with tall blind arcading capped by semicircular windows. The new
Black Eagle could produce 120,000 barrels a year, and it was 1880 before it became
profitable; it was demolished between 1972 and 1973.

Scamell's Cape Hill Brewery (Fig 4.44) in Smethwick, designed for Messrs Mitchell (later Mitchells & Butlers) in 1878, was a red-brick structure of around the same size as Burton's Black Eagle, and with a similarly tall chimney stack. These high stacks, often standing alone, were a feature of the series of large-scale breweries designed by George Scamell when in partnership with Frederick Colyer (1833–1914) from 1880 onwards. Colyer, who was trained in gas and hydraulic engineering, immediately produced a revised edition of Scamell's book (Fig 4.45), in which he recommended that 'the chimney-stalk should be of such dimensions as will ensure a good draught, the amount of this being in excess rather than the reverse'.[34]

Scamell & Colyer's first collaborative work was a new brewery for Eldridge, Pope & Co of Dorchester (Dorset), designed with the assistance of local architect

Fig 4.44
A commemorative watercolour of Henry Mitchell's Cape Hill Brewery, Smethwick, designed by George Scamell. The first brick of the new brewery was laid on 21 March 1878, and brewing commenced in July 1879.

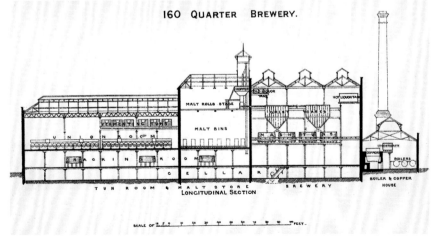

Fig 4.45
Scamell & Colyer's design for a 160-quarter brewery from their book *Breweries and Maltings* (1880). Note the long, horizontal Archimedean screw running between the malt mill to the grist cases, and the substantial amount of pumping this layout requires: from coppers to coolers, and thence the fermenting tuns and unions. A steam-powered hoist raises the filled casks from the cellar.

George Crickmay (1830–1907). The Dorchester Brewery (1880–1) was a feast of ornate polychromatic brickwork (*see* Figs 9.19 and 9.20), probably due to Crickmay, and was initially equipped with a 50-quarter plant. The internal layout allowed for the plant to be easily extended, and indeed it reached 80 quarters within seven years. The 130ft-high chimney was described by the visiting Barnard as 'one of the most perfect, and, at the same time, ornamental pieces of masonry, of its kind, we have seen'.[35] Its base carried the company's insignia and the shaft above was decorated with brick diapering; it terminated with a broader segment of brickwork around the top. The chimney survived when the brewhouse was burnt out in 1922 (then rebuilt to a slightly simplified design incorporating some original decorative elements) although the top of the shaft was removed in 1950. It has been retained in the conversion of the brewery to an arts, housing and commercial complex (2009–14).

The practice's next job was for Dudney & Sons of Brighton, whose Portslade Brewery (Fig 4.46) they designed in 1881. It too has a tall, detached chimney with a massive base, in this case sporting the company logo entwined with barley stalks and bunches of hops. Scamell & Colyer's Tadcaster Brewery (Fig 4.47, *see also* Fig 3.29), designed for John Smith's, opened in 1883. At 160 quarters the brewery had a greater capacity than most built during the 1880s; its fermenting room, measuring 154ft by 90ft, was the largest in England to use the Yorkshire square system (*see* next chapter). All the buildings were of Yorkshire stone and the 150ft-high octagonal stack tapered gently towards its ornate top.[36]

Scamell & Colyer's Clarence Street Brewery in Burton, a 50-quarter brewery put up in 1883 for the estate of the Warrington brewer Peter Walker, was much more externally decorative than their previous works and unusual in several other respects. For its size, its brewing capacity was small; the malthouse had a striking octagonal kiln topped by a weathervane in the form of a goat; the interior of the kiln was circular with a steam-driven central rake, unique in Burton; and the words 'Trustees of the late Peter Walker' in lettering almost a storey in height ran along near the top of the east and west sides of the brewery.[37] Other decoration included an ironwork

Fig 4.46
Dudney & Sons Portslade Brewery (1881), designed by Scamell & Colyer, showing one of the practice's typically decorative chimney bases. The brewery originally had a pitched roof.

crown on the brewhouse, and panels of tiles bearing images of hops and foliage
beneath the windows. The detached, 120ft-high chimney shaft was circular in cross
section on an octagonal base. This most distinctive brewery ceased to brew about
1925 and was demolished in 1976, aside from the Goat Maltings, which are due to
be converted to housing.

George Scamell outlived Frederick Colyer by 13 years, and was able to lunch
at the Black Eagle Brewery in Burton on 28 June 1927, the year of his death.
In conversation with one of Truman's directors it emerged that he had built
breweries valued at more than £700,000 over his entire career.[38] For comparison,
it was estimated that in the early 1870s, when Scamell was setting out in business as
an independent consulting engineer, the capital invested in UK breweries and
maltings was about £12,400,000.[39]

The ornamental brewery

George Scamell's brewery construction textbook made no mention of architecture
or embellishment, yet by the end of his career he and Colyer were designing highly
efficient but also decorative breweries that well deserved the label 'ornamental'.
From the 1880s onward brewers' architects produced buildings that ostentatiously
displayed the brewery's name and offered prospective customers an attractive image
of what otherwise might be thought of as a plain factory building. The ornament
often took the form of the brewery's trademark carried out in ironwork (for the
crown of the brewhouse), carved stone or occasionally terracotta, tiles or mosaic.
In addition the lucams, the oriel window of the brewer's room overlooking the yard,
and the gateway to the yard were all likely sites for decoration.

The greatest proponent of the inclusion of an architectural element in brewery
design was William Bradford (*see* Fig 4.52), whose breweries are discussed below.
His views were initially published in the catalogues of the first two Brewers'
Exhibitions, in 1879 and 1880, then more widely disseminated in the *Brewers'
Guardian* in 1885. He chided brewers with little regard to the appearance of their
brewery; 'the idea that anything is good enough for a trade building is a great

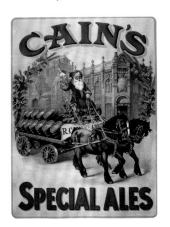

Fig 4.49
The grade II listed Hook Norton
Brewery, designed by William Bradford
& Sons and built between 1898 and
1900, is probably the practice's best
known work, an archetypal English
country brewery.

mistake', and regretted hearing clients remark, 'Mind, I don't care anything at all about the look of the place.' He also criticised earlier brewery designers:

> In passing through a town your attention is usually attracted by two or three buildings of large size towering above the rest, and they are generally the church, municipal buildings, and brewery, and, as a rule, the brewery is a most hideous-looking structure, without the slightest attempt at design from an architectural point of view; and, in many instances, the appearance could have been made really imposing with very little, if any, additional cost.

Fig 4.50
The town of Alton in Hampshire, seen from the air in 1928, with two large breweries close together on Turk Street. The tall, horizontally striped tower in the centre of the shot is Crowley's Brewery, and just beyond lies Courage's Brewery (1904), designed by William Bradford & Sons. Neither has survived, although Molson Coors still brew at Alton in a modern plant.

Fig 4.51
A pair of ornamental breweries dominate this postcard view of Alton: Crowley's (1901, demolished 1975) on the left, and Courage's to the right, with large lettering spelling out the firm's name mounted along the roof ridge (although blurred in this view).

The Breweries, Alton

He advocated some small expense on the brewery's exterior to ensure its attractive appearance, and suggested that the chimney shaft should be made a particular feature, indeed 'a thing of beauty'.[40] Six years later, speaking at the Institute of Brewing, he could look back at the days when 'a presentable elevation was considered superfluous' and contrast this with 'the present generation' of breweries. He emphasised the usefulness of a good image: 'In these days, when commercial offices are palatial, and many manufactories are imposing buildings, there is every reason why the brewery should be good-looking and important.'[41]

To judge by the number and variety of ornamental breweries erected from the 1880s to the early 1900s, Bradford's promotion of decent brewery architecture seems to have struck home. Of course, not all were either convinced or wished to go to any extra expense. In his 1894 paper read at the Institute of Brewing the brewers' engineer G T Harrap (a former boiler inspector) noted the tendency for brewers to commission architects with only a superficial knowledge of engineering, resulting in 'engineering absurdities perpetrated in breweries'. He suggested that it should be possible 'to arrange a pleasing elevation by simply making use of the natural grouping of the various buildings together with the structural details, thus saving the cost of nearly all added ornament which in the majority of cases weakens the structure'.[42] In practice, however, Harrap worked with the architect William Duffield, who had been an assistant in William Bradford's office during the 1880s, and together they produced several large and decorative breweries around the turn of the century.

Looking back at late 19th century breweries from the standpoint of 1932, Stovin Bradford – then in charge of William Bradford & Sons – commented, 'Until about 50 years ago breweries, as a rule, were just a collection of nondescript buildings, with no pretence to be otherwise. From that time, however, architectural effect, and improved internal arrangements, seem to have received the consideration they rightly deserve. It is now appreciated that clean, wholesome buildings, pleasant to the eye are a good advertisement.'[43] This chimed in with the inter-war vogue for a more genteel and respectable 'improved' public house.

William Bradford & Sons

William Bradford (1844–1919), founder of the third major brewers' design practice, came not from an engineering background but from the building trade. He was born in Devon, the fourth child of 13 in the family of a builder, Robert Bradford, and his wife Grace.[44] Initially William worked with his father; he married in 1866 and his son Stewart was born the following year, but by 1871 he was already widowed (he married again in 1872), and living in London. In the census he gave his profession as an architect, although we know nothing of his training. His five brothers also moved to the capital, where two were in the licensed trade and another, Robert Bradford (1850–1909), became a draughtsman in William's office.

William Bradford appears to have worked in the brewing industry before establishing his own architectural practice in 1879, when he gained his first brewery commission, for additions to Dashwood's Hope Brewery in East Grinstead (West Sussex). At this point his workload was mostly the design of small breweries or minor alterations to pubs and breweries, but he publicised his practice through the 1879 and 1880 Brewers' Exhibitions and his breakthrough came with a commission for Stansfeld's Swan Brewery (*see* Fig 4.3) in Fulham. Built between 1881 and 1882 this was

Fig 4.52

William Bradford (standing, far right) on the day of his daughter Agnes Evelyn's wedding in 1912, in the grounds of his Surbiton home. Percy Bradford stands next to William, whose wife Edith is seated between them.

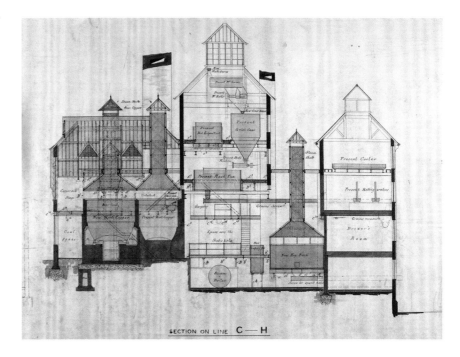

SECTION ON LINE C — H

a 50-quarter brewery with an ornate brewhouse and a 120ft-chimney shaft, which
was topped out in style on 12 January 1882. Bradford, the brewer and the
contractors congregated at the top of the Italianate chimney, where the cast-iron cap
was christened and 'bumpers of champagne were drunk' in a typical brewing
industry ceremony.[45] He ensured the Swan Brewery was well publicised in the trade
journals and his career never looked back.

He went on to be the leading brewers' architect of the late 19th century,
building or altering well over 70 breweries and maltings in locations throughout
England and Wales, although the majority of his works were in the south of
England.[46] His distinctive decorative style, easily identifiable today, featured
ironwork, variety in materials and fenestration (often including tiny, triangular
dormer windows), and picturesque grouping. Bradford's later works tend to be
marginally less ornate, but he always emphasised the brewery's name or trademark.
He was the only brewers' architect invited to speak at the inaugural Brewers'
Congress, held in 1885 in conjunction with the seventh Brewers' Exhibition, but
poor organisation resulted in such a small audience that he refused to speak; he had
a reputation for shortness of temper. His 1889 book *Notes on Maltings and Breweries*
continued his campaign for good brewery architecture while giving a detailed
practical guide to construction and plant arrangement.

Amongst his early works was Harveys Bridge Wharf Brewery (1881–2; Fig 4.54)
at Lewes (East Sussex), still a working brewery and the only one in England to be
listed grade II*. It was a small plant, only 15 quarters, but Bradford made 48 site
visits to oversee construction work. Although the picturesque tower was rebuilt
between 1985 and 1986 (*see* Fig 9.23), doubling the brewery's capacity, the new
detailing looked so convincingly Victorian that it was commended by the Civic
Trust.[47] On a rather larger scale was Field's Nottingham Brewery (Fig 4.55), where

Fig 4.54 (above)
Harveys Bridge Wharf Brewery (1881–2) in Lewes cost just over £8,000 to build. Brewing continued while construction was under way, as Bradford sited the new brewhouse in the yard, alongside the 1879 fermenting room; the first brew in the new building was put through in July 1882.

Fig 4.55 (right)
Nottingham Brewery seen during the late 1890s while the nearby Victoria Station was under construction. E W Field bought the brewery in 1879 and completely rebuilt it with a 60-quarter plant, using William Bradford as his architect. Brewing ceased in 1952; both brewery and station (clock tower aside) were demolished during the 1960s.

Bradford worked during 1882 to 1890 renewing buildings over the entire site,
including two brewhouses (25 and 60 quarters). At the main entrance Gambrinus,
the genial spirit of brewing, made a rare British appearance; the two huge doors
carried bronze panels of the figure – with his obligatory tankard – astride a cask,
executed in brass. The Gambrinus symbol originated in Europe but was taken up
most enthusiastically by American brewers, who used him in their advertising and
to decorate their brewhouses.[48]

During the 1880s the Bradford practice was involved in contracts throughout
England and in Wales (at Wrexham), the largest being the 80-quarter addition to
Simonds' Brewery, Reading in 1886. The 60-quarter brewery featured in Bradford's
book, and illustrated by a handsome engraving, was built in 1889 for the New
London Brewery Company (*see* Fig 4.4) on a site just north of the Oval cricket
ground. But in 1925 the company ceased to trade and the premises eventually
became a Marmite factory. In 1893 Bradford secured a much more substantial
contract, the almost complete rebuilding of the Cannon Brewery in Islington (many
of the buildings are extant). The office, fronting the street and with elaborate
double doors to the yard, went up in 1894 to 1895, and the massive fermenting
house to the rear during 1895 to 1898.[49] At the same time a scheme for a large new

brewery in Limerick, drawn up by Bradford for a group of London businessmen and reminiscent of the New London Brewery, failed through lack of support from potential investors.[50]

William Bradford did not make a great mark on Burton's buildings, most of which were in place before he began practice. His wine and spirits store built for Ind Coope around 1897 still stands on Station Street, and he may have worked on the same firm's brewery. However, the largest maltings he ever designed, the massive four-block, 39-bay, 600-quarter development for Worthington's on Wetmore Road in 1899, was burnt out and then demolished in the late 1970s.

The practice was officially known as William Bradford & Sons from mid-1898, although Stewart Bradford (1867–1903) – the only child from his first marriage, with a reputation as a bit of a rogue – was in the business by 1891. He was made a partner in 1900 alongside Percy Bradford (1877–1913), who had worked for his father from 1896 and become a partner in 1898; he assisted with the construction of the Tate Gallery while taking his articles. The firm's most influential partner turned out to be William's nephew, William Foster Stovin (1877–1940). William Bradford may have paid for his nephew's education, possibly always seeing him as the eventual heir to the firm, and Stovin worked as an architect in Wales before joining the Bradford practice around the turn of the century. He was probably involved with the largest single brewery commission to be carried out by the practice, the 150-quarter Star Brewery in Nottingham (1899–1900; Fig 4.58), which displayed Shipstone's star trademark in stonework, ironwork and as an ornamental clock face.

The 140-quarter Tucker's Maltings in Newton Abbot in Devon, designed by the practice in 1903, survives as a working floor maltings. Although impressive, Tucker's is less ornate than its perspective drawing in the *Brewers' Journal* suggests.[51] The Bradford practice was always well publicised, and must have made significant

Fig 4.57
A 1921 aerial shot of Style & Winch's Medway Brewery (1898, William Bradford) in Maidstone, showing the complete complex of brewery buildings laid out around the yard. Nearest the river is the seven-storey brewhouse, and to its left the fermenting house. Note also the extensive cask pyramids. All this was demolished after brewing ceased in 1965.

efforts to ensure frequent mentions in the trade press. We know little of its staff, but several future brewers' architects and engineers are likely to have passed through the office during their training.

William Foster Stovin was made a partner in 1905. His prominence is acknowledged in the modern naming of part of the former Mansfield Brewery (*see* Fig 4.39), built by Bradford & Sons in 1907 and converted after the brewery left in 1984, as the Stovin Bradford conference suite. William Foster Stovin changed his name by deed poll to William Foster Stovin-Bradford on 4 January 1919; William Bradford himself died at his home in Surbiton almost a month later, on 2 February 1919. He was in his 75th year. A staunch freemason, he was buried in Putney Vale cemetery, in a grave marked by a simple Celtic cross. Unusually for a specialist brewers' architect, he was accorded an obituary in *The Builder*; it commented 'there are few towns in which he has not left some mark of his work, most of his brewery buildings bearing to a marked degree an individuality quite his own'. And as the *Brewers' Journal* put it, he had designed and built 'some of the finest breweries in the kingdom'.[52]

Stovin Bradford, as he was known in brewing and family circles, continued to run the firm, in partnership with two sons from William Bradford's third marriage (in 1894), John 'Jack' Bradford (born 1895) – who had been made a partner prior to his father's death – and Arthur 'Bill' Bradford (1901–81). They put up a new fermenting house at Charrington's Anchor Brewery in 1920, and a warehouse at the Cannon Brewery in Islington between 1924 and 1925 (although it had been designed in 1914). Jack left the company in 1924 and Bill followed 10 years later, leaving Stovin in sole charge. His son William John Foster Stovin-Bradford worked in the family business, notably on the new office building (1929) at Shipstone's in Nottingham, where the firm had been involved since 1899. However, Stovin Bradford died in 1940 and by the end of the war William Bradford & Sons had ceased to trade.

Fig 4.58
An aerial photograph of Shipstone's Star Brewery in Nottingham, taken in 1928 just as a substantial extension to the brewhouse was being completed. The original brewhouse and the similarly styled (but rather less decorative) new buildings were all designed by William Bradford & Sons.

Beyond the big three

Due to the lack of practice records, it is impossible to say exactly how much of the available brewery construction and fitting-out work was carried out by the three major brewers' architectural practices: Davison, Inskipp & Mackenzie, Scamell & Colyer and William Bradford & Sons. A reasoned estimate using available sources suggests around 40 per cent of the total, with Bradford's being twice the size of its main competitors. This leaves us to consider who else was involved with brewery architecture around the turn of the century.

Another major player in London, where the majority of the larger firms were based, were the brewers' engineers Arthur Kinder & Son, a practice set up by Arthur Kinder before the 1870s. His son Harold became a partner in 1891 and ran the firm from around the turn of the century, when they built several substantial maltings including those at Langley (1898; *see* Fig 4.10) – a suburb of Oldbury (West Midlands) – for the nearby Showell's Crosswells Brewery, and at Romsey in Hampshire for Strong's Horsefair Brewery (1902). During the 1880s the firm built many small breweries, but by the 1890s they were taking on much larger contracts like Chandler's 120-quarter brewery (1893) in Bethnal Green, for which they also designed some of the plant. Their best-known work is the Blandford Brewery (1899–1900) put up for Hall & Woodhouse at Blandford St Mary in Dorset; the copper installed at the time was in normal use until January 2012.

The Bristol region was famed for its production of a wide range of industrial machinery, and was the base of several brewers' engineers, some of whom also designed breweries. The longest established was George Adlam & Sons, which began life around 1820 as coppersmiths and brass founders. George Adlam's sons, William and Henry, carried on the business, and William Adlam took a special interest in the commercial possibilities of the brewing trade. By the mid-1880s the firm was building and equipping several breweries annually, as well as manufacturing plant. Their largest 19th-century design contract was for the 150-quarter Cannon Brewery in Watford, erected for Benskin's between 1897 and 1901; it had a series of towers rising to eight storeys.

By the turn of the century George Adlam's grandson Edwin G Adlam was managing the firm, which became a private company in 1908 (and went public in 1928). They provided a complete design service to brewers, from preparing plans and arranging the building contract to making the plant and supervising its installation. The brewery supplied plans and plant for the Madras BBB Brewery Company, whose Madras brewery opened in 1913.[53] It was an offshoot of a London concern, British Beer Breweries, that had a licence to use an unusual heat-resisting yeast thought ideal for brewing in warmer climates. Adlam's continued in business until 1963; part of one of their works still stands on Parnall Road in Fishponds, north-east Bristol.

Also based in Bristol, at Castle Green, were Llewellins & James, a general engineering concern established in 1735. They specialised in brewery and maltings plant and construction from the 1860s, although they are better known as bellfounders. Their works, rebuilt (following a fire) between 1875 and 1877, was a splendid example of Bristol's fancy industrial style, and appeared on the front cover of their 1888 catalogue. It ran to over 230 beautifully illustrated pages and included designs for breweries, on the gravitation and pumping systems, and for maltings, as well as a wide range of plant. In 1891, due to 'increasing pressure of architectural business', Llewellins & James expanded their works and employed more staff.[54]

Overall they were involved in designing around 40 breweries, mostly during the 1880s, and supplying plant for many more.

Other architects specialised in maltings and occasionally worked on breweries, for instance Joseph Wood of Birmingham, who designed Morland's Brewery (1911–12) in Abingdon (Oxfordshire). Russell & Spence of Glasgow offered themselves as architects of breweries, maltings and distilleries, while Edinburgh's Peter Lyle Henderson (1848–1912) – known in Scotland as 'the brewers' architect' – worked on many pubs as well as several breweries around Edinburgh and Glasgow. We are still unaware of the architects of many breweries, even one as striking as Crowley's Brewery in Alton (1901) with its yellow and orange-striped brick tower (*see* Fig 4.51). The late 19th and early 20th centuries were not noted for advances in brewery construction methods, in contrast to the many innovations in brewing equipment, and by 1910 only a handful of large brewhouses were being commissioned annually. Inevitably, many brewery sites ended up with a mixture of architectural styles as elements were added and rebuilt over time.

Between the wars

Inside the typical brewery, little changed between the wars. There were some improvements to plant, but these were fitted into the traditional arrangement of vessels. It would still be some years before more modern production methods became the norm. Even the outwardly sleek and modern Guinness Brewery (1933–5; *see* Fig 3.56) at Park Royal in west London, a beautiful piece of industrial architecture by Sir Giles Gilbert Scott, contained outdated plant. The external look of the plant – modern, albeit not modernist – resulted from the brewery's view of construction: 'as we brewed to a high standard, so should we build to a high standard'. But Guinness decided the internal layout of the 'English Brewery' should be a replica of the 'new' Dublin brewery (built in 1898), 'a plant that had served the company so well for many years'. Although the company's head brewer commented

Fig 4.59

Laying the foundation stone of Mitchells & Butlers No 2 Brewery (1912–14) at Cape Hill in Smethwick. Completed just before the outbreak of war, it was one of the most modern breweries in Britain. Henry Mitchell (1837–1914), who jointly founded the brewery with William Butler (1843–1907), stands to the right wearing a flat cap.

that at the time of the first mash 'the brewery was 50 years out of date', it did prove to be an efficient plant.[55] After some vessels began to fail, the brewhouse was modernised in the early 1990s, only a decade before the end came in 2005 when the soaring redevelopment value of the land persuaded Guinness to move production back to Dublin.

Externally most alterations and extensions to breweries during this period were of traditional construction and appearance; Stovin Bradford, for one, did experiment with concrete construction but went back to the old materials. The plans for the new brewhouse (1936–9) at Greene King's Westgate Brewery (*see* Fig 3.54) in Bury St Edmunds were drawn up by the firm's consulting engineer and head brewer, in conjunction with their regular plant suppliers, Adlam's of Bristol and Briggs of Burton.[56] The brewery architect, W Mitchell, was on the committee overseeing the project, so probably contributed to the exterior design of the five-bay, plain brick structure. Its facade is dominated by three tall round-headed windows, running almost the full height of the brewhouse and allowing the plant to be seen from outside. Members of the Institute of Brewing, visiting in 1952, were 'greatly impressed with the robust and dignified architecture of the spacious, light, and well-ventilated building, the high efficiency of the plant'.[57]

By 1939 the number of breweries had dropped to only a quarter of those existing in 1915. Inter-war brewers generally turned to architects only to produce 'improved public houses' for their estates, in Tudorbethan, neo-Georgian or even daringly moderne style. Although Allsopp's sponsored an architectural competition in 1920 for a 'Model Public House', they were hoping for a 20th-century version of a Georgian tavern, not an outwardly modern design.[58] It was a time far removed from the boom years of the ornamental brewery, with but a few outstanding pieces of architecture, amongst them Park Royal and Nottingham's Home Brewery offices.

Fig 4.60
The mammoth Mitchells & Butlers No 2 Brewery seen during the 1920s, from a celebratory book published by the firm to mark the 50th anniversary of brewing at Cape Hill.

Home Brewery offices, Nottingham

The Home Brewery site, at Daybrook in north Nottingham, was developed by maltster John Robinson from 1875. By 1882 there was a six-storey brewhouse, and continued additions over the years resulted in a typical large urban brewery, an interlocking array of towers and chimneys (*see* Fig 4.65).[59] The firm spent over £788,000 on extending and improving its tied estate during the period 1919 to 1926, then appointed Cecil Howitt (1889–1968) of Nottingham as its consultant architect in the early 1930s; he completed his first three pubs for the brewery in 1937.[60] The following year Howitt was asked to draw up plans for the almost complete reconstruction of the brewery; this included erecting a large modern office block facing the main road.

Building began in 1938, with the intention of completing the offices by the end of 1939, but when war intervened the long, low office block still lacked its central tower; it was eventually added in the early 1950s. The design was similar to Howitt's 1931 head office for the Raleigh Cycle Company nearer the centre of the city, with two wings, a tower and a central entrance, for the drays in the case of the brewery. In the Raleigh office Howitt integrated art and architecture by adding a series of 28 relief panels along the wings, running between the upper and lower windows. Made from iron, they were cast at the Lion Foundry in Kirkintilloch (East Dunbartonshire) and showed cherubic figures engaged in various stages of bicycle production. Their designer was the Nottingham-born architectural sculptor Charles Doman (1884–1944), who was then teaching art in London.

Not surprisingly Howitt chose the same combination of sculptor and foundry for the Home Brewery office, although the three initial designs for the reliefs (Fig 4.61), perhaps suggested by the foundry in 1939, are nowhere near as lively as the Raleigh panels.[61] Two include figures but leafy hops, barley sheaves and the brewery initials dominate. They were soon replaced by Doman's proposed scenes from the brewing process, complete with playful cherubs. His three reliefs show four chubby little figures stirring the mash, clustered around a barrel and drinking at a table. The set of three is repeated in the same order four times on each 12-bay wing, with the mash tun designs flanking the central tower, followed by the barrel and then the drinking scene (Figs 4.62–4.64).

The Lion Foundry probably also provided the ornate pair of central wrought-iron gates, which gave access to the yard. At some point the black cast-iron reliefs were painted white with a pale-blue ground, making the images clearer from a distance. The brewery itself continued to expand, putting up a new brewhouse in 1972 to 1974 after demolishing an old maltings, but was acquired by Scottish & Newcastle Breweries in 1986 and closed 10 years later. The brewery buildings were eventually demolished to make way for a supermarket but the offices, listed grade II in 1993, remained and were later used by Nottinghamshire County Council, although they went up for sale in 2012.

Fig 4.61
One of three initial designs for the ornamental panels at the Home Brewery, possibly produced by the Lion Foundry of Kirkintilloch.

Fig 4.62
Stirring the mash, one of the Home
Brewery's cast-iron reliefs designed
by Charles Doman.

Fig 4.63
Filling the cask, shown on a relief at the
Home Brewery.

Fig 4.64
Enjoying the ale, shown on a relief at the
Home Brewery.

Fig 4.65 (below)

The Home Brewery, Nottingham, seen from the air during the 1950s when work on the central tower of the new offices was being completed. The entire brewery is visible to the rear, including a large maltings block immediately behind the offices and the tall brewhouse tower. This mostly comprises the brewery buildings, designed by local architect and engineer Herbert Walker (b1846) and built between 1880 and 1881.

Fig 4.66 (above right)

The Home Brewery offices in Nottingham, seen when in use by Nottinghamshire County Council. The area behind the office block, once occupied by the brewhouse and ancillary buildings, is now a car park.

Later 20th-century breweries

Continued rationalisation in the brewing industry produced few notable buildings during the 1950s and 1960s, when shed-style beer factories became the norm and the brewing process underwent radical change, typified by the introduction of closed fermenters. First used in the early 20th century, they became commonplace in the 1960s, often in the form of a vertical, cylindrical vessel with a conical bottom: the cylindroconical fermenter. Scottish & Newcastle's Fountain Brewery in Edinburgh, modernised in 1973, pioneered computer-control for the entire brewing process, which eventually came to be housed in one vast space rather than in the traditional series of linked structures.

The new beer factories were so large that greenfield sites were necessary. In 1979 Whitbread opened the Magor Brewery near Newport in south Wales, on a site chosen because of its good motorway access and plentiful water supply. The £51,000,000 plant was designed by Frederick Gibberd & Partners as a series of pavilions, each housing a separate part of the brewing process.[62] The brewery is still in action, unlike the £90 million Courage Brewery, designed by the firm's own architects' department and built beside the M4 near Reading in 1979. This was rather more elegant than a shed; its stainless-steel vessels could be seen from the motorway at night through the brewhouse's glass curtain walling.[63]

Away from the beer factories, there were a few architecturally exceptional buildings. One was the bottling hall added to Ind Coope's Romford Brewery between 1960 and 1961 by contractors Sir Robert McAlpine and Sons. Clear-span shell-concrete arches stretched over four huge sheds, giving unobstructed floor space and allowing the new hall to be built over and round the existing bottling plant, which continued in production until construction was complete. Although not an especially early use of shell concrete in England, at Romford its design was particularly elegant and effective. However, the building was demolished in 1998 to make way for a superstore.

A good candidate for the most unusual 20th-century brewery design was the ziggurat-style structure (Fig 4.67) put up by the Danish company Carlsberg Breweries from 1971 to 1973 in Northampton. The site was the former Phipps Northampton Brewery, acquired in 1960 by Watney Mann, Carlsberg's partners in the venture. The Danish architect Knud Munk designed the new riverside plant, with Ove Arup & Partners as engineers and management consultants. Its most striking feature is the stepped glass wall on the southern facade of the concrete and steel brewhouse, through which the plant can be seen; to the rear is a long, low shed, containing the fermenting hall. There was no technical reason for the vertical layout of brewing vessels, but it succeeds in drawing attention to what happens inside the brewery.

Finally, two sophisticated Suffolk sheds. Michael Hopkins Associates produced an elegant design solution for the racking plant built in 1980 for Greene King at their Westgate Brewery in Bury St Edmunds. The site was a water meadow, subject to occasional flooding, so the concrete floor was raised on piles to allow the water to flow safely beneath. Not far away, the Adnams distribution centre (2005–6) near Southwold, by architects Aukett Fitzroy Robinson, has a claim to be our greenest warehouse. It has an array of environmentally sensitive elements, including the first commercial use of hemp in Britain; hemp, lime and chalk blocks were used for all the walls. Most noticeable – in a building designed to minimise visual intrusion – is the gently curving roof, covered in earth and bearing a carpet of grass and wild flowers. When built, this was the biggest green roof in Britain at around 0.42ha.

Present day building in the brewing industry tends to be limited to small alterations and additions, both for the remaining regional brewers and the growing number of microbreweries. A significant number of micros occupy buildings of historic architectural interest, and we may yet see a microbrewer building a 21st-century version of an ornamental brewery, with the same aim as the Victorian brewers, to increase trade and improve public image.

Fig 4.67
The unusual stepped glass facade of the Carlsberg Brewery (1971–3) in Northampton, which allows us to see something of the mysterious brewing process going on within. Designed by Knud Munk to express the best of Danish architecture, it won the Financial Times Industrial Architecture Award in 1975.

5 Inside the Brewery

Fig 5.1

The mash tun room at Shipstone's Star Brewery, Nottingham, around 1900. Note the system of wires and pulleys for raising the tun covers, and the mashing machine (right, pointing upward between two tuns) which can be rotated to direct the grist and hot water mix into either tun.

Fig 5.1

The mash tun room at Shipstone's Star Brewery, Nottingham, around 1900. Note the system of wires and pulleys for raising the tun covers, and the mashing machine (right, pointing upward between two tuns) which can be rotated to direct the grist and hot water mix into either tun.

The forerunners of modern brewing equipment were the domestic washing copper and wooden cask. The copper – a large laundry boiler originally made of copper, later iron – functioned during brewing as the water and wort heater. Brewing was a relatively simple process that could be carried out, often single-handed, at home or in a small brewhouse. As brewing became more commercial, the utensils slowly grew larger and more complex, but were still recognisably domestic. Truly industrial-scale vessels only arrived with the massive 18th-century city breweries.

Several examples of domestic brewhouses and their original equipment (often in part) remain on country estates, but only a single Victorian pub brewhouse has survived complete with its kit, at the Golden Lion in Southwick, near Portsmouth. This late 19th-century brewhouse (*see* Figs 1.2–1.4) supplied only the village pub and a small off-licence trade, and was run by one brewer with an occasional assistant. When the last brewer, Dick Olding, retired around 1956 Southwick Brewhouse was abandoned; by the 1970s the building was in a state of considerable decay, but it was restored between 1982 and 1985 and is now a museum, basically a single room housing most of the brewing process. The equipment is simple (Figs 5.2–5.4): the copper is encased in brick and heated by coal fire from beneath, just like a domestic copper, and the wooden mash tun and fermenting vessels are

Fig 5.2 (above)
A view inside the Victorian wooden mash tun at Southwick Brewhouse, showing the mechanical masher and its revolving rakes above the perforated false bottom.

Fig 5.3 (right)
The Southwick Brewhouse grist case located above the mash tun. Hot local spring water, heated by steam from the ground-floor boiler, was fed into the mash tun and then mixed with milled malt dropping down from the grist case.

Fig 5.4 (right)
The coal-fired open copper at Southwick Brewhouse, enclosed in its brick jacket. The copper was emptied via the large tap to the left of the stepladder, the wort flowing away along the moveable wooden trough to the hop back.

Fig 5.5 (far right)
The grist case above the mash tun at Sarah Hughes Brewery in Sedgley. The brewery was established in 1921, but no brewing took place for almost three decades after 1958. Much original equipment, including the grist case, was eventually restored and brewing resumed in 1987.

unlined. These utensils could well have been made by local metalworkers and coopers. Industrial brewing, however, required large-scale vessels, pumps and other machinery; specialist brewers' engineering firms eventually evolved to meet this demand.

The Stag Brewery and Richard Moreland

The size and complexity of Victorian commercial brewing equipment is well illustrated in the drawings of working plant at Watney's Stag Brewery in Pimlico (Figs 5.6 and 5.7), produced by the engineers Richard Moreland & Son, probably around 1870. Their 26 detailed sections and elevations show a wide variety of machinery, including lengthy Archimedean screws and an array of cogwheels and axles allowing power to be transferred between horizontal and vertical motion. The vessels range from a closed, convex-bottomed copper through mash tuns

Fig 5.6
A drawing produced by London firm Richard Moreland & Son for alterations at Watney's Stag Brewery, Pimlico, towards the end of the 19th century. The plant was worked by a beam engine, and included three mash tuns of differing sizes, each fed from two grist cases. This section looking south shows fermenting tuns and storage vats.

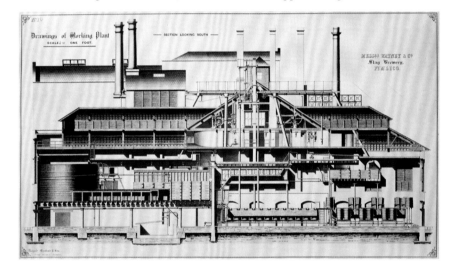

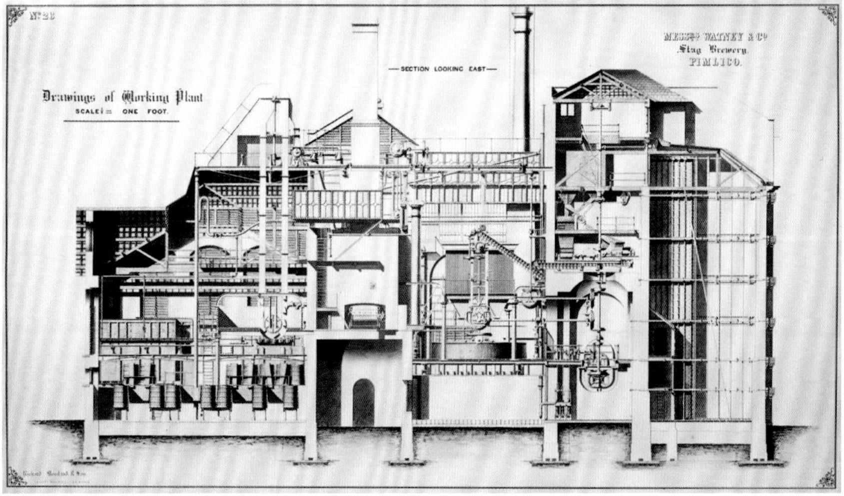

Fig 5.7
This Moreland drawing for the Stag Brewery shows two Archimedean screws (centre right) transferring grist between the mill and a grist case above a mash tun, and a bucket elevator in a double tube (centre left) rising high above the roof of the brewhouse. Note also the shafts and gear wheels (right) driven by the beam engine.

around 8ft in height to rank upon rank of fermenting tuns. It is likely that Moreland's provided the machinery as part of the substantial improvements made to the brewery from the 1860s onward.

The firm of Richard Moreland & Son originated with Richard Moreland, who was born in Clerkenwell in 1805; he was apprenticed to millwright Thomas Cooper of Old Street in 1819. The two formed a partnership in 1831, manufacturing gearing and grinding machinery (as well as treadwheels for prisons), and soon 'had all the principal London and country breweries and distilleries on their books'.[1] After the Barclay, Perkins Anchor Brewery was badly damaged by fire in 1832, Cooper & Moreland were called in to plan its reconstruction. By working night and day, Moreland designed and executed the job in only six months.

Thomas Cooper died in 1834 and Richard Moreland bought the business; they continued at the same Old Street workshop using the original tools, which were rapidly becoming outdated. They were reluctant to invest in new tools and fell behind other firms which brought in modern appliances, only changing their ways in 1856, perhaps due to the influence of Moreland's son (also Richard Moreland), who was taken into the business the following year. The firm soon became known as Richard Moreland & Son. After the Stag Brewery contract they moved away from brewery engineering, and Richard Moreland senior – their specialist in this field – retired in 1886; he died in 1891.

In 1897 Moreland's converted into a limited liability company, as many other brewing and engineering firms did around the end of the century. Although they chose not to remain dedicated brewers' engineers, other plant manufacturing concerns sprang up wherever the concentration of brewers was strong enough to warrant it. A wide range of these engineers' historic vessels, notably coppers and mash tuns, still survives in today's older working breweries, often marked by a manufacturer's trade plate which may also give the date. Plant was often bought second-hand, and also modified according to the theories and whims of the head brewer. The 19th-century plant manufacturers built on a tradition of craft metalworking skills originating with the medieval trade guilds.

Coppersmiths

A list of crafts 'exercised in London from times of old' and drawn up in 1422 included the coppersmiths. Amongst other things, they made pots and pans from sheet copper, large washing vessels and assorted basins for professional purposes. Some of these must have been used by the brewers of the day, and by the 18th century the chief business of coppersmiths was said to be making boilers and stills for breweries and distilleries.[2] Their workshops mostly lay along the banks of the Thames, where the main centres of sugar refining, brewing and distilling were located. There were 72 coppersmiths working in London in 1790, mostly in small workshops or at home, although this began to change in the early 19th century when bigger employers, with more capital, were able to expand. The 1831 census reported a total of only 486 coppersmiths in England, Scotland and Wales, almost all in the London area and Scotland. Pontifex, one of the major London firms, employed 30 journeymen and 23 apprentices by 1841. An apprentice to a brewing specialist might be sent to work in a brewery as well as his own workshop. Just like the coopers, when an apprentice coppersmith finished his time there was a ceremonial meeting to 'hammer him out', a noisy occasion with all hands hammering on anvils and the apprentice being pelted with anything mucky available.

By the 1860s the London trade had begun to specialise, with individual workshops concentrating on anything from tea urns to washing coppers; some firms supplied all the requisites of country house kitchens. And of course there were the brewing copper makers, and the makers of stills. Brewing work tended to come in bursts, usually in the winter, presumably so that new plant could be installed in the summer when brewing was suspended. Brewers' coppersmiths were paid a piecework rate (rather than by the hour) for making coppers and hop backs. At the turn of the century there were 933 coppersmiths in London, although most of them were employed on marine repair work, and around 30 in Burton.

The Pontifex family

The brothers William and John Pontifex, from the village of Iver in Buckinghamshire (about 20 miles from London) set up rival London coppersmith companies that contributed many elegant copper vessels to breweries at home and abroad. The story of the firm set up by William Pontifex (1766–1851), the older of the two, began when he was taken on by a relative, Richard Jones, as an apprentice in 1781. Jones was in business as a coppersmith in London producing a wide range of goods including brewing coppers; by the time of his death in 1788 the works was in Shoe Lane, close to the River Fleet. William Pontifex took over the business, which Jones had left to his wife Mary, by paying her an annuity, and traded as Jones & Pontifex. After Mary's death in 1793 he traded under his own name, making copper plates for engravers as well as brewing coppers and stills; he also bought, sold and repaired second-hand coppers (Fig 5.8).[3]

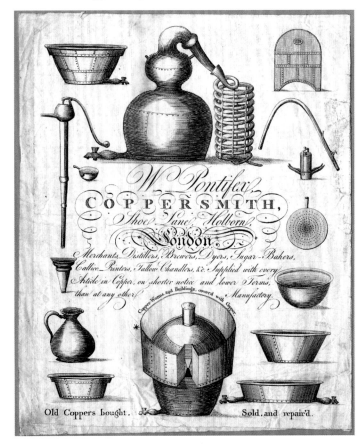

Fig 5.8
A fine array of copper vessels shown on William Pontifex's draft trade card dating from about 1796. The brewing copper at bottom centre is equipped with his own energy-saving apparatus, an invention that Pontifex said would condense steam and improve hop flavour.

Fig 5.9

Well over 30 men employed inside
Pontifex's Shoe Lane works around 1806,
before its great expansion during the
1830s. Towards the rear several men
hammer a large vessel to render
it dense and firm, a process known
as planishing.

As the Pontifex works expanded in the early 19th century (25 men were employed at Shoe Lane by 1804) William entered into several changing partnerships at a number of different premises; his younger brother Russell Pontifex (1775–1857) was a partner from 1806 to 1813. William also took on apprentices including three of his sons: Edmund in 1805, William junior in 1809 and Alfred in 1814. The pre-eminence of the firm was emphasised by the publication of an aquatint showing the interior of the Shoe Lane works around 1806 (Fig 5.9); it was then in the hands of William and Russell Pontifex, and Edward Goldwin. The publishers were two artists, William Henry Pyne and John Claude Nattes, who collaborated on a series of etchings documenting the trades at the start of the 19th century.[4] Their print of the Pontifex works was unusual in that it was larger than others in the series, and an aquatint rather than an etching. Pyne and Nattes may have thought their view of the copper works would sell more in colour; it certainly shows off the curious vessels very nicely.

At this point one of the firm's major competitors, at least in its brewery work, turned out to be one of William's younger brothers, John Pontifex (1772–1841). Having served his apprenticeship, John established his business as coppersmith and vatmaker around 1800 at 55 Shoe Lane, close to his brother's works at 46–8 Shoe Lane. He quickly became prosperous, took on several apprentices, and advertised himself as a coppersmith, back-maker, brewers' millwright and brewers' architect. His trade card displayed an example of his brewery design, a fine elevation of a 12-bay brewery, along with a wort copper and a mash tun.[5]

The firm run by John Pontifex was more of a specialist brewers' coppersmith than his brother's much bigger Farringdon works, from which William Pontifex senior retired in 1820, leaving Edmund Pontifex (1791–1870) and William Pontifex junior (1793–1870) in control. They tripled the size of the factory during the 1830s

Fig 5.10

The coppersmiths' shop at the Farringdon Copper, Brass and Lead Works, illustrated in the *The Penny Magazine* of 25 June 1842. In the foreground a man uses a machine to bend a copper pipe into the form of a heating coil. To avoid distortion, the pipe is filled with lead before bending; the lead is melted out afterwards, leaving the coil intact.

and from 1839 traded as Edmund & William Pontifex & J Wood. Production at their Farringdon Copper, Brass and Lead Works was described in detail by George Dodd in one of his articles on visits to London factories, first published in *The Penny Magazine* in 1842 (Fig 5.10).[6] The main floor of the factory was about 200ft long, split roughly evenly into lead and copper manufacture. In the copper department, after adjusting to the 'din and clatter', he reported 'Men wielding large hammers are on every side fashioning vessels and articles of copper: here a sugar-pan, there a sugar-filtering cylinder, in one place a boiler, in another a copper, in a third a still, in a fourth a worm.' The works could provide everything a brewery might need in the way of utensils, not only in copper but in iron and other metalwork, along with wooden vessels, and the firm's draughtsmen (who worked on one of the upper floors) provided the necessary plans and working drawings.

John Pontifex died in 1841; his estate included four small London breweries, one being the Stag Brewery in Enfield. Two nephews, Henry Pontifex (1800–87) and Charles Pontifex (1807–76), sons of his brother Daniel, then carried on the business, having both been apprenticed to John.[7] Their partnership lasted two decades before they split up around 1860, Charles becoming a vatmaker (Charles Pontifex & Sons) while Henry continued as a brewers' coppersmith, trading as Henry Pontifex & Sons, and took part in the 1862 International Exhibition in London. There were around 7,000 exhibitors in the show's industrial section alone, the Henry Pontifex & Sons stand being part of the massive class 31, devoted to iron and general hardware; this had well over 400 entries (Fig 5.11).[8] They showed both brewing and distilling equipment.

Four years after the exhibition the firm left Shoe Lane, moving to their newly built Albion Works (1866–7) in York Way, opposite King's Cross station. The buildings, which still remain, include an office, warehouse and several workshops,

Fig 5.12

Nameplate on the older of the two Ram
Brewery coppers. The pulley wire is
attached to the manhole-like cover of
the copper's low-level opening.

now converted for other uses (*see* Fig 9.18).[9] They were then, albeit briefly, one of the most successful coppersmiths in London. Meanwhile back at Shoe Lane, the Farringdon Works had shown at the 1851 Great Exhibition, and Edmund Pontifex retired in 1853. The business was carried on by his son, also Edmund, and retained the same name, although it was often referred to simply as Pontifex & Wood (which indeed it became in 1888). Both branches of the family had displays at the inaugural Brewers' Exhibition in 1879, Pontifex & Wood offering their 'Farringdon' refrigerator, described as a 'cooling wall', while Pontifex & Sons also showed several refrigerators as well as their new steam cask washer. Pontifex & Wood became regular exhibitors, showing a 350-barrel copper for Combe's Wood Yard Brewery in 1883, but five years later family debts caught up with the firm, and it was wound up in 1888. Receivers carried on the business, around 1892 selling the goodwill to a Derby company, Haslam Foundry and Engineering, pioneers in manufacturing refrigeration equipment, who retained the Pontifex & Wood name.

The Albion Works had also gone into decline. Henry Pontifex & Sons still managed to put on an imposing display at the 1891 Brewers' Exhibition, but the denouement came three years later when the firm was wound up and its remaining assets sold to Pontifex & Wood (actually Haslam's). Ironically, although this was the first time the two strands of the family coppersmiths had been united, none of the Pontifex family were now involved. A small announcement in the October 1894 *Brewers' Journal* confirmed that the business of Henry Pontifex & Sons was being transferred from the Albion Works to the Farringdon Works.[10]

In 1896 Pontifex & Wood left Shoe Lane, moving to the Union Foundry in Derby, where they continued in business until the early 1960s. This left the Farringdon Works nameless, so its mortgagees bought the goodwill of Henry Pontifex & Sons, also adopting the name. After the Shoe Lane works was destroyed by fire in 1911 a new Farringdon Works was erected in Tyseley, east Birmingham, and an office block,

Pontifex House, put up on the site of the old works. Henry Pontifex & Sons continued to trade as brewers' engineers until the late 1940s.

There is a curious coda to this story. An engineering firm named H Pontifex & Sons was established in Leeds in 1796 to supply copper vessels to the chemical industry, and traded continuously from that date. It seems likely that there is a connection with the Pontifex firms in London, but this is unproven. The Leeds concern manufactured bespoke vessels of all types, in 1933 making a stainless-steel fermenting vessel – said to be the first of its kind in the UK – for the local Tetley's Brewery.[11] However, they closed in 2010, bringing to an end over two centuries of Pontifex involvement in the brewing industry at home and abroad. Their remaining machinery and vessels, such as the two Victorian Pontifex & Wood coppers surviving at the former Ram Brewery in Wandsworth, are to be treasured (Figs 5.12 and 5.13).

Fig 5.13
Two Pontifex & Wood coppers, dating from 1869 and 1885, still remain at the former Young's Ram Brewery site in Wandsworth. Both are the same shape, with a concave indentation running from the dome down towards the base, where an angled opening allows hops to be added.

Brewers' engineers

Of course there were many other brewers' engineers, although few as long lasting as the Pontifex firms. Advertisements at the back of the first volume of Barnard's *Noted Breweries*, published in 1889, are a good guide to the major English firms of the time. Pontifex & Wood illustrated their 'Pontifex' patent refrigerating machine, and offered to give estimates 'for every description of brewery plant'. Also based in London were G J Worssam & Co, Henry Stopes, and C Pontifex, who pointed out that he was a senior partner of Pontifex & Sons. Outside London were three Burton firms – Buxton & Thornley, Robert Morton, and Briggs – who each took entire pages (or a double-page spread in the case of Briggs & Co) and Wilson & Co of Frome in Somerset. Several Scottish and one Irish firm of engineers also advertised in the book, not surprising as Barnard had recently completed a tour of British and Irish distilleries.

A wider selection of engineering firms took stands at the Brewers' Exhibitions, including specialists in water supply, malting plant, casks, ventilation, refrigeration, bottling plant and engines, both steam and gas. The nationally known concerns such as Llewellins & James and George Adlam & Sons, both of which were able to fit out entire breweries, could be found alongside smaller firms such as R Ramsden & Son, and J J Pike & Co, both from Haggerston in north London, or H Roberts & Co of Mile End. Unusually, the latter firm showed a model of a 10-quarter brewery at the 1888 Melbourne Centennial Exhibition, bringing it back to display at the 1890 Brewers' Exhibition. Even these smaller firms did business with the major breweries, although they were often highly specialised, frequently offering buyers items they had patented themselves. The network of engineering suppliers which evolved to meet the demands of late Victorian brewers must have provided employment for thousands, yet we know little of it aside from advertisements and reports in trade journals, along with a few surviving artefacts.

G J Worssam & Son

One of the larger London firms was G J Worssam & Son, a brewers' engineers and coppersmiths based at Wenlock Road, just north of Old Street. George Jarvis Worssam (1814–79) began his career as a millwright, working with his brothers for Samuel Worssam & Co, makers of woodworking machinery at their Oakley Works in Chelsea's Kings Road. In 1843 he became works manager for the brewers' engineer Richard Moreland, but left to found his own firm of specialist millwrights and pump repairers in 1849. He was soon granted several patents, and throughout its entire history the firm continued to patent improvements to machinery. George's son Henry Worssam (1846–1915) joined the firm in 1863 and it became G J Worssam & Son in 1874. It was Henry who guided the firm towards brewers' engineering, adding a coppersmith's shop to the works. His younger brother Ernest Worssam (1853–1916) joined Whitbread's Brewery in 1874 and was head brewer from 1898 to 1912.

Towards the end of the 19th century the firm was a regular exhibitor at the annual Brewers' Exhibitions, their displays emphasising machinery of their own design. Although Worssam's main business was plant manufacture and supply, at its peak the firm was capable of designing and fitting out complete small breweries, for instance the new Steam Brewery for Newland & Nash of Bedford in 1906; its maltings still survives.[12] Henry Worssam's three sons all joined the firm, and although one was killed in the Great War, Ralph and Cecil guided Worssam's until it was taken over by Vickers Ltd in 1945. One of the fourth generation, Leslie Worssam, son of Cecil, continued to work in the brewery engineering division of Vickers until 1985.[13]

During the independent life of G J Worssam & Son, which lasted just under a century, its products found their way into many breweries at home and abroad. They specialised in bottling plant, for the dairy as well as the brewing industry. In 1909 Tooth & Co's Kent Brewery of Sydney bought some of Worssam's products, which may well have been bottling machinery. The city's Powerhouse Museum holds a handsome brass maker's label from equipment supplied to Tooth's – Australia's second-oldest brewery – which lost its bottling plant to a fire in 1903.[14]

Burton's brewers' engineers

The prodigious growth in Burton's breweries during the middle and late 19th century was accompanied by the expansion of brewers' engineering works in the town. By the turn of the century there were five major firms and another, Pickering Brothers of the Union Foundry, closed around 1890.[15] In addition the Thornewill & Warham works provided engines for many breweries, as we shall see in the next chapter. The three best-known Burton firms were Buxton & Thornley, Morton's and Briggs, the latter still in existence today.

Buxton & Thornley were based at the Waterloo Works, which was founded about 1865 and stood immediately east of what is now the Town Hall. They made a wide range of machinery and copper, brass and iron goods, including their own patent 'Burton steam pump', which the *Brewers' Journal* described as 'almost a household word in breweries'; customers included Bass, Peter Walker and Truman's.[16] In advertising the firm promoted the pump's economy, adaptability and simplicity: 'The pumps are easily fixed, and can be attended to by an ordinary workman.' Two of their water pumps and a steam engine (*see* next chapter) were

Fig 5.14
Buxton & Thornley three-throw water pump (three single-acting pumps side by side) on display at the National Brewery Centre. The electric-powered pump was one of a pair installed in 1901 at Worthington's Wetmore Maltings in Burton to provide water for steeping the grain.

sold to the Hook Norton Brewery (Oxfordshire) in 1899, and are still in everyday use. A Buxton & Thornley pump and an engine (1889) can also be seen at Claymills Pumping Station, just north of Burton, built between 1884 and 1886 to process the town's brewing effluent. One of the driving forces behind the firm's success was Peter Thornley (c 1844–1912), who invented a series of improvements to steam engines. Buxton & Thornley was taken over by Briggs & Co in 1912.

The firm which eventually became today's Briggs of Burton plc was established in the mid-18th century; by 1840 coppersmith Thomas Bindley had a works in Burton's High Street. Samuel Briggs became his apprentice about 1865 and was a partner by the early 1870s. They set up the Burton Copper Works in nearby Station Street to make brass and copper brewing plant, initially selling their wares to local brewers, and then further afield; in 1885 they opened a London office. In the same year the firm won a medal for their brewing machinery at the International Inventions Exhibition held at South Kensington, using this fact prominently in their advertising. Around this point Thomas Bindley died, and the firm became S Briggs & Co. By the 1890s they were recognised as one of Britain's leading brewers' engineers, and expanded to a new works in the former Moor Street Brewery in 1900. Here they operated a foundry, assembly shop and design offices.

Briggs became a limited company in 1911, and after taking in Buxton & Thornley bought up Thornewill & Warham (with their New Street works) and Shercliff's both in 1929, making S Briggs & Co Ltd the biggest engineering firm in Burton. William Briggs was by then in charge of the company, his father Samuel having died in 1928. They gave up the Moor Street works in 1956, but stayed on at the larger New Street site until 1988, when they bought Robert Morton & Co and moved to Morton's Trent Works in Derby Street, where they remain, still producing equipment for the brewing industry.

Fig 5.15
On display in the brewhouse at Tetley's of Leeds in 2008 was the last brewing copper to be manufactured in copper by Briggs of Burton. The 135-barrel copper was made in 1966.

Robert Morton was born in 1859 in Stockton-on-Tees, where his family owned a foundry. He moved to Burton by 1876, establishing his brewers' engineering firm around 1880. They sold six cast-iron 80-quarter mash tuns to Barclay, Perkins in 1891, and rapidly became renowned for their horizontal and vertical refrigerators, although the firm was more than simply a plant manufacturer, as Morton's advertised in 1898: 'Breweries erected complete – plans and estimates given.' Like Briggs, Morton's was a firm with worldwide reach; a limited number of historic vessels and machines manufactured by both companies still survives, in Britain and abroad, as well as many modern plant installations.

Dealing with the malt

At the brewery, the first pieces of machinery our malt encounters are the malt screens and mills, the iron or steel rollers of the malt mills combining with the screens to ensure the malt is of the exact specification required by the brewer. The mills can be of various designs, usually incorporating from one to three pairs of

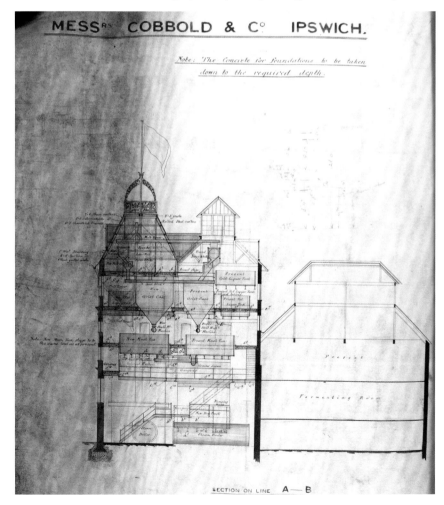

Fig 5.16
One of William Bradford's 1903 drawings for the Cliff Quay Brewery in Ipswich, showing positions of the old and new malt mills, with space for a third to be installed. An elevator brings the malt up from the hop and malt store, connecting with a malt or Archimedean screw which transfers it to the mills, each having a screen and a pair of rollers.

Fig 5.17
Malt mills at Mitchells & Butlers Cape
Hill Brewery, Smethwick during the
1920s. The mills are driven by line
shafting, and on the floor below are huge
grist cases to collect the output.

rollers. The screen is normally a rotating cylinder through which the malt passes, leaving through around three sets of differently sized apertures. Dirt and dust are removed via the smallest holes, then larger sizes of malt, eventually leaving any residue of foreign bodies, such as stones, to be deposited from the end of the cylinder. Many combinations of mill and screen are possible, but cleanliness is essential. This type of machinery was not specific to brewing – mills and screens were agricultural implements used by grain merchants – however, two major agricultural engineers did advertise their wares specifically to the brewing industry as well as the broader market. They were Nalder & Nalder of Wantage (Oxfordshire), and Robert Boby of Bury St Edmunds (Suffolk).

Nalder & Nalder, founded in 1857, manufactured all sorts of steam threshing and grain handling machinery, and became a limited company in 1866. Their base was the Challow Iron Works (1840) at East Challow on the western edge of Wantage, at least part of which still stands, an elegant nine-bay limestone range with a central ornamented tower. In 1883 the firm's 'patent rotary malt screens, so well known and extensively used throughout the trade' were displayed at the Brewers' Exhibition.[17] Their rotary-action machinery was regarded as long lasting because of its lack of vibration; it was also relatively quiet in operation.

Although Nalder & Nalder were successful in the brewing world, Robert Boby (c 1816–86) of the St Andrews Works in Bury St Edmunds was acknowledged to be the leading manufacturer of screening and dressing machines. He started out as an ironmonger in the early 1840s, but his invention of a self-cleaning screen in 1855 propelled his firm to the fore. They expanded to produce a wide variety of agricultural implements, many directed at the brewing industry, and by the time of Boby's death his firm had sold over 14,500 grain cleaners and separators.

The business was incorporated in 1898 as Robert Boby Limited and by 1906 it employed more than 300 men; an advertisement from that year boasts of selling over 40,000 screens. In 1927 the company was taken over by Vickers, although it continued under its own name as a subsidiary, but the works were closed in 1971. However, one workshop building – now known as the Boby Building – survives, having been moved to the Museum of East Anglian Life at Stowmarket in Suffolk.

Mashing

After the milling stage, our grist awaits mashing stored in a wooden or iron grist case, a hopper positioned above or beside the mash tun. If the grist and hot water are mixed in a machine before entering the mash tun, then the grist case is located to the side of the mash tun, opening out into the mashing machine; otherwise, the grist falls directly into the tun.

The most commonly used external masher is the Steel's masher, which was patented in 1853 by the somewhat acerbic Glasgow mechanical engineer and brewer James Steel (1792–1891), later a partner in Steel, Coulson & Co. One of Steel's many inventions, it is a horizontal cylinder containing an Archimedean screw or a rotating axle with rakes attached.[18] Grist and water are fed into the cylinder, and mix together before being expelled into the mash tun. The cylinder itself is often a handsome copper construction, decreasing in breadth towards the mash tun; a fine example dating from about 1900 is still in use at Hook Norton Brewery (Fig 5.22). Most brewers' engineers made their own versions of the Steel's masher, for instance Elgood's North Brink Brewery in Wisbech retains a 1910 Steel's-type machine by Worssam's of London.

However, it was not the only type of external masher; a self-acting masher with no moving parts was invented by Alloa brewer Charles Maitland (c 1819–98) in 1863. The so-called Maitland patent mash tun (although the masher was the innovative part) comprised two small, concentric vertical cylinders, the inner one being perforated. Grist was sent down through the inner tube and water through the

Fig 5.18
A mash tun and segmented cover seen at Gale's Brewery in Horndean, just before closure of the brewery in 2006. All buildings apart from the red-brick brewhouse tower (1869) have been demolished, and the site developed for housing.

outer, so that jets of water hit the falling grist, lessening the need for mechanical stirring within the tun.[19] As with the Steel's masher, devices using this principle are still in use today. Machines based on these patents and others, for instance E R Southby's self-acting masher of 1880, were manufactured by most brewers' engineers, although Steel's was the most frequently advertised.[20]

Now for the mash tun, a large vessel of circular cross section, originally made of wood (often oak), and later of copper or iron. Although a cast-iron mash tun was in use by 1808, wooden mash tuns were still popular at the end of the 19th century. Copper linings could be added to wooden or cast-iron mash tuns. Mash tun covers could be made of wood or copper, be flat or domed, and for convenience have a lifting or sliding section for opening. Large tuns might have a cover hung on chains with counterbalancing weights, so that it could be easily lifted (see Fig 7.26).

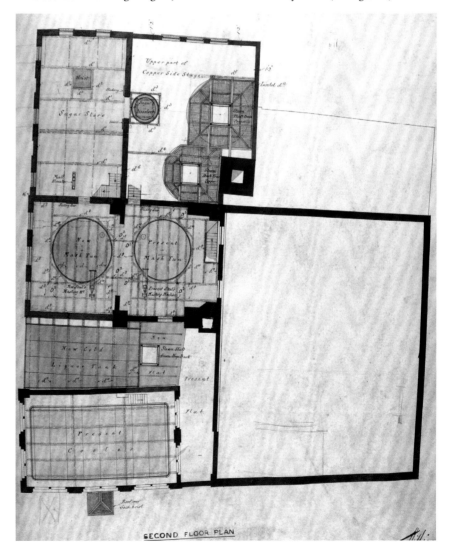

Fig 5.19
William Bradford's 1903 plan for doubling the brewing capacity at the Cliff Quay Brewery in Ipswich. An additional mash tun is to be installed on the second floor, along with a second Steel's masher.

SECOND FLOOR PLAN

Fig 5.20
Three of the four mash tuns at Wolverhampton's Springfield Brewery seen in 1991, just as the brewery was closing. The tuns were installed by Robert Morton & Co of Burton in 1896. The brewery was gutted by fire in 2004 and the remains await redevelopment.

Fig 5.21
A system of pulleys and chains hoists the wooden mash tun covers at Mansfield Brewery, seen in this 1933 photograph. The output of the mashing machine can be directed into either of the two tuns visible, which probably date from 1907 when the brewhouse, designed by William Bradford & Sons, was built.

Fig 5.22
The Steel's mashing machine (centre), dating from around 1900, stationed between a pair of mash tuns at Hook Norton Brewery. The L-shaped copper cylinder can be rotated about its long axis, allowing the mixture to be expelled into either tun. Note the belt drive (top right), part of a line shafting system that transfers power from the steam engine, on the ground floor, throughout the brewery.

Fig 5.23
A gleaming underback at St Austell Brewery, located beneath a wooden mash tun made by Llewellins & James of Bristol.

Fig 5.24

Raking the mash in a large mash tun at
Brakspear's Brewery, Henley-on-
Thames, during 2000; brewing ceased
two years later.

Fig 5.25
The 1914 (left) and 1916 mash tuns
at Shepherd Neame's Brewery in
Faversham. The tuns, made of gunmetal
and English oak, were reconditioned in
1949 and 1960 respectively, and are still
in regular use.

The tun has a double floor, the upper plates (or false bottom) perforated to let the
wort run through to the underback – a smaller open copper vessel – below, while the
spent grains are collected on the false bottom above.

Originally, mixing the mash inside the tun was carried out by men with 'oars' or
wooden stirring implements, but an internal mechanical masher was invented by
Matterface in 1807. It was a complex piece of plant (often known as a porcupine
because of its spikiness) with a vertical shaft running through the mash tun, from
which one or more arms radiated, each carrying a set of revolving rakes. 'Thus the
contents of the tun are thoroughly roused in every part' as Walter Sykes put it in his
1897 treatise on brewing.[21] This system was popular, although as ever with brewery
machinery, there were several other methods of mixing the mash.

The oldest mash tun still working regularly is at All Saints Brewery in Stamford,
Lincolnshire, where the 1876 mash tun produces fruit beers. At the St Austell
Brewery in Cornwall, a mash vessel of 1893 is used not for its original purpose but to
infuse hop cones in hot water, making 'hop tea'; their 1913 mash tun still works
normally. At Wainfleet in Lincolnshire, Bateman's 1898 mash tun only operates for
seasonal brews. The 1914 mash tun at Hall & Woodhouse (Blandford St Mary,
Dorset) was in full operation until 2012, and the two mash tuns (1914 and 1916)
made of oak and gunmetal (an alloy of copper, tin and zinc) at the Shepherd Neame
Brewery (Fig 5.25), Faversham (Kent) are both used regularly.

The copper

Our wort now goes to the copper, or brewing kettle as it is known in America. Coppers, as the name suggests, were normally made of copper but by the mid-20th century were generally stainless steel. Early coppers were completely open, but these were eventually superseded by closed coppers, either flat-topped or more usually domed, with vents and a porthole that can be opened to add hops. Domed coppers were introduced from the early years of the 19th century but took some time to be accepted; indeed, the major Burton brewers retained their open coppers into the 20th century (although they were five or six times smaller than the closed coppers used in the great London breweries).[22] At Belhaven Brewery in Dunbar (East Lothian), founded in 1719, every batch of wort was boiled in a single open copper well into the 1960s, severely limiting brewing capacity.

Originally the copper was heated externally, directly from beneath by a wood or coal fire; the bottom of the copper was convex, protruding up into the large, basin-shaped vessel. Next, from around the 1870s, came steam heating in two forms, internal and external, the latter requiring a copper with a concave lower section and cylindrical upper part. Surrounding the bottom was a larger iron steam jacket, with room between the two for hot, high-pressure steam to circulate.

Fig 5.26 (above)
This 1893 steam-heated copper at St Austell Brewery is still occasionally used for brewing. St Austell's larger 1914 copper (originally coal-fired) was replaced by a stainless-steel vessel in 1998; its 1947 copper cover is now on display in the visitor centre.

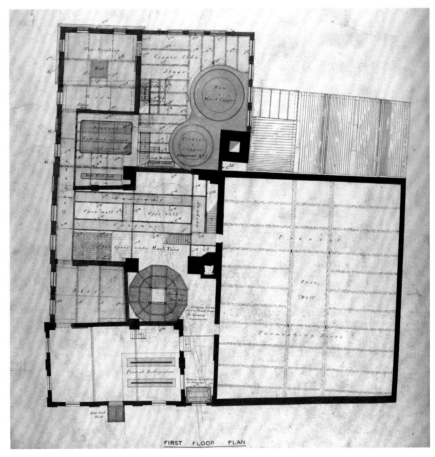

Fig 5.27 (right)
William Bradford's 1903 plan for extensions to the first floor of the Cliff Quay Brewery in Ipswich, showing the positions of the old and (larger) new wort coppers, next to the hop weighing room. Both coppers were convex-bottomed and about 12ft in height, extending through two floors.

FIRST FLOOR PLAN

Fig 5.28
A celebratory photograph taken during the installation in 1873 of a new 1,000 barrel copper at the Star Brewery in Romford. Seated is the Star's head brewer C P Matthews.

Fig 5.29 (right)
Inside the copper at Arkell's Kingsdown Brewery in Swindon. The heated wort is pumped up the central column and spews out into the copper from the 'mushroom' at the top, creating an intense but even 'rolling boil'.

Fig 5.30 (far right)
The 1779 domed copper seen at Brakspear's Brewery in Henley-on-Thames in 2000. Its wooden cladding bears the mark of engineers and coppersmiths Bennett, Sons & Shears from the Farringdon Works in London's Shoe Lane, a firm known for its copper brewing vessels and which was active between around 1785 and 1891.
The upper part of the copper was moved to the Wychwood Brewery of Witney in 2004, and is probably the oldest working vessel at an English brewery.

In 1868 E & W Pontifex and Wood's Farringdon Works made a steam-jacketed copper 12ft in diameter for the Mortlake Brewery, London; it was then the largest ever made (or 'hammered up') from a single sheet of copper, and weighed in at 1 ton 18cwt. Even bigger were the 'two enormous brewing coppers' made by Llewellins & James in 1897 for an Australian brewery. Such was their size that neither railways nor shipping companies would carry them, so they were taken by road from Bristol to London, mounted on two drays. Each load weighed about 4½ tons and took up a large part of the roadway.[23]

An internally steam-heated copper was fitted with a coiled pipe mounted inside the vessel through which the steam passed (Fig 5.32). Modern coppers often use

Fig 5.34 (left)

Cleanliness is vital in brewing, as shown by this dramatic shot of a man working inside a copper. It was taken in Manchester during the 1950s by Walter Nurnberg (1907–91), who used tungsten lighting to create images reminiscent of 1940s American films. His work transformed industrial photography and gave a boost to post-war industry.

Fig 5.35

The old copper room at Tolly Cobbold's Cliff Quay Brewery, Ipswich, seen in 2010 when the building was becoming derelict; redevelopment plans were agreed in 2013. On the right is a boiling copper installed at Cobbold's Harwich Brewery in 1723, then brought to Ipswich in 1746, where it was eventually used as a sugar dissolving vessel; it was probably England's oldest brewing vessel to survive in a working environment. However, by 2012 all the Cliff Quay brewing equipment had been stolen.

Fig 5.36

After boiling in the copper, the hot wort passes through a hop back, which has a perforated base to sieve out the spent hops. The large vessel on the left, at Bateman's Brewery in Wainfleet, is the hop back; on the right is the wort receiver and sugar dissolving vessel.

this method, although nowadays they are gas (or sometimes oil) fired. Even more sophisticated are tubular heat exchangers or calandria, where wort is circulated through external pipework to be heated before being pumped back into the copper.

A few early coppers survive, notably a 1779 copper dome from Brakspear's (now at Witney, *see* Fig 5.30 and p 150) and the two splendid Pontifex & Wood vessels of 1869 and 1885 at the old Ram Brewery site in Wandsworth (*see* Figs 5.12 and 5.13), where redevelopment is to take place shortly, probably including a brewery museum. The 1885 open copper at Wadworth's Northgate Brewery, Devizes in Wiltshire is used for seasonal brews (*see* Fig 5.31), and a little-used 1893 copper remains at the St Austell Brewery (*see* Fig 5.26). Very unusually, the Caledonian Brewery in Edinburgh still has two of its original open coppers, dating from about 1869, which are direct fired by gas. And a final rarity: at the little Stanway Brewery, in the old country house brewery of Stanway House in Gloucestershire, the two coppers are directly wood fired. The brewhouse operating occasionally on the Shugborough estate in Staffordshire is also wood fired.

Fig 5.37
Combe's Wood Yard Brewery in Covent
Garden, photographed around the 1870s
to 1880s. Before the use of refrigerators
became commonplace, open coolers
required a huge amount of ventilation,
provided by louvres and other openings,
normally located at or near the top of
the brewhouse.

Cooling and refrigeration

After boiling in the copper, the temperature of the wort is reduced in a cooler –
latterly known as a coolship – which was originally a large, shallow (5–8in in depth)
rectangular open vessel located high up in the brewhouse tower, where louvre
windows provided good ventilation (Fig 5.39). They could be wood or iron, but
were generally copper, and later vessels were deeper. From the mid-1880s
refrigerators were beginning to replace, or at least work alongside, flat coolers; this
eventually allowed a more compact arrangement of plant.

These refrigerators were metal heat exchangers, invented by Jean Louis
Baudelot in 1859, in which circulating cold water passed through a series of tubes,
the wort flowing over them in a thin layer. Initially they were horizontal but took up
so much space they were replaced with vertical refrigerators, such as those patented
by Robert Morton, but there were many variations. Larger breweries had banks of
vertical refrigerators. The modern version of the refrigerator is the paraflow, a plate
heat exchanger where the hot wort travels in the opposite direction to the cooling
fluid. It was invented in 1923 (for use in milk production) by Richard Seligman
(1878–1972), founder of the Aluminium Plant & Vessel Company (later APV).
It was soon adapted for brewing; by late 1925, seven British breweries were using
paraflows, five years later the figure was more than a hundred, and they rapidly
became ubiquitous.

Mechanical refrigeration was a boon for lager brewers because of their need for
long-term cold storage, and its basic principles had been understood for centuries
before being practically developed towards the end of the 1800s. It relies on
compression of gas, thus producing heat, then rapid decompression so that heat is
taken from the environment. In 1868 Truman's Brewery in London installed two
ice-making and refrigerating machines manufactured by Siebe Brothers of
Lambeth.[24] They were used mostly to chill water before being sent through the

Fig 5.38
The top of the fermenting house at the
Bass Old Brewery (rebuilt in 1876), seen
around the turn of the century. To the
rear is a vast open cooler, measuring
47ft by 39ft, where the hot wort initially
lies to be aerated. It then runs on to the
horizontal refrigerators (foreground), to
complete cooling before fermentation.

Fig 5.39
Steam rising from the open copper wort
cooler at Hook Norton Brewery.
It was in regular use until 2004, and still
survives in its original position, near
the top of the lower brewhouse tower.

Fig 5.40
A rare surviving pair of early
20th-century open copper wort coolers
at Elgood's Brewery in Wisbech.
Now disused, they have been replaced
by an enclosed plate heat exchanger.
To the rear is the timber-cased
1950s copper.

Fig 5.41
Vertical refrigerators made of copper tubing, seen at Mitchells & Butlers Cape Hill Brewery between the wars. The hot wort cools as it trickles over the tubes, through which cold water passes.
To ensure the wort remains pure, air in the room is filtered during refrigeration.

normal refrigerators; Allsopp's of Burton bought two of the Siebe Brothers patent machines in 1872. But the most significant contributor to refrigeration technology was the German engineer Carl von Linde (1842–1934), who in 1873 invented artificial (or mechanical) refrigeration while working for the Spaten Brewery in Munich. The ice blocks formed in this process were used to cool the brewery's cellars. By the 1880s most German breweries made their ice mechanically, and artificial refrigeration was a critical factor in the spread of lager brewing worldwide.

Fermentation

Now our wort is cool, we can move on to fermentation, which for porter was famously carried out in huge wooden vats. It seems they were first erected at London's Red Lion Brewery, St Katherine's, in 1736, and were made by the brewery's own coopers.[25] These vats were commonplace after 1760, and mostly made within the brewery, although Guinness of Dublin, who continued using large-scale vats long after they had become unfashionable elsewhere, bought at least some of theirs from brewers' engineers and coppersmiths James Oxley & Co of Frome. In the 1860s they made a dozen vats holding a total of 30,000 gallons for Guinness (probably for their number seven vat house), and Oxley's already had an order for 20 more vats of the same size for Dublin.

Fig 5.42 (right)
Stout vats at the **Bass New Brewery** (1863–4) in Burton, seen around 1900. The 16 vats, each holding about 500 barrels, mostly contained the firm's Special Stout while it matured. Bass also produced the stronger Imperial Stout and Extra Stout.

Fig 5.43 (below)
The extensive square room at Bass Old Brewery around 1900, with a few of its 114 fermenting squares. Each square is 6ft deep and holds 2,200 gallons of beer. After several days in the squares, the beer is sent to one of three union rooms to be cleansed of yeast.

There were also specialist vatmakers such as Powell & Layton, who we first hear of in Southwark during 1763. Around the start of the 19th century their firm came into the Carty family, and by 1861 as was employing 46 men. T R Carty & Son took over Charles Pontifex's vatmaking business in 1897, moving to Peckham in 1921, where they continued as England's best known vatmakers until closure in 1989. At that point there were probably around 10,000 wooden vats, tanks and drums still in use, although many in industries other than brewing. Carty's customers tended to be loyal; the records of orders from Brakspear's Brewery in Henley-on-Thames can be traced back through Carty's books to 1799. One of their largest orders came in 1935 when 11 square, kauri pine fermenters and 17 oak storage vats were supplied to the new Guinness Brewery at Park Royal, doubling Carty's annual turnover.[26]

Fig 5.44
Fermenting tuns at Melbourn Brothers All Saints Brewery in Stamford, photographed by the engineer and windmills expert Rex Wailes (1901–86) in 1963. On the centre tun (number three) is a board carrying a description of the contents, including its batch or 'gyle' number and the type of beer, in this case IPA (India Pale Ale).

Fig 5.45
In the foreground of this turn-of-the-century postcard is the impressively well-ventilated fermenting house added to Fox & Sons Oak Brewery in Green Street Green (a suburb of Orpington) by William Bradford & Sons in 1897. The brewery employed about a hundred people, but debts forced its closure in 1909, and the site was cleared in 1938; it is now 'The Oaks' housing estate.

Aside from the massive porter vats, fermentation normally took place in much smaller, open-topped round or square cross-section vessels – 'rounds' and 'squares' – generally made from wood (often English oak) but sometimes stone or slate. Their capacity could usually be measured in tens of barrels, although during the late 1880s the engineer Robert C Sinclair designed six slate fermenters for Groves & Whitnall's Regent Road Brewery in Salford, each holding 214 barrels, the largest of their kind in Britain at the time.

Brewers experimented with fermenting vessels built from glazed bricks and tiles, brick lined with glass plates, wood lined with lead or copper, and enamelled iron plates, but 'none of these have stood the test of experience'.[27] Rounds were made very like barrels, of wooden staves held together with iron hoops, while squares were built up from wooden planks; both were flat-bottomed vessels. A standard fermenter had a built-in attemperator, a coil of copper piping through which cooling water flowed, and a smooth interior finish so it could be cleaned efficiently.

During the fermentation cycle, yeast has to be skimmed from the top of the vessel, some of it being used for later fermentations. There are numerous methods of skimming yeast, one of the more modern being vacuuming it off, and consequently wide variations in fermenting equipment. The Yorkshire square system originally used square fermenting tuns, with a capacity of about 30–50 barrels, made from stone or slate slabs; modern squares are stainless steel and often round (Fig 5.46). Above the main square is a second compartment (the yeast trough) with a circular hole cut through the centre of its bottom. As the wort ferments it gushes upward through the hole then overflows back into the larger vessel below, leaving the yeast to be collected in the trough. When Barnard visited John Smith's Tadcaster Brewery he saw the largest stone square fermenting room in England with 173 squares each holding 25 barrels.

The best-known yeast removal system is the Burton union (Fig 5.47), which was neither invented in Burton nor peculiar to it, but became associated with the town through its high-quality pale ale production, and is still in use at Marston's Brewery.[28] It comprises a double row of casks connected together in sets (normally of 24 casks) and mounted on a frame, which discharge yeast and beer via 'swan's-neck' pipes into a long overhead trough. The yeast is removed and the beer returned to the casks, and so the process continues until fermentation is complete. This

Fig 5.46
These six round, stainless-steel open fermenters, actually Yorkshire squares in function, were installed in the new brewhouse at the Black Sheep Brewery, Masham in 2006, helping to increase the brewery's capacity by almost two-thirds.

Fig 5.47
Yeast swirls along the troughs in the union room at Bass No 2 Brewery (formerly the New Brewery) in Burton during the 1970s. Note the swan's-neck pipes protruding from the rows of casks.

Fig 5.48

Open fermenting squares in use during 1964, even as closed fermenters were becoming the norm. They eventually evolved into tall, narrow metal vessels with automatic temperature control, allowing them to be used to store and condition the beer after fermentation. These tanks can have a capacity of up to several thousand barrels.

system developed from Warrington brewer Peter Walker's 1838 patent, which crucially mentioned the top trough, but was otherwise rather different from union sets in practice. His work built on much previous experimentation and was in turn improved by the Burton breweries.

Not only were union sets expensive, and difficult to clean, but they required a sizeable floor area: one of Robert Davison's fermenting rooms at Allsopp's New Brewery (1860) held around 1,200 casks, but this was exceeded four years later at the Bass New Brewery (1864) with the biggest union room in Burton, housing 1,456 casks. Around 1890, when the use of unions was at its peak, about 11 per cent of beer brewed in the UK was fermented in Burton unions, and an estimated 85 per cent of those union sets were located in Burton itself.[29] Both E & W Pontifex and Wood, and Llewellins & James specifically advertised their union sets, but any of the major brewers' engineers would have supplied them, or indeed most of the work could well be done in a brewery's own cooperage.

The cost of a brewery

Once our beer has fermented to the brewer's satisfaction, it is given time to mature (conditioned) and transferred (racked) to casks, keg or bottles. All this involves further equipment, and of course the brewing process as a whole requires power, as we shall see in the next chapter. From hoisting the malt into the brewery, through to sending the beer out in casks, there was huge scope for the brewers' engineers to sell their wares, but it is difficult to estimate the financial significance of the 19th-century brewery engineering market.

Despite William Bradford thinking it 'simply absurd' to give general estimates for brewery construction and fitting out linked to capacity, Scamell & Colyer did exactly that, although qualifying their figures by pointing out that costs were approximate and site-dependent.[30] They based their estimates on work they had actually carried out, and combining the costs of building and plant, a 10-quarter brewery worked out at £3,650, a 70-quarter brewery at £20,150 and a 160-quarter brewery at £68,000. Generally the cost per quarter fell as the size of the brewery increased, ranging from £480 to £224, although there were anomalies. It is impossible to disentangle construction and plant costs, but fortunately they gave a single estimate relating to plant only, for fully equipping a 15-quarter tower brewery; this was about £1,800, or £120 per quarter.[31] The combined cost of plant and building for a 16-quarter brewery (with Burton unions rather than standard fermenters) was given as £5,300, so we can say that for small breweries at least, the plant may constitute around 40 per cent of the total cost.

The trade papers were very coy about money, but did report on the 50-quarter Swan Brewery (*see* Fig 4.3) in Fulham put up for Stansfeld's by William Bradford in 1881 to 1882: 'we believe the total cost is only about £30,000'.[32] At around £600 per quarter, these lavish premises were at the top end of Scamell & Colyer's range. Rather more economical was Bradford's new brewhouse (1881–2) at Harveys Bridge Wharf Brewery (*see* Fig 4.54) in Lewes, where Pontifex & Wood supplied most of the 20-quarter plant, along with James Oxley of Frome. The whole thing cost just over £8,000.[33] Using our 40 per cent figure, the plant manufacturers might have made a little more than £3,200 out this single contract.

We know from trade journals and other contemporary sources that during the 1880s nearly 1,300 quarters-worth of new brewery buildings were erected in the UK. However, the size of these structures is mentioned in perhaps only one in ten of these reports, so the true figure could well be of the order of 13,000 quarters. With plant costs at about £120 per quarter, then an extremely rough estimate for the total value of plant contracts during the decade is £1,560,000. Annually this is £156,000 or the equivalent current spending worth of over £7.5 million in today's money.[34] For comparison, the annual profits of a single brewery, Georges & Co of Bristol, averaged almost £39,000 during the 1880s.[35] If we take into account the additional value of plant renewals and alterations at existing breweries, as well as design fees for brewers' engineers who provided architectural services, we can see that brewery engineering was a substantial industry, albeit nowhere near as financially significant as brewing itself.

Old plant in a new world

Changes in brewing technology throughout the 20th century, and the availability of new materials like stainless steel, had a great impact on the shape and size of brewing equipment. The Crawley aluminium fabricators APV carried out a series of large-scale orders for Guinness during the 1950s, culminating in 1959 with the on-site construction in Dublin of what was then the world's biggest beer fermenter, a stainless-steel mammoth of 8,016 barrel capacity (well over 4.6 million half-pint bottles).[36] National-scale brewers brought in items such as the rocket-like, silvery cylindroconical fermenters which altered the external appearance of the typical brewery from the 1970s; they are particularly noticeable in Burton, where small forests of them cluster beside the older buildings. They were just one of many plant innovations aimed at reducing processing time; others include the lauter tun (which separates wort from mash solids, enabling faster throughput) and the whirlpool (replacing the hop back). However, many traditional brewers hung on to their older plant, perhaps modernising it by lining vessels with steel or plastic; Tetley's Brewery in Leeds retained its Yorkshire square fermentation system but slowly replaced the slate squares with stainless-steel vessels on much the same principle from the 1960s onward, finally getting rid of the old squares in 2008 (then closing the brewery in 2011).

Fig 5.49

A massive fermentation tank makes its way through Burton during the 1970s. It is about to cross the railway bridge, midway through its slow, half-mile journey from the Trent Works of Robert Morton & Co to the Bass breweries on Station Street. The Station Hotel is extant, but no longer a pub.

Fig 5.50 (right)
Still extant in a disused part of the
Old Truman Brewery in Spitalfields is
this 1971 ceramic tile mural, with its
accurate representation of
contemporary brewing equipment.
Particularly noticeable are the
cylindroconical fermenters (top left).
The tiling was designed by Gordon
Smith & Partners and made by
Pilkington's+Carter of Manchester
and Poole.

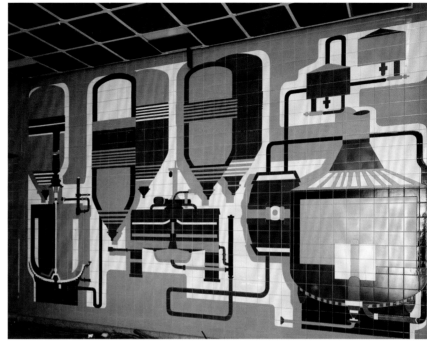

Fig 5.51 (below)
One of three 100-barrel glass-lined
steel maturing tanks is squeezed into
Eldridge Pope's Dorchester Brewery
around 1960. They were each 10ft high
and almost as wide, too big for the
railways, and had to be transported
by road.

There has always been a strong second-hand market in brewing kit. The rise of microbreweries from the 1970s combined with the disappearance of many older concerns resulted in a certain amount of traditional brewery plant migrating to new breweries, notably the Black Sheep Brewery at Masham in North Yorkshire. This opened in 1992, housed in a maltings previously used by Lightfoot's Wellgarth Brewery. The heart of the new brewery – a late 1940s copper, mash tun and hop back made by Ramsden's of London – came from Hartleys Brewery in Ulverston (Cumbria), which had just closed (Fig 5.53). Three Yorkshire squares were acquired from Hardys & Hansons in Kimberley (Nottinghamshire), and another three, dating from about 1890 and probably the oldest equipment at Black Sheep, from Darley's at Thorne (South Yorkshire). Although Black Sheep completed the installation of a new brewhouse in 2006, most of their original vessels still continue in operation.

Similarly in 2002, following the closure of Brakspear's Henley Brewery, the Wychwood Brewery of Witney in Oxfordshire (founded 1983) took on the brewing of Brakspear beers, and the original Brakspear fermenters and 1779 copper dome (see Fig 5.30) were moved to Witney in 2004. The fermenting vessels work on the 'double drop' system, with two circular fermenters suspended well above six square wooden vessels; the wort begins fermenting on the top level, then after 16 hours is allowed to drop down to the squares below (leaving any solids behind), where the process is completed.

Modern brewing kit also has substantial second-hand value, in the growing market for small-scale plant brought about by the growth of craft brewing firms. About a hundred brewpubs in the Firkin chain were established during the two decades following 1979. After they closed in 1999, the brewing plant – most of it wooden clad – was removed and later sold in Britain and worldwide. Former Firkin equipment can now be found in France, Denmark, Australia and further afield.[37] Part of the appeal of Firkin kit was aesthetic, a significant point for those microbrewers whose brewery is on show to their customers.

Traditional brewers often keep disused vessels on display, sometimes in a small museum area, as a visitor attraction. Of course, shiny coppers work best in this respect. In front of Greene King's visitor centre in Bury St Edmunds is a copper made by Briggs of Burton (see Fig 3.54), while outside the National Brewery Centre in Burton stands a copper from the Bass New Brewery. When Okells Brewery moved to their new home

Fig 5.52
A rather battered but still glamorous 1929 copper at Robinson's Unicorn Brewery, Stockport, takes centre stage in the visitor centre. Made by coppersmiths Robert Morton & Co of Burton, the 200-barrel copper has been partly dismantled in order to show off the internal pipework of the calandria. It was retired from use in 2010.

Fig 5.53
The Black Sheep Brewery's first set of
brewing equipment is located in the
double-height kiln area of the former
Lightfoot's Brewery in Masham. At the
top is the grist case, then the mash tun,
hop back (between the horizontal pipes)
and the late 1940s copper.

outside Douglas (Isle of Man) in 1996, they took with them a copper dome from their previous premises, and mounted it as a shelter above the pedestrian entrance to their warehouse. Redeveloped breweries are also home to occasional pieces of heritage equipment, like the copper in the centre of Burton's former Everard's Brewery (now Burton Village) and part of a boiler built into housing at the former Wethered's Marlow Brewery.

Perhaps the most enjoyable means of using these vessels is to turn them into seating, as in the Vats Bar at Kendal's Brewery Arts Centre (in the old Whitwell, Mark premises), or the café attached to the Adnams store near their Sole Bay Brewery in Southwold. Here are two gleaming copper-lined, wooden fermenting vats made by Carty & Son in 1925 (Fig 5.54), both of sufficient size for a couple of tables and several chairs to fit inside. Enter through openings cut away from the vat walls, then eat and drink within the brewing vessel, as the Victorians so enjoyed doing.

Fig 5.54
One of two modified Carty & Son fermenting vats, previously in use at the Sole Bay Brewery, decorating the café at the Adnams Cellar & Kitchen Store in Southwold.

6 Powering the Brewery

Fig 6.1

Men at work: Tamplin's Phoenix
Brewery, Brighton in 1897. Workers roll
casks around the yard, but pulleys and
an ornate ironwork hoist (incorporating
the brewery's phoenix symbol) are used
to lift them on to wagons for delivery.
Another hoist, possibly steam powered,
hauls sacks up through the brewhouse.

From ancient hand-powered brewing through wind, water and horse power to the eventual introduction of steam engines, gas and electricity, the provision of power – and its cost – has been crucial to the profitability of the brewing industry. Early brewing was hard physical labour, part of the daily domestic grind. Similarly in commercial breweries there was much hauling of weighty sacks, pumping of liquids and shifting of casks, as well as the heavy work of mashing: the mash initially had to be stirred, and afterwards the soggy, dense mass of spent grain had to be dug out of the tun.

In mashing, when the grist and hot water were first mixed, it was essential to ensure even heat distribution and to break up resistant lumps of grist. The mash was raked and stirred (a process sometimes known as rowing) using implements called

153

Fig 6.2

A brewster watches four men mashing
with oars at a brewery in Soissons,
north-east of Paris, in a watercolour by
Jean-Louis-Joseph Hoyer (1762–1829)
dating from around 1800. A fifth man,
to the rear, appears to be working
a pump, and the one visible oar is
lattice shaped.

Fig 6.3

Workers at an Edinburgh brewery and
maltings around the 1870s show off the
tools of their trade. They hold assorted
shovels and rakes used for turning the
grains during malting, while a small sled,
for moving casks, is propped up against
the man with the dog.

oars (Fig 6.2), which were indeed oar shaped although with a larger blade; later oars had a lattice design that could be pulled through the mash more easily. In the 1730s William Ellis, who probably had some experience in a great London brewery, noted the mash for a strong beer being 'work'd by several Men with Oars for about half an Hour'.[1] The Scottish beer and wine writer W H Roberts described how the process of mashing 'is performed with the greatest care, until every ball or lump is broken, and the whole uniformly mashed'.[2] Once mashing was complete and the wort drained off, the tun had to be cleaned out and the grain disposed of, normally as animal feed.

This and other heavy work in the brewery was carried out by a small band of strong general labourers (usually Irish), about whom we have little information as they rarely appear in financial records. We do know that Barclay, Perkins employed between 75 and 100 such men during the 1790s, each earning just under a pound a week, while Truman's employed 94 in 1772. Whatever the details of their wages, they were small beer in comparison with the total cost of malt or casks to the brewer, and the industry as a whole was not a great user of labour.[3] This did not prevent brewers from casting around in search of labour-saving devices, as even a willing and cooperative workforce needed rest, whereas machinery did not. Burdensome physical tasks in the brewery fell into two main groups, those requiring rotary motion, such as stirring or grinding, and others needing horizontal or vertical propulsion, including pumping and lifting. As we saw in chapter 4, gravity could be harnessed by means of the tower system of brewing, but brewers had always looked to natural resources – wind, water and animals – to provide extra power. When their breweries became more industrialised and vessels increased in size, the need became ever greater.

Wind and water

The Weevil Brewery (*see* Fig 3.21) in Gosport, on the western shore of Portsmouth Harbour, was ideally situated to benefit from the wind's energy, unlike many urban breweries. By 1716 its water was being pumped from a well by a four-sailed, open-trestle post mill in front of the cooperage. The Admiralty bought the Weevil estate and brewery in 1751, around the time that another well came into use, rendering the windmill redundant. In 1760 the Admiralty approved the construction of a windmill to work the second well, but it appears that a horse mill provided the power instead. The original windmill was demolished in 1786 after being damaged by high winds.[4]

Although records of brewery windmills are sparse, the Weevil windmill is typical in that it powered a water pump rather than brewing or grinding machinery, just like the small four-sailed tower mill still standing in open countryside at Haigh to the north-east of Wigan. This wind pump was built in 1845 to supply water to John Sumner's Haigh Brewery. The brewery closed soon after being taken over by Greenall Whitley in 1931 and the windmill was left to become derelict, but its sails and machinery were restored in 2011.

England's best known brewery windmill is at Bateman's Salem Bridge Brewery in Wainfleet, but it never powered the brewery. The six-storey brick-built tower mill dates from around 1820 and was used to grind corn. When it became part of Bateman's, soon after the First World War, its sails were in such a poor state they were taken down and the mill transformed into a bottling shed; no milling machinery survives. However the tower, topped by a weathervane in the shape of a beer bottle, has become an iconic symbol. In contrast, Kingsford's Windmill Brewery in Dover was powered by its mill, this one originally built in 1798 to pump water. The brewery bought the mill in 1829 and converted it to extract water from its own well and to power malt-grinding machinery; the mill's four-sailed form was a dominant presence on the skyline next to the brewery chimney. Although the Windmill Brewery ceased trading during the 1880s, most of the buildings survived until demolition in 1983, although the mill probably disappeared before the First World War.

Few urban breweries can easily make use of water power, and indeed being located next to a river can be a mixed blessing, as recent inundations at Harveys in Lewes (the Ouse flooded the brewery in 2000) and Jennings Castle Brewery in Cockermouth, Cumbria show. Jennings, situated right at the confluence of the Derwent and the Cocker, suffered devastating floods in 2009; casks were found as far downstream as Workington.

But historically, water has been a useful and free power source, after the initial cost of installing a water wheel (*see* Fig 2.3). Smaller rural breweries might well have milling as a sideline and be built on the bank of a stream, so water power could drive the grindstones. This was the case at Letheringsett, a small Norfolk village on the River Glaven. The 18th-century brewery, which had its own on-site maltings,

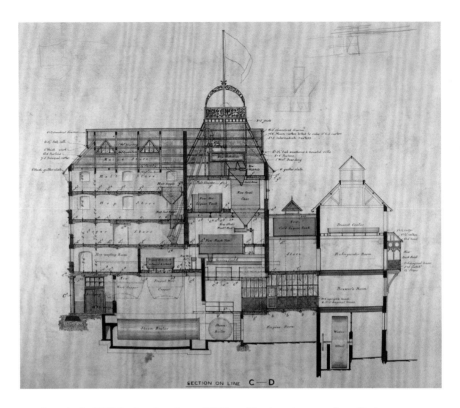

SECTION ON LINE C — D

was bought in 1780 by local maltster William Hardy, who soon installed a water wheel beside the brewery to power the previously horse-driven malt mill. Hardy then spotted an opportunity to expand into flour production and in 1784 began grinding corn; eventually the brewery had a complex milling system involving three wheels. Morgan's Brewery of Norwich bought Letheringsett Brewery in 1896 and used it for soft drink production until a fire in 1936, although most of the buildings still survive.

Only one of England's traditional breweries still obtains part of its power from a water wheel. The working wheel is at Donnington Brewery near Stow-on-the-Wold in Gloucestershire, which occupies a rural site converted to a corn mill around 1580, when two 12ft-diameter wheels were installed. It became a brewery in 1865, remaining completely water powered until 1959. A single overshot wheel functions now, driving small pumps and machines. At Palmers Brewery in Bridport, Dorset, the 18ft-diameter undershot water wheel (Fig 6.5) is still in working order, but gradually became redundant after mains electricity reached the town in 1930. It was made at Thomas Helyear's foundry on West Street and installed in 1879, replacing an earlier wheel.

In Oxford, the water wheel at the old Morrell's Lion Brewery (Fig 6.6) has outlived the brewery, which closed in 1998 and was converted to housing. It drove a former horse wheel and worked in combination with two steam engines to power the brewery machinery, the overall design allowing the water wheel or either engine to drive any part of the plant. The water wheel itself, 13ft in diameter and 3ft 9in wide, is undershot and may date from the mid-18th century or before.[5]

Fig 6.5 (above)
The water wheel at Palmers Old Brewery in Bridport is stamped 'T Helyear Bridport 1879'. The wheel's sophisticated (but difficult to manufacture) design, with curved buckets for greater efficiency, was based on improvements published in 1825 by the French engineer Jean-Victor Poncelet (1788–1867).

Fig 6.6 (right)
Looking north up the Wareham Stream in Oxford, with Morrell's Lion Brewery and its water wheel on the left. Today the view is somewhat changed from Henry Taunt's 1920 photograph; although the wheel and the lower buildings survive, modern flats have replaced the tall brewhouse and chimneys.

Horse power

Horse wheels of various forms, and occasionally horse treadmills, were used in agriculture and industry from medieval times. The horse wheel comprises a vertical shaft on which is mounted horizontally a large-diameter wheel at a level high enough for one or more harnessed horses to be attached to it. The shaft taking power from the wheel, by means of a gear, is usually positioned above the wheel. Simple but very effective, horse wheels powered London's great common brewhouses, and by the mid-18th century breweries throughout the country were deriving a great deal of their power from this source. Pumping, lifting and milling could be accomplished via the horse wheel using gears and shafts to drive the relevant machinery, but it could not – at least initially – be adapted for all the

brewery's needs. Mashing was still carried out by hand until after the steam engine was introduced from the mid-1780s onward. James Walker of Dover filed the first patent for a mechanical mashing rake in 1787, intending it to be horse driven.[6]

Such was the efficiency of steam power that industrial horse wheels were all but abandoned by the start of the 19th century. Barnard, in his series of brewery visits around 1890, found only one working example, although not actually powering brewing machinery. It was 'an old-fashioned ponderous horse-mill, used to this day for grinding malt for the retail trade' at Hall & Woodhouse's Ansty Brewery (Dorset), in a malthouse built in 1786.[7] The Ansty Brewery closed about 1900, when the firm moved all production to a new brewery at its Blandford St Mary site.

However, Barnard never visited Morrell's Brewery, where the 15ft-diameter horse wheel was still intact when steam engine expert George Watkins (1904–89) inspected their machinery around 1949. He noted that the wheel's maker was Francis Anding of the Albert Iron Works in Uxbridge, and suggested that along with the rest of the machinery it dated from between 1830 and 1850, describing it as 'a splendid example of brewery plant'.[8] As with many breweries, including Whitbread's at Chiswell Street, the steam engines (and water wheel in this case) drove the plant through the horse wheel (Fig 6.8).[9] This arrangement, particularly popular in the early years of steam, ensured that in case of a steam engine breakdown, horses could easily be brought in as temporary replacements. Similarly the pre-1820 engine house at Steward & Patteson's Pockthorpe Brewery in Norwich was put up beside the horse wheel and next to the brewhouse.[10]

We have a good description and drawing of a horse wheel, albeit one used to pump water rather than directly power brewing, from Gosport's Weevil Brewery (Figs 6.9 and 6.10). Here John Smeaton designed horse-powered pumps in 1780 and, using the same plan, in 1788; the latter remained in use until about 1861. In fact these can more accurately be described as horse engines, as the 20ft-diameter wheel, gearing and transmission lay below the level of the two horses, which walked around a 32ft-diameter path. Each circuit measured about 100ft. Substantial foundations of the 1788 structure still remain, now covered by modern buildings.[11]

Fig 6.8

This 1817 diagram of a brewery from the *Edinburgh Encyclopedia* shows the direct linkage, via gearing and a shaft, between the steam engine and the horse wheel. The steam engine drives the plant through the wheel, which connects to the malt mills, Archimedean screw, mash tun and water pump.

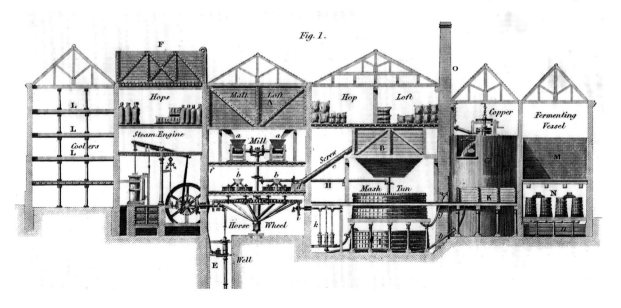

Fig 6.9
Section through John Smeaton's 1780 design for the horse engine at the Weevil Brewery in Gosport. The pair of horses drove a beam engine, housed to the right, which pumped water from an adjacent well.

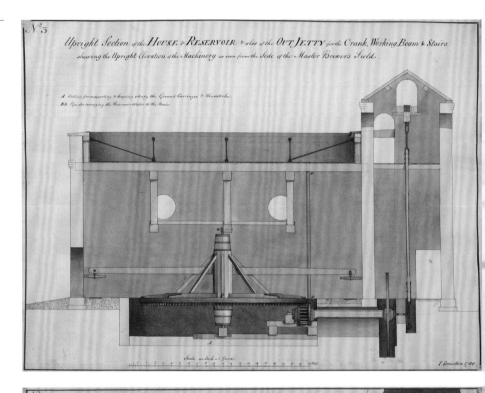

Fig 6.10
Plan of John Smeaton's 1780 design for the horse engine at the Weevil Brewery in Gosport, showing the construction of the horse wheel and the transmission mechanism, via gearing, to the beam engine and pump.

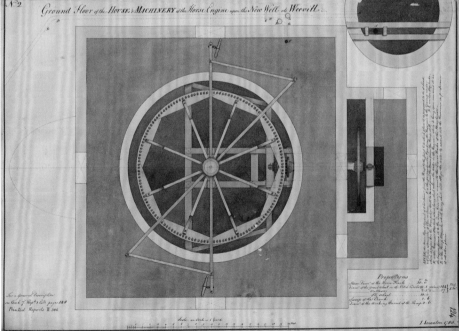

Fig 6.11
The annual dray horse parade outside the main gateway of William Stones Cannon Brewery in Sheffield, seen on 9 June 1902. Such parades always attracted a good crowd to see the impeccably turned out animals, although in this case the spectators appear more interested in the photographer, while the draymen seem unimpressed by the delay.

Fig 6.12
The loading stage at Shipstone's Star Brewery, Nottingham, around 1900. For easy loading, the raised platform is roughly the height of the dray floor. Note, to the rear, the brewery dog surveying the scene from a barrel.

Although horse wheels and engines from the agricultural sector are on view at several UK museums, there are no brewery horse wheels to be seen, all swept away in the move to steam power and subsequent brewery rationalisation. But in Antwerp, the Brouwershuis (Brewers' Building) of 1553 to 1554 still houses an intact horse-driven treadmill which powered a water scoop, raising water from below into reservoirs within the building. From there it was distributed to the city's breweries through a pipe network. The Brouwershuis was built by the entrepreneur Gilbert van Schoonbeke (1519–56) as part of an expensive but ultimately successful plan to promote industrial development in Antwerp.[12]

Behind the dramatic disappearance of horses from inside the brewery lay the problem of costs. The mill horse, so-called as they often drove malt mills, was not a valuable commodity. Towards the end of the 18th century a mill horse was valued at a maximum of £5, and often a lot less; in contrast, the colossal, glamorous dray horses were worth about ten times as much. They had in common their running costs: feed, stabling, and the wages of farriers, blacksmiths and wheelwrights who looked after them. By 1780 a large brewery needed over 20 mill horses, machinery having increased in size to the point where 4 horses were required to turn the wheel, rather than the original one. In 1786, one of Whitbread's brewers estimated the annual cost of a mill horse to be at least £40, and found that by installing a steam engine he could save annually a sum equivalent to 24 mill horses; this was roughly the cost of installing the engine, which itself was cheap to run.[13] A tempting prospect indeed, and from the late 1780s the mill horses – the unsung heroes of the Georgian brewing industry, endlessly trudging round and round in the bowels of the brewhouse – were replaced by steam engines.

Boulton and Watt's steam engines

Pumping engines had been available to brewers for some years, but were uneconomic propositions because horses still had to be kept to power the malt mills. It was the attraction of mechanised rotary motion that ensured a series of orders for Boulton and Watt from the final years of the 18th century. The first seven breweries to install their rotative steam engines were all in London, Henry Goodwyn's Red Lion Brewery leading the way with an order in May 1794. Goodwyn's was a four-horsepower engine, although measurements of power at that stage were approximate. The second order – just a month later – came from Samuel Whitbread, and by virtue of his position as the nation's leading brewer, it gained much publicity. The 10-horsepower engine began operating in 1785, was inspected by King George III and Queen Charlotte on their visit to the brewery in 1787, and thereafter became one of London's great curiosities, as the *The Picture of London* over-enthusiastically reported: 'One of Mr. Watt's steam-engines works the machinery. It pumps the water, wort, and beer, grinds the malt, stirs the mash-tubs, and raises the casks out of the cellars. It is able to do the work of 70 horses, though it is of a small size, being only a 24-inch cylinder, and does not make more noise than a spinning-wheel.'[14]

The process of fitting a steam engine into a working brewery was tricky. Even though installation normally took place during the summer break from brewing, much to-ing and fro-ing between the brewery's own engineers and the Boulton and Watt team was required. The usual arrangement was for the brewer's engineers to send plans of the brewery to Boulton and Watt, who responded with detailed drawings of the engine and its fittings. The brewer's contractors then built the engine house, advised by Boulton and Watt, who sent a supervisor to oversee the actual installation and early running of the engine. They sent out as much of the engine as possible in prefabricated form, so as to lessen the chance of the parts being ruined on site by local fitters, who might feel their local knowledge was more relevant than the manufacturer's drawings.[15]

Installation of a 10-horsepower rotative engine at Barclay, Perkins during the summer of 1786 suffered several mishaps, from parts being delayed by shipping or even completely mislaid, to Boulton and Watt changing their on-site supervisor mid-contract. The job, due to be completed by August, was only finished in November (Fig 6.13).[16] With some minor modifications, this massive beam engine remained in service at the brewery until 1884, when it was replaced by a 125-horsepower horizontal engine made by James Watt & Co. The original 1786 engine, although partly scrapped, was obtained by the National Museum of Scotland in 1886; after being completely refurbished in 1999 it is now on display in Edinburgh (Fig 6.14).

The first brewery outside London to invest in a Boulton and Watt engine was Shepherd's (now Shepherd Neame) at Faversham, who purchased their engine in 1789 and promptly began to advertise themselves as the Faversham Steam Brewery. James Watt himself retired around 1800, when his fundamental patent expired, thus allowing other firms to develop and manufacture steam engines, and the business was taken on by Watt's and Boulton's sons. Altogether Boulton and Watt had provided engines for over 30 breweries by the 1820s, including Guinness in Dublin, who bought their first stationary steam engine in 1808.[17]

All the major breweries were mechanised by the early 19th century, but several rural and smaller concerns retained their horses for some years. Matthews & Canning's Anchor Brewery in Chelsea, for instance, was still working with a two-horse wheel in the 1840s, but had installed a six-horsepower engine by 1854.[18] However, brewers who did decide to convert to steam generally found their engines to be reliable, economic and extremely long-lasting.

Fig 6.13 (below left)
Boulton and Watt's sectional drawing of the 10-horsepower steam engine installed at the Barclay, Perkins Anchor Brewery, Southwark in 1786. Steam is piped to the engine cylinder from the boiler on the right; the up-and-down motion of the beam then turns the wheel which drives the brewery plant.

Fig 6.14 (below right)
The 1786 steam engine from Barclay, Perkins Anchor Brewery on display in 2012 at the National Museum of Scotland, Edinburgh. The engine is 31ft high and weighs just under 20 tons. Its boiler would have stood to the right, beyond the supporting wall.

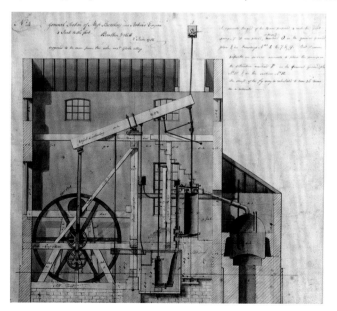

SECTION ON LINE E—F

Fig 6.15

William Bradford's 1903 alterations to the Cliff Quay Brewery show the efforts made to remove steam, a by-product of boiling the wort. Two wooden steam shafts, each about 30ft high, provide ventilation and prevent steam entering areas where it would be unwelcome, particularly the fermenting house. Note also the ornate ironwork crown, typical of Bradford's designs.

The 1785 Whitbread beam engine was finally decommissioned in 1887 after 102 years of service, and would have been scrapped had Professor Archibald Liversidge, an English-born academic from the University of Sydney, not been visiting London at that point. Liversidge was one of the founders of the city's Technological, Industrial and Sanitary Museum (forerunner of the Powerhouse Museum) and saw the engine as an ideal exhibit. Whitbread's agreed to donate the engine and it was partly dismantled before being shipped to Australia, where, due to lack of funds, it languished in storage. It was eventually restored and put on display at the new Powerhouse Museum in 1988. A final accolade for the engine came when its image, along with portraits of engineer James Watt, entrepreneur Matthew Boulton and their Soho Manufactory, were chosen for the reverse of the British £50 banknote issued in November 2011.

The steam-powered brewery

The early steam-powered breweries were great visitor attractions. Whitbread's, having set up their engine in 1785 to power pumping and grinding, the following year contemplated adding cask cleaning and other cleansing works to the list of tasks driven by steam, causing their brewer, Joseph Delafield, to remark: 'The brewhouse, as the possession of an individual, is and will be when finished still more so, the wonder of everybody by which means our pride is become very troublesome being almost daily resorted to by Visitors, either Strangers or Friends to see the Plan ... .'[19] There was a sense of wonder at the 'ingenuity of contrivance' employed by the brewers to link all their new-fangled machinery to the engine using

Fig 6.16
The transfer of rotative motion from horizontal to vertical by means of meshing gears can be seen in this photograph of mash tun rake driving machinery at Combe's Wood Yard Brewery in London around 1875. It was probably taken as the building was being converted to a warehouse and the plant dismantled.

Fig 6.17
Cask washing at the brewery of Davis, Strangman & Co in Waterford, established in 1792. The image was shot around 1900 by the local commercial photographic studio of A H Poole. High-level line shafting drives at least six machines. Although the power source is out of view, it was probably a steam engine as we see hot, steaming water available on tap from a pipe running above head height.

an array of shafts, axles and wheels.[20] There were mechanical rakes of various designs for mashing the malt, more powerful pumps, improved lifting gear, powered Archimedean screws and more. Brewing was no longer a wood-based craft but one requiring engineering and metalwork expertise.

Even by the 1840s visitors could still be bewildered by a great brewhouse: 'the pumps, pipes, rods, and other apparatus are so thickly arranged on every side'. But they had learned to take almost for granted the presence of steam; George Dodd, on his tour of Barclay, Perkins around 1842, saw two steam engines (of 30 and 45 horsepower) and simply commented that 'The construction of these engines, and the mode in which power is communicated from them to various parts of the establishment, resemble those generally observed in large factories, and need not claim particular notice here.'[21] It was during the next phase of steam power, the change from direct-fired to steam-heated coppers during the 1870s, that some breweries thought it profitable to identify themselves as a 'Steam Brewery'. The public once again equated the use of steam with being modern; breweries were as proud of their conversion to steam heating as they had been of their original steam engines.

All this steam was provided by sturdy boilers and men toiling away in the heat of the stoke holes (Fig 6.22), shovelling coal into furnaces (although the process of bringing coal to the stoke hole had been partly mechanised by Barclay, Perkins before 1842, using a track system, and some breweries eventually invested in mechanical stokers).

Fig 6.20 (above)
The vertical boiler at the restored Victorian brewhouse at Southwick in Hampshire. Still in working order, it was last used to power brewing on 26 May 1985, when a special ale was produced to celebrate completion of the brewhouse's refurbishment.

Fig 6.21 (above right)
The Southwick Brewhouse boiler was manufactured by Lumby's of Halifax, whose Greetland Boiler Works also made cisterns and safes. In 1900 the firm advertised itself as the world's largest maker of wrought-iron boilers, but it went into liquidation in 1960.

Fig 6.22 (right)
Workers feed coal into the furnaces of three huge Lancashire boilers in the stoke hole of Shipstone's Star Brewery, Nottingham around 1900.

Boilers were simply tanks of differing designs, which allowed flames to heat water and produce steam. Inefficient early boilers could only work at low steam pressure, and were soon replaced by the Cornish boiler, introduced by Richard Trevithick junior about 1812, with a single furnace tube surrounded by a cylinder of water. William Fairbairn's Lancashire boiler, available from 1844, had a double furnace tube, and was typically 8ft across by 30ft long. Both these designs were very strong and durable.

The engine makers

Once James Watt's patent expired – and to an extent before, as there was a certain amount of piracy – numerous companies began to manufacture improved steam engines, some of which were bought by the growing number of breweries. The same companies often went on to develop gas engines in the last quarter of the 19th century, and eventually electric motors. Of course these engines in turn replaced steam power, but several original brewery steam engines still survive, for instance the 25-horsepower Buxton & Thornley steam engine sold to Hook Norton Brewery in 1899. Still in daily use, it was a replacement for an engine dating from around 1880, although the two were used together for some time.

Rather than going to nationally known manufacturers like Buxton & Thornley of Burton, smaller brewers often obtained their engines from the local ironworks. The Ram Brewery in Wandsworth took delivery of an A-frame beam engine made by the local firm Wentworth & Sons in 1835. It was a Woolf compound engine, designed by the Cornish millwright Arthur Woolf (1766–1837), resident engineer at Meux Reid's Griffin Brewery on Liquorpond Street during 1796 to 1806, where he experimented with boiler design. The Woolf compound engine incorporated two cylinders with different pressures and was widely adopted in the mid-19th century.

Fig 6.23
The horizontal single cylinder steam engine at Southwick Brewhouse. It was restored, along with all the brewing equipment, from 1982 to 1985 by volunteers from Southampton University Industrial Archaeology Group, working under the guidance of Hampshire Buildings Preservation Trust and the chief brewer and chief cooper from Gale's Brewery in Horndean.

Fig 6.24
Hook Norton's 1899 steam engine seen in 2002. It was manufactured by the Burton firm Buxton & Thornley. Thornley was a personal customer of the brewery. The engine is still in regular use; note the number of belts driven by line shafting.

Fig 6.25
The second well room at Shipstone's Star Brewery in Nottingham, seen about 1900. The engineers and ironfounders E Timmins & Sons of Runcorn supplied the well's pumping machinery in 1884, so this area predated the alterations carried out between 1899 and 1900. Beneath the brewery were three extensive cellars excavated from solid rock.

The Ram Brewery engine originally drove four pumps and a vertical shaft from which power was taken to drive milling and mashing machinery over several floors. This 1835 engine – which was still in working order at the start of the 21st century – is still in place at the former Ram Brewery site, along with an 1867 steam engine also made by Wentworth's.

Harveys of Lewes also went to a local firm for what was probably their first steam engine, a four-horsepower horizontal engine made by James Jackson of Brighton in 1856. It was replaced by a Pontifex & Wood steam engine when the brewery was rebuilt in 1881; this powered the brewery until the early 1960s, and is still preserved there. Likewise Barnsley Brewery went to Needham, Qualter, Hall & Co of the town's Railway Foundry for their engine in 1874; although it was possibly only the third engine to be built by the firm, they had previously patented several improved designs. This engine is now on display at the Markham Grange Steam Museum near Doncaster. Another still remaining at a brewery is the engine supplied around 1900 to Wadworth's of Devizes by George Adlam & Sons of Bristol; it was restored in 2004 (Fig 6.26).

Bass, too, went to local supplier Robey & Co for the tandem compound engines (Fig 6.27) required to power their range of eight new malthouses at Sleaford, Lincolnshire in 1905, but in this case Robey's happened to be one of Britain's best-known steam engine manufacturers. The firm, founded in 1854, employed over 500 people by 1871 at their huge Globe Works on the southern edge of Lincoln. The two Sleaford Maltings engines were mirror images of one another, and powered

Fig 6.26
Wadworth's Northgate Brewery (1885) in Devizes was probably powered only by hand and horse until around 1900, when this horizontal single-cylinder steam engine was installed by Adlam's of Bristol. The engine drove a hoist, the well pumps and other plant until superseded by electric power about 1940, and was restored in 2004. The brewery's architect, John A Randell of Devizes, was also responsible for the 'full size' model *Stonehenge As It Was* shown in 1894 at the Woodhouse Park exhibition venue in London's Shepherd's Bush.

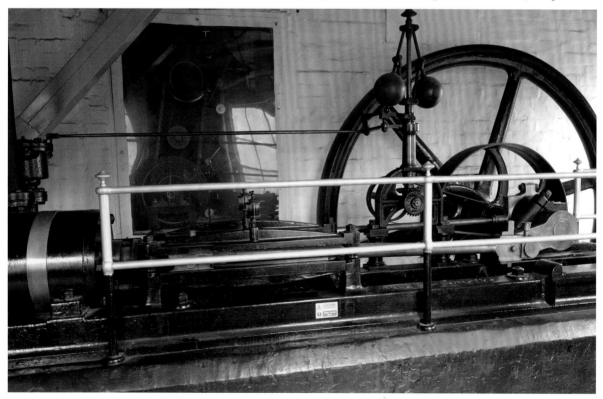

hoists, pumps, screens and ventilators throughout the maltings, via line shafting (rotating shafts) driven from a 13ft flywheel. The engines worked until the maltings closed in 1959, and one is now on display at the National Brewery Centre (Fig 6.28), along with the front plate of a double-tubed Manchester boiler, patented and manufactured by Daniel Adamson & Co of Newton Moor Iron Works near Manchester. Three more Robey engines were bought by Truman's Black Eagle Brewery, London in 1899. They drove cask hoists until the last of the three was retired in 1970. Two have survived on public view, one being donated to the Kew Bridge Steam Museum, the other finding its way to the Robey Trust in Tavistock.

Fig 6.27
The Robey & Co tandem compound engines at the Bass Sleaford Maltings, photographed by steam engine expert George Watkins in 1970; the engines and shafting cost £9,238. The maltings began operating in 1906 and worked until 1959, initially providing about one-fifth of the malt used by Bass.

Fig 6.28
The two Robey engines from Sleaford Maltings were removed during the 1970s. One is now on display at Forncett Industrial Steam Museum near Norwich, while the other (shown) went to the National Brewery Centre in Burton. Both are in working order and still run regularly.

Thornewill & Warham

Thornewill & Warham of Burton differed from other steam engine manufacturers in that they were specialist brewers' engineers. The firm's roots went back to at least the 1730s when Thornewill's were making iron goods. By the 1780s the business had expanded considerably from its New Street base, and they were probably the major supplier of iron hoops (for beer casks) to local brewers. After 1800 their foundry work and engineering became much more significant, and by 1849, when Robert Thornewill and J R Warham signed a partnership agreement, the firm was capable of manufacturing steam engines for Burton's brewers. In 1861 their New Street Works employed 178 people, as many as the town's largest breweries.[22]

Thornewill & Warham built most of the locomotives used by Burton breweries from 1860 to 1880 (Ind Coope was one of the first brewers to order them), and acquired a national reputation for their steam engines, which they increasingly exported. They also moved into constructional engineering; much of the ironwork used in the building of the town's breweries between 1850 and 1890 was supplied and erected by Thornewill & Warham. The firm could also completely fit out a brewery, as they did in 1868 at the Vale of Mowbray Brewery in Leeming, North Yorkshire, for Plews & Sons. They were told by John Plews 'to spare no expense in making the plant as perfect as possible', supplying engines, machinery and mash tuns, as well as engines and plant for the Plews maltings.[23]

Greenall Whitley's Wilderspool Brewery (Fig 6.29) in Warrington bought two Thornewill & Warham single-cylinder steam engines in 1884. They were located in a power house lavishly decorated with ceramic tiles and marble, and powered the brewery via a flat belt from the 8ft 6in-diameter flywheel until 1962. The engines were kept in working order until brewing ceased in 1990, then were removed in 1996, prior to the buildings being converted to offices, and are now on show at Markham Grange Steam Museum.[24]

Fig 6.29
Greenall Whitley's Wilderspool Brewery in Warrington, as it was at the end of the 1970s; the corner office block, with its unusual round tower, is grade II listed. After the modern brewery buildings were demolished in 1993, the two Thornewill & Warham engines were removed, which involved lowering them about 9m to the ground from their ornate second-floor engine room.

Gas and Electricity

Gas lighting, using town gas produced by the destructive distillation of coal, was widely available from the mid-19th century. Gas firing for boilers and coppers was introduced in the mid-1880s and was commonplace within a decade. Perhaps even more significant was the use of gas in engines; the German engineer Nikolaus Otto patented the first commercially successful internal combustion engine in 1866, and three years later Crossley Brothers of Manchester acquired the rights to manufacture and sell these gas-fuelled engines throughout Britain and its colonies. By 1880 they had made around 1,300 engines and improved the design.[25] They went on to produce all sorts of engines, many of which were bought by breweries, but their initial gas engine was an ideal replacement for smaller steam engines.

Electric light soon began to replace gas; during Barnard's brewery tours in the late 1880s, he found that most of the major breweries (and some of the smaller ones) were already well equipped with electric lighting, 'by far the best illuminant for breweries, as it is absolutely pure'.[26] The Vaux brewery in Sunderland, for instance, put in electric lights during 1884, and Joule's Brewery in Stone (Staffordshire) around 1885, the latter finding they saved time and money. Once installed, the running costs of gas and electric lighting were roughly comparable, but the use of gas lights and the resultant dirt incurred the annual cost and trouble of whitewashing, painting and cleaning.[27] The most extensive system of electric

Fig 6.30

Tending the engine at Shipstone's Star Brewery, Nottingham, probably during the 1960s. The gas engine, made by Crossley Brothers of Manchester, may date from the early 20th century.

lighting seen by Barnard was at the Guinness Brewery in Dublin, with a total of 526 incandescent lamps. However, the *Brewers' Journal* still felt that installation of electric lighting was worthy of note even in 1890, when Bramley Brewery near Guildford went over to the new light source. Their system was powered by the same engine that drove the brewery plant.[28]

The next stage, of course, was to electrify the actual brewing machinery. An early example came in Norwich, where Bullard's Anchor Brewery added a mineral water manufacturing plant to their premises in 1897; significantly, 'a feature of the factory is the fact that the motive power is entirely supplied by electricity'.[29] Although there were many further experiments, the brewers' engineers Arthur Kinder & Son claimed that their new Brampton Brewery in Chesterfield (Derbyshire), built in 1903, was the first in England to be completely electrically driven. The same firm's Langley Maltings (1898; *see* Fig 4.10) was also electrically powered.[30]

In 1907 Percy Bradford, a partner in brewers' architects William Bradford & Sons, spoke enthusiastically about electricity – both for lighting and power – to the Institute of Brewing. He pointed out that it was often cheaper than gas, while 'in point of convenience and cleanliness it is unrivalled'. His firm had designed and were about to erect a new brewery in the Midlands (this was probably the Mansfield Brewery) 'in which the whole of the machinery will be driven by separate electric motors'; all the brewer had to do when he wanted to grind or mash was switch on the relevant motor. Although Bradford's audience did not wholly share his enthusiasm, thinking electricity might just be an American fad, it turned out to be the way forward.[31]

In Burton, the Bass steam cooperage was converted to an 'electric cooperage' in 1916, using the supply from Burton's power station, and the firm continued with its electrification programme throughout the 1920s and 1930s. Electrification of the Bass New Brewery at a cost of £4,579 was said to have produced an annual saving of £3,800 for Bass.[32] The use of electric power by brewers slowly increased, and it became normal for larger establishments to have their own generating or power stations.

7 Burton upon Trent – Beer Capital of Britain

Although Burton's beers had acquired a national reputation for excellence by the end of the 17th century, the buildings of the industry were still small, really domestic, in scale. The beer was generally produced by the town's publican brewers in brewhouses attached to inns, many along High Street and Horninglow Street, near the Great Bridge over the River Trent. Burton's pioneering common brewer was Benjamin Printon, an entrepreneur and an incomer (from London), who established a small brewery by the western end of the bridge in 1708; he employed three men. From the 1720s a concentration of breweries arose in this area; they were only marginally bigger than the pub-brewhouses and were unconnected with inns. By the 1740s several of the old pub-brewhouses were being enlarged and converted into premises suitable for common brewers, although still with only a single copper.

Merchant brewers including Samuel Sketchley from Nottingham and Benjamin Wilson (1714–1800), probably from the Derby area, came to Burton and made a good living through taking on small brewhouses and expanding their trade. Wilson's High Street brewery, established in 1742, employed 30 men by 1750 and produced 1,000 barrels annually.[1] He retired in 1773 leaving his sons, notably Benjamin Wilson (1751–1812), to run the business and two more brewhouses were opened, although he saved money by hiring malthouses when required rather than building his own. By purchasing Sketchley's Horninglow Street premises in 1790, Wilson upped his brewing capacity to 4,500 barrels; impressive for Burton but still trivial by London standards.

A few late Georgian townhouses remain (although altered) from this point in the industry's development, including 181 Horninglow Street and 136 High Street. These houses were both home and workplace, adjoining their brewhouses. One brewhouse-cum-malthouse from around 1774 has also survived, on the north side of Horninglow Street (to the rear of 183–4); this initially belonged to John Davies-Greaves before being acquired by Francis Thompson about 1815. This merchant brewer's yard and buildings were converted to offices in the early 1990s as Anson Court.

Worthington, Bass and Allsopp

Leicestershire-born William Worthington (1723–1800) came to Burton in 1744 to work as a cooper, attracted by the lucrative but risky Baltic export trade in beer. He worked at Joseph Smith's small pub-brewhouse on the High Street's east side and bought the premises in 1760, adding a second brewhouse the following year. By the 1780s he was probably brewing about 1,500 barrels a year, although much of his profits came from trading in timber and iron. William's two sons William (1764–1825) and Thomas (1766–1805) joined him in the business, making a significant early contribution in 1791 by marrying the two daughters of Henry Evans, owner of the brewery immediately opposite. This enabled Worthington's to expand on to the west side of the High Street, where they eventually built the brewhouse and cooperage, while retaining William's townhouse on the east side with stores and maltings to the rear.[2]

Meanwhile the wagon carrier William Bass (1717–87) had bought 136 High Street in 1777, along with a brewhouse and malthouse, where he started to brew in a small way. Following William's death, his son Michael Thomas Bass (1759–1827) went into partnership in 1791 with Musgrave's (who had taken on Printon's brewery in 1729) in order to expand overall brewing capacity. Next, John Ratcliff – who already worked for Bass – joined the partnership in 1796 (Musgrave left in 1797), and Bass & Ratcliff put up a new brewhouse which was in full swing by the end of 1797.[3] It stood on the long plot behind 136 High Street, stretching down to the riverside, close to Worthington's premises on the south side.

Just north of Bass was a brewhouse owned by Benjamin Wilson, then Burton's leading brewing concern. Samuel Allsopp (1780–1838), the son of Wilson's niece, played an increasing role in the firm from 1800, and indeed bought out most of Wilson's interest in 1807; the rest of the business passed to Allsopp on Wilson's death five years later. But it was not a propitious time to be a brewer in Burton, as the Baltic trade had gone into serious decline, brought about by the Napoleonic wars. With few, if any, tied houses, the town's brewers were forced to look to the home trade as a substitute, with all the transport difficulties – roads, canals – that entailed; at the time, it took about a week for a cask of ale to make the journey from Burton to London. Rising costs and uncertain markets resulted in dwindling trade; by 1822 only five brewing firms, all specialist brewers rather than merchant brewers, remained in Burton.[4] These were Allsopp's, Bass & Ratcliff, Worthington's, Thomas Salt (who bought Clay's brewery on the High Street around 1800), and John Sherratt's, a modest concern to the south of Burton's centre.

The surviving brewers concentrated on slowly expanding sales to London and south Lancashire while trying to revive their exports. In the early days there was not much in the way of new building at the breweries; when necessary, extra plant was squeezed into existing premises. The Bass brewhouse, for instance, held 4 mash tuns in 1804 but 10 in 1809, with a concomitant increase in storage facilities. By 1819 however, when Michael Thomas Bass's son Michael Thomas Bass junior (1799–1884) was working as an apprentice in the firm, there had been significant extensions on the riverside site: the Bass & Ratcliff property included two brewhouses, three tun houses, three cool houses and three malthouses.[5]

India Pale Ale

The key to Burton's future brewing prosperity turned out to be a completely different product from the sweet, strong, nut-brown beer the town's brewers exported to the Baltic. From the mid-18th century the East India Company had purchased supplies of strong, hoppy, pale ale to ship out to India. It was good business for the small brewery run by George Hodgson on the River Lea at Bow; his October-brewed pale ale was taken down the Lea by barge and loaded on to the Company's ships in the docks at Blackwall, near the mouth of the Lea. This arrangement worked well until 1821, when the brewery's then-owners tried to export the pale ale themselves, cutting out the East India Company altogether. It proved to be a poor decision; the Company retaliated by finding a new source of supply, Allsopp's of Burton.

Early in 1822 Samuel Allsopp was invited to London by a Company representative, who persuaded him that the potential India trade could replace the lost Baltic exports, if only he was able to brew a suitable substitute for the 'India beer'. It was fortuitous that Burton's well waters were ideal for pale ale production, and after some experimentation, the first Allsopp pale ale went out to India in 1823. Its rapid success was no secret, and Bass & Ratcliff and Salt's soon started to brew pale ale themselves. The India trade built up steadily, with Bass and Allsopp to the fore; Bass, with their newly expanded brewery, were the greatest beneficiaries. By 1830 Bass's output had reached 10,000 barrels per annum, and throughout the 1830s Bass and Allsopp's were exporting a combined annual total of around 6,000 barrels of pale ale. This level of production involved frequent extensions to buildings and improvement of plant. In addition to the expansion of the existing breweries, new players arrived and began businesses; there were nine firms in Burton by 1834.

Although many of the newcomers started in a modest way, the overall
impact on the town was significant; by 1840 around 350 men worked in
brewing, and the annual output was about 60,000–70,000 barrels. Even by this
point the major breweries had become much more than a series of small
brewhouses. Viewed from the east, across the meadows of the Hay, the High
Street breweries – particularly Bass (Fig 7.2), Allsopp (Fig 7.3) and Salt (Fig 7.4)
– were now a substantial mass of interconnected buildings in ranges up to four
storeys in height, sporting several tall chimneys. This implied the presence of
furnaces and boilers heating multiple coppers, and possibly even steam engines.[6]
Industrial-scale brewing had reached Burton.

Bass & Cos Brewery, Burton on Trent.

Allsopps & Co's Brewery, Burton on Trent

Salt & Co's Brewery, Burton on Trent

The railway arrives

The Birmingham and Derby Junction Railway (the Midland Railway from 1844) opened its line through Burton in August 1839, cutting down to 12 hours the time taken to send a cask to London; the cost of carriage also decreased dramatically. Burton's pale ale was already being drunk in the home market, where it was referred to as 'Indian beer' or 'pale ale as prepared for India'.[7] The first mention of India Pale Ale in print occurred in the *Liverpool Mercury* in 1835, after which the term spread slowly until the Burton firms were able to capitalise on the arrival of the railway and sell their bright, bitter beer in London quickly and cheaply.[8] In 1841 first Bass then Allsopp advertised their East India Pale Ale in *The Times*, and the drink became hugely fashionable and popular, so much so that several London and regional brewers set up branches in Burton in order to compete. Later, towards the end of the 19th century, the discovery of 'Burtonisation' – the treatment of water so that its chemical constituents resembled those of Burton's well water – allowed Burton-style beers to be produced anywhere.

The effect on Burton's breweries was considerable. Bass's output (now under Michael Thomas Bass junior, who had taken over after his father's death in 1827) grew from fewer than 15,000 barrels in 1834 to over 80,000 in 1849, by which time the brewery, although constantly extended, must have been creaking at the seams. The new partnership, set up in 1835, of Bass, John Ratcliff's son Samuel, and John Gretton looked to the future from the 1840s by buying land west of the High Street for potential expansion. Immediately north of the Bass Brewery, Allsopp's rebuilt

Fig 7.5

Detail from a map of Burton originally published by Bass in *A Visit to Bass' Brewery* (1902). Numbers 1–19 mark Bass sites (shown in red); other locations, indicated by letters A–P, have been added.

Key

1 Old Brewery
2 Middle Brewery
3 New Brewery
4 Central offices
5 Steam cooperage
6 Repairing cooperage
7 Shobnall ale stores
8 Dixie ale stores
9 Middle Brewery ale stores
10 Shobnall cask-washing sheds
11 Dixie cask-washing sheds
12 Middle Yard cask-washing sheds
13 Engineers' shops
14 Grange pumping station
15 Shobnall Maltings
16 Anderstaff Lane Maltings
17 Plough Maltings
18 New Brewery Maltings
19 Middle Brewery Maltings
A Allsopp's Old Brewery
B Salt's High Street Brewery
C Burton Brewery Company
D Allsopp's New Brewery
E Ind Coope's Burton Brewery
F Worthington's High Street Brewery
G Trustees of the Late Peter Walker Clarence Street Brewery
H Truman, Hanbury & Buxton's Black Eagle Brewery
I Everard's Trent Brewery
J Marston's Albion Brewery
K Allsopp's Shobnall Maltings
L Cooper's Crescent Brewery
M Worthington's Wetmore Maltings
N Charrington's Abbey Brewery
O Salt's Walsitch Maltings
P Worthington's Hay Maltings

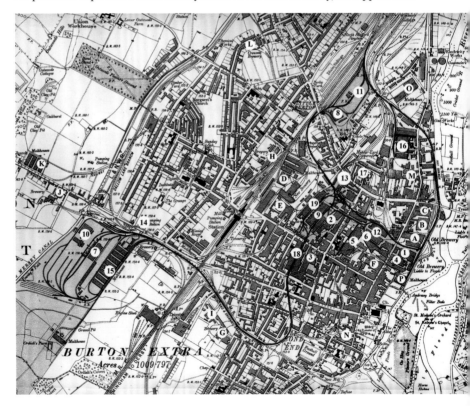

Fig 7.6
Early 20th-century postcard view of the
Trent Bridge, with Burton Brewery
Company's premises to the left (with
two chimneys, left of the church steeple)
and part of Salt's Brewery on the far left.
The Burton Brewery Company site was
cleared in 1962, while Salt's was
demolished in 1956.

their brewery from 1842 to 1843, producing a handsome nine-bay brewhouse in a curious combination of country house (pilasters, pediments) and functional (repeated round-headed arcading) styles; it was the first completely modern brewhouse in Burton. An interesting newcomer was the Burton Brewery Company (Fig 7.6), founded in 1842 by Henry and Thomas Wilders, with premises at the north end of the High Street, just beyond Salt's Brewery; by 1861 it was the town's third largest brewery.

The first industrial breweries

But all this was merely a prelude to the dramatic expansion of the industry in Burton during the period 1850 to 1880, when the town became almost totally enveloped by breweries and its roads were constantly criss-crossed by trains hauling wagon-loads of casks. During these three decades the town's brewing industry trebled in size every 10 years in terms of output and employment, putting a huge strain on communications and services, particularly the water supply.[9] The erection of new breweries, maltings, cooperages, stores and engineering shops called for a higher degree of engineering and managerial competence than had been required when brewing was nearer the domestic in scale.

In 1854 the Old Brewery, as Bass, Ratcliff & Gretton's orginal premises became known, was powered by six steam engines and lit by gas, but it was still inadequate for the firm's needs, and they had begun work on the New Brewery, standing to the north of Station Street, in 1853. At this point it appears that Bass were still reliant on in-house expertise for the planning and design of their breweries and maltings, including the first malthouse (1852) at the Scutari site, near to the New Brewery.

It again displayed the blind arcading that was to become so strongly associated with the industry's buildings in Burton; this originated in the design of the working buildings on country estates, and became a classical industrial motif, used at earlier breweries including Simonds of Reading and Cobb's, Margate.

The New Brewery eventually took over five years to build, much too long at a point when its capacity was urgently needed. It may have been this delay which caused Bass to bring in what we would term a project manager, building surveyor Robert Grace (c 1795–1869) from Derby, who had moved to Burton by 1856 to live at 131 Station Street, in the midst of the Bass estate. We know little of Grace, whose wife was Burton-born, except that he arrived when Bass had no other leading architect or engineer, and left to be succeeded by the firm's first chief engineer and architect in 1867. By the time of the 1861 census Grace describes himself as an architect and surveyor, and in that year he also designed a small, 10-quarter brewery and maltings for Hardy's at Kimberley.[10]

Fig 7.7 (above)
Looking west along the Bass Middle Yard cask-washing sheds; a postcard view from the interwar years. The extensive Middle Yard lay between the Bass Old and Middle Breweries, and was linked to both by the private rail system.

Fig 7.8
Another view of the Bass steam cooperage, showing the mezzanine floor on the left, above the huge wood piles. This turn-of-the-century postcard was part of the series 'Famous Breweries of Burton' published by local printers W B Darley to cash in on public fascination with the brewing capital.

Fig 7.9
A postcard showing the famous Bass cask pyramids; the single 13-high heap to the rear of the lamppost contains over 3,700 casks. In 1873 the value of casks owned by Bass was a massive £200,000.

The Breweries from the River, Burton-on-Trent

Fig 7.10

The Bass water tower (1866) and Old Brewery from the Trent on an early 20th-century postcard. Railway wagons crowd the Hay Branch tracks, which pass the Old Brewery ale loading bank, and to the north (right) we see the chimneys of Allsopp's Old Brewery.

He had no time for other work away from Burton, as Bass undertook a huge building programme during the 1850s to 1860s while Grace was designing and overseeing new construction. The firm completed the New Brewery in 1858, put up the Delhi Maltings on the south side of Station Street (1858–9), erected additional malthouses at the Scutari Maltings (1861–2), then the Wetmore Maltings (1862–4) in Anderstaff Lane, ale and hop stores (1863–4), the steam cooperage (Fig 7.8) (1863–7) and the water tower (Fig 7.10) at the Old Brewery in 1866. Crowning all this was the third Bass brewery, the state-of-the-art New Brewery of 1863 to 1864, next to the Delhi Maltings; on its opening the former 'New' brewery became known as the Middle Brewery.

There was more still to come, but around 1866 Grace retired, secure in the knowledge that a successor to his post had been identified. He moved across the Trent to the pleasant eastern suburbs of Burton, where he died in 1869, aged 74. Robert Ratcliff, from the brewery, was one of his executors. Of Grace's buildings, a small part of the New Brewery remains, along with a section of the Wetmore Maltings (now converted for office use) and the landmark water tower, marooned on the Hay minus its brewery. By the time Robert Grace left Bass, the brewery's annual output had leapt to 600,000 barrels, a monument to his part in the company's development.

Of course, even as Bass was expanding, so were its competitors. In 1856 the first brewery from the London area, Ind Coope of Romford, arrived in Burton, buying a brewery already being put up for William Middleton near the station, and completing it to their own specifications. A fine office block in Classical style was then added about 1865, and alterations (perhaps designed by William Bradford) made to the fermentation block between 1896 and 1898. Ind Coope was by far the most successful of the incoming brewers, and their Burton Brewery – although not used for brewing since 1947 – is still for the most part extant, the best remaining

Fig 7.11
A postcard view of the Ind Coope Brewery, with the water tower prominent between the chimneys. The Midland Railway and Great Northern Railway wagons carried full and empty casks, and removed spent hops. The brewery yard was congested, with little siding space, and it was often late at night before all the casks were cleared.

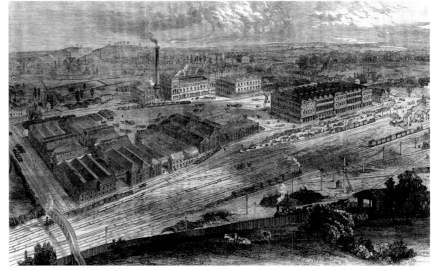

Fig 7.12
Allsopp's New Brewery shown, with some artistic licence, in *The Illustrated London News* of 1 November 1862. The main block on the right (extant and grade II listed) was the fermenting house, which included the great union room and racking hall. To its left, bathed in sunlight, was another union room and the brewhouse itself, next to the chimney, while the buildings in the left foreground comprised several ranges of maltings.

example of a Victorian brewery in Burton (Fig 7.11). The water tower, topped by a decorative tank manufactured by engineers Haslam & Co of Derby (who were eventually to take over the Pontifex firms), is an outstanding landmark in the town centre.

Immediately west of Ind Coope, Bass's great rivals Allsopp's put up what was described as the 'largest single brewery in the world' from 1859 to 1860.[11] Their New Brewery (Fig 7.12) stood beside the main railway line – from which it can still be seen – and was designed by London architects Hunt & Stephenson. The brewing plant, planned by Robert Davison with Allsopp's own engineers, included 'all the modern appliances, machinery and vessels' as Barnard put it. Allsopp's continued to brew at their Old Brewery, and made significant enlargements on both sites during the 1860s and 1870s. An array of other breweries, from medium-sized to very small, had opened in Burton by 1869, bringing the total to 29; the number of brewing companies was rather fewer, as some owned multiple breweries. But Bass and Allsopp remained dominant; in 1861 the pair employed two-thirds of the town's 3,000 brewery workers.[12]

Railways in Burton and beyond

Although the railway reached Burton in 1839, moving the beer between brewery or ale store and station remained problematic throughout the 1840s and 1850s. Most casks had to be hauled slowly through the streets for loading into wagons standing on sidings near the station, and as the trade increased, so did congestion problems. The roads filled with brewers' carts, or floaters as they were popularly known – low-slung two-wheeled platforms drawn by a single horse – which could take about a dozen casks. Towards the end of the 1850s the Midland Railway had to ask brewers not to send casks to the station after midday as they could not handle the traffic.[13]

Tooth's Crescent Brewery, on the north-east edge of Burton, hit on a solution in 1855 when they became the first of the town's brewers to gain permission to run a railway line across the public roadway. The level crossing connected the two split sections of their site.[14] This, however, was a horse-drawn railway or tramway, and (partly due to warring railway companies) it was 1860 before work could begin on building what eventually became an intricate steam-hauled rail network running around and through the breweries, with connections to the main line (Fig 7.13). Bass alone had 12 miles of track, and a special carriage for conveying awestruck visitors around the various brewery premises. The lines ran down the Hay riverside (Fig 7.14), out to Dixie in the north and Shobnall in the west, to various wharfs and depots, and across the town's main thoroughfares including High Street and Station Street. By around 1890 there were 32 level crossings, with 3 on Station Street alone, 1 each for Ind Coope, Bass and Worthington's tracks.[15] Local people naturally complained about delays caused by trains crossing the roads, just as in previous years they had been annoyed by hordes of floaters clogging up the streets.

Ease of access to the main line encouraged growth in the number of brewery agencies and stores set up to boost sales away from Burton; agencies were worked by independent traders on commission while stores were run by the breweries themselves. These networks originated in pre-rail days. Allsopp's agencies in London, Liverpool, Manchester and West Bromwich were probably the first, dating from 1808, while Bass established agencies around 1830 in London and Liverpool.[16] The Bass network had become thriving and profitable by the mid-1840s, when over half Bass sales were made through its stores and agencies.

Fig 7.13
Burton from the air in 1952, looking
south-west towards the passenger
railway station. The Guild Street branch
line runs across the right-hand corner of
the photograph, with the Bass private
line peeling off leftward between the
Scutari maltings (with chimney) and the
ale and hop stores. The Bass Middle
Brewery occupies the centre of the
frame, with the steam cooperage and
Middle Yard to its left.

Fig 7.14
The Hay railway sidings inundated
during the floods of August 1912.
A Worthington's steam engine (made by
locomotive builders Hudswell, Clarke &
Co of Leeds) hauls its load past the
Burton Brewery Company (far right)
and Salt's premises, with the Hay signal
box just visible (centre) and the Old
Breweries of Allsopp's and Bass beyond.

Once greater quantities of ale could be shipped more quickly and cheaply by rail, the larger Burton brewers rushed to rent or buy stores or create agencies around Britain and abroad. These ale stores could be very substantial structures, as shown in a Bass publicity booklet published in 1902, which illustrated 8 of their 29, including the Newcastle upon Tyne stores, the company's second or third most profitable after London.[17] It occupied a vast warren of vaults located in the undercroft of the Forth Banks goods station, south of the city centre, with access for drays through arched openings in the sandstone wall running along Pottery Lane. The vaults, which were also used by Walker's of Warrington in the 1880s, are extant. This is an unusual survival, as most stores at a distance from their breweries – in contrast to those nearby or at integrated sites – have been lost.[18]

In terms of profit and physical size the most significant stores were in London, usually near a railway company terminus. Haydon Square goods station was opened by the London & North Western Railway (LNWR) on 12 March 1853. With a main entrance off Aldgate High Street, it was one of several goods stations in the Fenchurch Street area. Four months later Allsopp's opened their new depot in Haydon Square (Fig 7.15); ale could be loaded on to wagons at Burton during the afternoon, and delivered to Haydon Square by 7 am the following morning. The stores occupied a range of massive brick warehouses up to eight storeys high, some newly built, others formerly used by the East India Company. There was a direct rail connection to the station, and the stores were fitted out with turntables and hydraulic cranes that lowered wagons into the cellars.[19]

From 1854 to 1856 the LNWR enlarged its goods facilities beside the Regent's Canal in Camden, just west of what is now Camden Lock Market. The works included construction of an L-shaped set of brick-built vaults, partly running alongside the canal. The vaults, some of which still survive, were built as an ale store for Allsopp's, who leased the space; at over 100,000sq ft, it was about five times the size of the Haydon Square premises, with a capacity of nearly 70,000 casks.

Fig 7.15
Inside Allsopp's newly opened ale store at London's Haydon Square goods station, as shown in *The Illustrated London News* of 16 July 1853.

Three express trains arrived nightly from Burton to replenish the Camden stores, which by the late 1880s employed around 70 men and 53 horses. In comparison, Worthington's stores at Broad Street goods station (just west of Liverpool Street Station) had stabling for 30 horses.

It was difficult for the railways to keep up with the volume of beer trade emanating from Burton during the 1860s and 1870s. By 1865 Bass was one of the Midland's most important customers, but the railway still had no access over its own lines to the London market, and had to rely on agreements with other companies. To remedy this, in 1860 the Midland had begun building its first St Pancras goods depot immediately north of the Regent's Canal, on what is now Camley Street. It opened in 1865, along with a huge beer store the Midland built for Bass on the opposite side of the canal; the two were connected by a line running across the canal to the north end of the roughly triangular store, which stood on the King's Road (now St Pancras Way). Bass rented the store, which was said to hold 160,000 casks, from the Midland and its successors until the 1960s.[20] The London Ale Stores, as it was known, was a massive brick warehouse stretching for 10 bays or so along each side and up to five storeys in height, with a lower range to the south housing double-height offices. A large sign on the curved corner facing King's Road proclaimed the function of the building and displayed the Bass triangle and diamond trademarks. The goods depot was demolished in the 1970s and the site of the stores is now occupied by an anonymous modern building.

One ale store which famously has survived is the undercroft of St Pancras passenger station train shed, which opened in 1868. The Midland's consulting engineer, William Henry Barlow, designed the platforms to run at a high level, enabling the tracks to cross the Regent's Canal. This left a void beneath, which Barlow originally intended to fill with spoil from tunnel construction. But such a valuable space had a better use, as he later explained:

> The special purpose for which this lower floor has been arranged is for Burton beer traffic; and in order to economize the space to the utmost, it was determined to use columns and girders, instead of brick piers and arches, making the distances between the columns the same as those of the warehouses, which were expressly arranged for the beer traffic. Thus, in point of fact, the length of a beer barrel became the unit of measure, upon which all the arrangements of this floor were based.[21]

In the undercroft around 800 uniform cast-iron columns were laid out on a grid plan spaced at 14ft 6in, a multiple of the height of a standard Burton beer cask (Fig 7.16). Hydraulic lifts gave access from the tracks to the 'vault', in which beer could be kept at a constant temperature. The stores were used by Salt & Co (Burton's fourth largest brewery in the 1870s), the long frontage to Pancras Road being topped by an advertisement for their ales (Fig 7.17). Aside from storage for about 40,000 casks, the vault housed Salt's offices, sampling rooms and bottling store.

Salt's stayed until around the turn of the century, after which the St Pancras store was used by Burton brewers Marston, Thompson & Evershed. From the 1950s beer traffic on the rails began to dwindle, as road transport took over, and by the 1960s the vaults were used only as an underground car park (Fig 7.18). The future of St Pancras itself came under review in 1966, but restoration eventually followed and the vaults now function as the Eurostar passenger reception; happily, the iron columns remain visible, a reminder of the undercroft's original purpose.

Fig 7.16
Navvies work on construction of the undercroft at St Pancras Station around 1867. The grid of cast-iron columns is clearly visible.

Fig 7.17 (below)
Looking south along the east facade of St Pancras Station. Up to about 1914 its parapet carried a lengthy sign advertising 'Salt & Company East India Ale & Burton Ale Stores'. The shot was taken, probably during the 1960s, by German emigré photographer John Gay (1909–99).

Fig 7.18 (right)
The undercroft of St Pancras Station trainshed, still in use as a beer store although plastic crates are taking over from wooden casks. The photograph, by C E Lee, probably dates from the late 1950s. Eurostar passengers wait in this area today.

Burton reaches its peak

When Bass moved into the London Ale Stores in 1865, their architect Robert Grace was on the point of retirement, having overseen a vast increase in the firm's activities. His replacement from 1867, who was given the title of chief engineer and architect, was William Canning (1823–c 1896), who originally came to Burton in 1846 to work as a railway engineer and surveyor. During the 1860s he was site engineer for construction of the Hay Branch, which ran down the riverside past the Bass Old Brewery, and shortly afterwards was appointed head of the Bass engineer's department. The post carried enormous responsibility, as the department's tasks ranged from buying and maintaining all machinery and plant, through erecting and repairing buildings, to purchasing coal, coke and building materials. In short, it was the driving force behind the brewery.

Fig 7.19
An unusual advertising poster of c 1870 for a beer garden, probably in Antwerp, selling Allsopp's beers. Their pale ale continued to be popular abroad into the 20th century, especially in Belgium, where it was not superseded by lager. Note the garden's provision for stout-drinking cyclists.

Fig 7.20
Massive pillars mark the entrance into the Bass Old Brewery from the High Street, in a postcard view from between the wars. In the centre, below the office clock, is a loaded floater, a low-slung two-wheeled cart. The Old Brewery was rebuilt in 1876.

For major projects, such as construction of the seven linked ranges of malthouses at Shobnall from 1873 to 1876, Bass employed outside contractors working under the chief engineer's supervision. Shobnall Maltings were said by Bass to be the largest in the world owned by a single firm, and Barnard certainly enjoyed their statistics: '4,000,000 bricks, 7,000 cubic feet of timber, and 400 tons of ironwork were used'. The huge complex also included cask-washing facilities and a large ale store. At the same time as the maltings were going up, Canning was also overseeing the complete reconstruction of the Old Brewery, which was completed in 1876. Although the smallest of the three Bass breweries, it was the one normally shown to visitors, being the most modern. There were 7 mash tuns, 8 coppers, 114 fermenting squares and 3 union rooms, the latter containing over 2,100 casks in all, each holding 150 gallons.[22]

In the mid-1870s Bass and Allsopp were easily the biggest breweries in Burton, but competition within the town was increasing, partly due to an influx of London and regional brewers. Between 1871 and 1872 the London brewer Charrington's bought and rebuilt Meakin's London & Burton Brewery, which stood in the south of the town near the site of Burton Abbey. The design of the Abbey Brewery, a five-storey brewhouse with an ornate lucam, was by brewers' architects and engineers Martin & Hardy of Nottingham, a small practice but one which had long connections with the brewing and malting industries. The practice also designed the Albion Brewery (Fig 7.21) at Shobnall, put up for London firm Mann, Crossman & Paulin from 1873 to 1875, another relatively small-scale (for Burton) brick-built brewhouse. The firm retreated to London in 1896, once Burtonisation of water

Fig 7.21
Looking south-east over Marston's
Brewery on Shobnall Road, in an aerial
shot taken during April 1921. The kiln
roofs of Allsopp's Shobnall Maltings
(1879, demolished 1978) are visible in
the lower foreground, and in the
distance is the huge Bass complex
including (from the top down) their
Shobnall Maltings (demolished 1979–83),
ale store and cask-washing facilities.

rendered brewing in Burton unnecessary, and in 1902 the Albion Brewery was sold to J Marston, Thompson & Son (later Marston, Thompson & Evershed), a recently amalgamated local concern.

Another new arrival from London was Truman, Hanbury, Buxton & Co, whose Black Eagle Brewery (1874–6) stood on the west side of the main railway line, almost opposite Allsopp's New Brewery. The design was by George Scamell, who in 1883, in partnership with Frederick Colyer, put up the Clarence Street Brewery south of Burton's centre for Walker's of Warrington (*see* chapter 4). Not far north of Clarence Street was the Kimmersitch Brewery (later Trent Brewery), designed by Leicester architect John Breedon Everard for Liverpool brewer Thomas Sykes in 1881, around the same time that Worthington's rebuilt their brewhouse (Fig 7.23). They used Nottingham architects Robert Evans and William Jolley, who are better known for their church architecture; Thornewill & Warham designed and carried out all the ironwork of the five-storey structure.

By the end of the 1880s, the result of all these developments and more was a total of 32 brewers in Burton, operating from 36 breweries. We can see now that the town's brewing industry had reached its peak, with annual production at a record high of 3,025,000 barrels and over half the working population employed in the industry. The output of eight different companies topped 100,000 barrels a year, but Bass were out in the lead, the largest brewing company in the world, on 980,000 barrels. About one-third of the town's land was taken up by the brewing, malting and ancillary industries. The statistics are staggering, and it is no wonder that the town was one of the great curiosities of the late Victorian era.[23]

Fig 7.22 (above)

Maltsters from Bass, seen around 1890 outside malthouse No 3 at Shobnall. As well as the seven (later eight) malthouses, Bass built two rows of six terraced cottages for their workmen at Shobnall, and these still survive as Bass's Cottages on Shobnall Road, now adjacent to the huge silos of the modern Molson Coors drum maltings.

Fig 7.23 (right)

A postcard view of Worthington's Brewery in 1909, with their No 4 locomotive waiting by the covered ale bank. To the rear (left of the chimneys) is the elegant brewhouse, built between 1880 and 1882 and incorporating a few elements of the previous building; it was demolished in 1968.

Fig 7.24

While a guest of Michael Arthur Bass at Rangemore, the as yet uncrowned King Edward VII visited Burton. On 22 February 1902 he was shown round the Bass Shobnall Maltings, the steam cooperage and the Old Brewery. There he began the mash which eventually resulted in King's Ale, first released in 1905.

The photograph shows a plaque commemorating the event, although not fixed to the King's Mash Tub (a tall mash tun, No 2) but to a smaller tun No 1; the plaque is now at the National Brewery Centre, attached to another tun No 2.

The town in decline

William Canning, who as chief engineer had guided Bass through some of their greatest years during the 1870s and 1880s, was joined by an assistant, Herbert Arthur Couchman (1863–1941), in December 1890. Canning, who by then was living in one of the Station Street houses, remained as chief engineer until June 1892, when Couchman succeeded him. The new chief was a Londoner, born in Tottenham, where he was apprenticed as a mechanical engineer.[24] It is unlikely that he had been in Burton long before he became Canning's assistant, but he quickly settled into the job, designing an eighth malthouse for Shobnall Maltings in 1891. He put up an additional ale store at Shobnall in 1895, but in that year was replaced as chief engineer by William Baker Ollis. Couchman's renowned strictness with the workforce had proved too much for the company. However, he was retained to pursue his engineering interests, just as before, while Ollis dealt with administration.[25]

Herbert Couchman was an energetic, versatile and meticulous engineer, becoming personally involved with the construction of everything from locomotives to churches in his time with Bass. He built the Plough Maltings on Horninglow Street (1899–1902), not as a floor maltings but a mechanical drum maltings. This was a precursor to his Sleaford Maltings (1903–7) in Lincolnshire, 8 massive

WOMEN ALE LOADERS.

Fig 7.25

Women rolling casks at Bass during the First World War, when labour was so short that, for the first time, the firm had to employ female workers in areas such as the bottling stores and maltings. By 1916, the Bass workforce in Burton was 2,774, of which 140 were women.

Fig 7.26 (right)
A fine array of counterbalancing weights on this Bass mash tun. The brewery had its own coppersmiths' department; by 1890 there were 28 copper wort coppers shared between the three Bass breweries.

Fig 7.27 (above)
A Bass union room on the eve of the First World War. The three union rooms at the Old Brewery held more than 2,100 casks. Note the wooden top troughs; later these would be metal.

Fig 7.28
The vast industrial ruin of the Bass Maltings (1903–7) at Sleaford, seen in summer 2013. Each of the eight ranges, plus central water tower and engine house, stretches northward towards the railway line; the buildings are much deeper than they are wide, making the whole a massive site. A mixed use redevelopment of the huge complex has stalled due to difficulties with road access.

Fig 7.29
This timeless shot of malt being wheeled into the screening room at the Bass New Brewery could have been taken at almost any point from the 1930s to the mid-1960s; the old-fashioned equipment includes line shafting driving the screening machine. Even in the early 1960s malt was still moved around the breweries on the 26-mile private rail network, by then outdated and expensive to operate.

Fig 7.30
Firemen fight the blaze at the Bass Wetmore Maltings in 1978. Much of the 5-acre complex survived, including the water tower and the sole Bass chimney stack now remaining in Burton, and the malthouses were later converted for office use.

red brick ranges (out of 16 originally planned) with a central engine house, water tower and chimney (Fig 7.28). Although this was a floor maltings, the movement of grain throughout the complex was mechanised.

When Couchman retired in 1917, leaving some fine buildings behind him, Bass was still in reasonable health, but the number of breweries in Burton had declined, reflecting the troubles of the industry in the UK as a whole. Only 17 breweries remained in Burton by 1911, and the amalgamations and closures continued well into the 20th century. Bass merged with Worthington's in 1927 (although Worthington's carried on operating separately until the brewery was closed in 1967), and Ind Coope merged with Allsopp's in 1934; Allsopp's Old Brewery was largely demolished from 1937 to 1938. By 1950 there were only five brewing firms left in Burton.

There were many more demolitions: Salt's (Fig 7.31) in 1956, the Bass Middle Brewery brewhouse in 1960, Scutari Maltings in 1964, Worthington's Brewery in 1968, the Abbey Brewery in 1970, Bass Old Brewery in the early 1970s, Allsopp's Shobnall Maltings in 1978 and much of the Bass New Brewery from 1984 to 1985, to mention only a handful. Bass merged with Mitchells & Butlers in 1961, then with Charrington United Breweries in 1967, to form Bass Charrington. The company was bought by Interbrew in 2000 and sold to Coors, now Molson Coors Brewing Company (UK) Ltd, in 2002. Thus Molson Coors, a firm with its origins in North America, came to control all but one of the remaining industrial-scale breweries in Burton. The odd brewery out was Marston's, acquired by Wolverhampton & Dudley Breweries (now Marston's plc) in 1999 and still brewing, indeed still using the Burton union system.

Burton upon Trent today

Despite all the demolitions, and many lost opportunities for regeneration schemes, there is much to see in Burton today, including breweries and maltings, converted former industry buildings, five microbreweries and of course the National Brewery Centre (*see* chapter 9), housed in the former Bass joiners' shop and adjacent buildings on Horninglow Street. Not surprisingly, several microbreweries occupy former brewing or malting industry premises, including Burton Bridge Brewery (founded 1982) in an old maltings; Black Hole Brewery, established 2007 in the former Ind Coope bottling stores; and the Tower Brewery, set up during 2001 in an old engine house-cum-water tower at Salt's Walsitch Maltings (*see* Fig 3.59).

We can see a good variety of historic and modern brewing-related buildings on a walk between the railway station and the National Brewery Centre; this brief description only outlines what is visible on the ground. Head east from the station along Station Street, passing the former Allsopp's New Brewery (now The 107 Building) on the left, then Ind Coope, and remnants of the Bass New Brewery to the south. At the T-junction turn left into High Street, passing a series of Victorian and earlier brewery offices belonging to Bass and Worthington, with the 1866 water tower to the east. At the next T-junction go left into Horninglow Street, passing the old merchant brewer's yard (Anson Court) to the north and 181 Horninglow Street, a Georgian brewer's house, to the south. The Plough Maltings are to the north after the Guild Street crossing, opposite the National Brewery Centre.

A more in-depth examination of the town would include a walk west from the station, through King Edward Place and south along the Trent & Mersey Canal to Shobnall, taking in Marston's Brewery. Then return to the centre via Burton Village (the old Kimmersitch Brewery), Clarence Street and the Goat Maltings. In addition, to the north of Horninglow Street, follow Wetmore Road, Wharf Road and Hawkins Lane to see a variety of converted and unconverted maltings. There is much more to see – for instance Thornewill & Warham's delightful iron-built pedestrian bridges across the Trent, and Claymills Victorian Pumping Station – but suffice it to say that there is more to modern Burton than rows of grey cylindroconical fermenters would suggest.

8 Beyond the Brewery

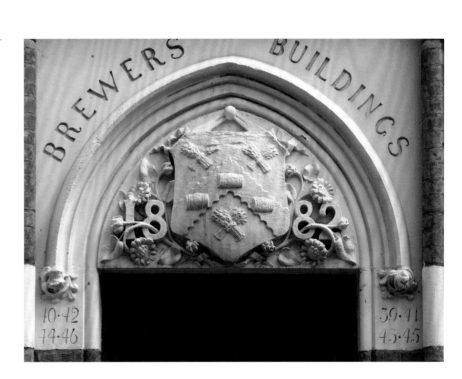

The broader architectural heritage of brewing and malting includes not only industry-specific buildings, from oast houses to public houses and everything in between, but a wide range of other structures put up with brewing profits. Beyond buildings, many causes and institutions were supported by philanthropic brewers. With breweries to be found in almost every UK town and city in the late Victorian era, this aspect of brewing's heritage amounts to a substantial intervention in the wider world.

Providing for the workforce

Firstly, edging slightly beyond the brewery itself, we might look at housing supplied for the industry's workers and their families. Typically, relations between brewer and employees were characterised by an old-fashioned but mostly successful paternalism, resulting in a generally contented and cooperative workforce. This approach is exemplified by Greene's Brewery (later Greene King) in Bury St Edmunds. Here, Edward Greene began buying and building property for his workers in the late 1850s, when the firm's finances allowed. As he said in an 1865 speech 'I hold it to be every man's duty to look to his cottages.' The first went up in 1859, and over the next 25 years another 40 were acquired or built, so that by 1887, and the amalgamation with King's Brewery, over half the workforce occupied low-rental company houses. The pick of Greene's cottages were the 16 comprising Maynewater Square (1868), just south of the brewery and still extant; they were considered locally to be model dwellings.[1]

In Essex, the earliest-known housing provided for brewery or maltings workers was at Mistley, where Richard Rigby (1690–1730) built a small planned industrial village in the early 18th century to service his port, which included two malthouses. The first housing for Essex brewery workers was put up by the Gibson family during the 1840s in Saffron Walden, where they owned what became the Anchor Brewery.[2] This Tudor-style terrace of five houses is unusually decorative for brewery workers'

Fig 8.2
Brewers Buildings in London's Rawstorne Street are three blocks of model dwellings put up by the Brewers' Company and designed by their own surveyor Edward H Martineau (1823/4–1901). The first block (1–24) was built between 1871 and 1872, the second (25–34) between 1876 and 1877 and the third (35–46) between 1882 and 1883. The colourful Gothic facade hides flats which were gloomy and fairly cramped, but were renovated in the 1980s.

accommodation, which was usually fairly plain, like the late 19th-century terraces and semi-detached houses built for Dudney's Southdown Brewery workers in Portslade, East Sussex.

Perhaps because they so often lack distinguishing features, we do not know as much as we should like to about the pattern of house building for brewery workers, although as in other industries, the larger concerns were more likely to be substantial providers. Watney's, for instance, erected Castle Buildings (1882–3) and Alexandra Buildings (1880s), both handsome four-storey terraces of model dwellings, just east of the Stag Brewery, along with a club room and library. The brewery closed in 1959 and redevelopment of the Stag site was intended, leaving the housing in limbo; their 'future seems highly uncertain' as the 1973 planning polemic *Goodbye London* put it.[3] However, both survive, unlisted although in a conservation area.

Certainly no major model villages were built by brewers, whose labour requirements were not as great as most other processing industries, although Guinness toyed with the idea. The company's chief medical officer, John Lumsden, spent the summer of 1904 investigating English garden villages, including the industrial examples of Cadbury's Bournville and Lever's Port Sunlight.[4] On his return he recommended building a similar village on the outskirts of Dublin, but the Guinness board demurred, pointing out that their workers already had many benefits, which indeed they did; free medical care for employees and their families dated from 1870, and company pensions, initially contribution-free, had been provided since 1860. However, Guinness eventually did build on part of Lumsden's suggested site. It was not a complete model village but what Lumsden described as 'excellent cottages', along with the brewery sports ground; the Guinness Athletic Union was founded in 1903.

The closest an English brewery came to creating an industrial village was probably the Mann, Crossman & Paulin development at Shobnall on the outskirts of Burton. Their brewery went up between 1873 and 1875 at the centre of the 30-acre site, as well as 'four handsome villas for the foremen of the departments, a row of twelve model cottages for the workmen, and a house for the foreman cooper'.[5] Eventually came a house for the head brewer, a hotel (now the Albion pub) and – in 1888 – a small brick mission church, known after its consecration in 1898 as St Aidan's. Shobnall Grange, dating from the 17th century, was used as the manager's house. Pevsner describes this disparate collection as a model village, which perhaps exaggerates the company's original intentions.[6]

Although much reduced, brewery housing continued to be built in the 20th century. The outstanding example is Mayflower Green, seven humble cottages in Stratford-upon-Avon, put up in 1938 for workers at the nearby Flower's Brewery, which – as we shall see later – had a history of philanthropic activity. A monopitch-roofed modernist terrace, Mayflower Green now looks like a prototype for much small-scale post war housing. The cottages were designed by Stratford architect F W B Yorke and his beer-drinking son F R S Yorke, who had published his influential *The Modern House* four years earlier.[7] Later he became part of the successful practice Yorke Rosenberg Mardall, but always remained particularly proud of Mayflower Green.

Brewer paternalism often extended to the provision of sports clubs and facilities for the workforce, Christmas dinners or parties, and occasional excursions. August 1890, for example, saw about 100 employees of the New Westminster Brewery

Fig 8.3

A cricket match in progress during the 1920s at the Mitchells & Butlers works ground in Smethwick, with a good view of Cape Hill No 2 Brewery. The pitch was one of three provided by the company (one survives), and significant matches in the Birmingham & District Cricket League could attract 2,000–3,000 spectators to the ground. In all the M&B sports grounds covered 25 acres.

Company enjoy a day at Brighton, while Hastings was the chosen destination of Thorne's Nine Elms Brewery. The latter trip ended with a dinner, during which 'an envelope with a money bonus was handed to each man'.[8] The legendary Bass railway trips, which at their peak around the turn of the century transported around 10,000 workers annually to the seaside, began modestly in August 1865 with a visit to Liverpool. These day trips ran every year from 1883, the numbers involved eventually becoming so large that only four resorts – Great Yarmouth, Blackpool, Scarborough and Liverpool (for New Brighton) – could host them. Organisers at Bass negotiated free or reduced entry to the local entertainment venues, and the sheer scale of the trips generated good publicity for the resorts concerned.[9]

Brewers in the community

The philanthropic works of many brewers affected the entire community, not just the workforce; Barnard suggested that 'among manufacturers, brewers stand pre-eminent for their unbounded and princely liberality'.[10] Their good works ranged from the erection of swimming baths, libraries and art galleries through donations to hospitals and local universities to the funding of churches and chapels. Occasionally these activities had an impact on the national and even international stage, a prime example being the continued generosity of brewer Charles Flower (1830–92), who established the Shakespeare Memorial Theatre in his home town of Stratford-upon-Avon. Flower took over from his father as head of the family brewery in 1863, and while modernising and enlarging the firm found time to become deeply involved in local civic life. As the tercentenary of Shakespeare's birth approached in 1864, the idea of a monument was mooted locally, but Flower opposed this; his vision of a suitable memorial entailed building a theatre that would attract crowds to the town to celebrate both playwright and plays in Shakespeare's original environment.

Fig 8.4

A postcard view of the original
Shakespeare Memorial Theatre in
Stratford-upon-Avon; the site and
almost all the funding were provided by
local brewer Charles Flower. The Swan
Gallery (left of the tower), shortly to be
refurbished by the Royal Shakespeare
Company, was the only part of Flower's
building works to survive the 1926
fire intact.

Fig 8.4

A postcard view of the original Shakespeare Memorial Theatre in Stratford-upon-Avon; the site and almost all the funding were provided by local brewer Charles Flower. The Swan Gallery (left of the tower), shortly to be refurbished by the Royal Shakespeare Company, was the only part of Flower's building works to survive the 1926 fire intact.

Flower donated a site for the theatre and organised an international campaign to raise funds and support for his brainchild. Despite ridicule from the British press, which regarded Stratford as being too remote to support serious theatre, an architectural competition was held in 1876. The commission was won by two young architects, Edward Dodgshun (1854–1927) and William Unsworth (1851–1912), who had both carried out part of their training with the arch-medievalist William Burges. Perhaps this had some influence over the built outcome; the Shakespeare Memorial Theatre, which opened in 1879, was a fabulous concoction of Gothic imagery and Elizabethan half-timbering, all topped by a soaring tower (Fig 8.4). Flower footed most of the bill, which came to well over £20,000, and went on to fund the associated library and gallery, also by Dodgshun & Unsworth, that were added in 1881.

The picturesque theatre was popular with the public (although actors disliked the church-like interior and the cramped backstage facilities), but lasted less than half a century before a disastrous fire burned it almost to the ground on 6 March 1926; only the library and gallery survived. Performances were moved to the local Picture House, also owned by the Flower family, while Charles Flower's nephew, Archibald Flower, led the fundraising campaign to build 'the most modern and best equipped theatre in the world'.[11] This time most of the donations came from American supporters, and the new theatre opened in 1932. The shell of the 1879 theatre was redeveloped as the Swan Theatre in 1986, its entrance being through Charles Flower's original library and gallery, now known as the Swan Gallery. Although this is the only building remaining from his original project, the broader consequences of his philanthropic drive lay with the establishment of the theatre and its company in the town of Shakespeare's birth.

Another unusual survivor from this philanthropic era is the Electric Palace cinema and opera house in Bridport, put up by the local brewery owner John Cleeves Palmer (1854–1928) in 1926 in an attempt to bring opera to Dorset. The cinema facilities were included to subsidise the work of the local operatic society.

The simple structure was enlivened during the late 1930s by the addition of a mural scheme (Fig 8.5) running throughout the foyer and auditorium (the latter now overpainted), the work of local artist George Biles (1900–87), who designed Palmers' pub signs from 1918 until shortly before his death. He worked from a studio off East Road in Bridport, producing his trademark double-sided signs with a different picture on either face; he also painted wooden road signs for the town during the 1950s and 1960s.

Again a brewer's personal interest, not opera in this case but collecting glass, ceramics and art, resulted in the gift to the community of the town house of Cecil Higgins (1856–1941), the Bedford brewer, along with his adjoining Castle Brewery maltings. Higgins offered the house to the town in his will in order to provide a home for his collection; the Cecil Higgins Art Gallery, as it was eventually known, opened in 1949. The gallery merged with nearby Bedford Museum in 2005, and after a major redevelopment project the combination reopened in 2013 as The Higgins. The brewery courtyard forms its main entrance, and the maltings still has a distinctly industrial appearance.

A major gallery – the Walker Art Gallery (1874–7, architects Cornelius Sherlock and H H Vale) – was just one of several substantial gifts made to Liverpool by local brewer Andrew Barclay Walker (1824–93), who owned breweries in Warrington and Burton. The gallery, which originally housed contemporary art exhibitions, cost over £50,000 (Fig 8.6). Walker, whose public services were recognised in 1877 with a knighthood, lived in the Liverpool suburb of Gateacre, where he provided the village green and other facilities; his mansion, Gateacre Grange (1866, now apartments) was also designed by Sherlock. Although he added an opulent

Fig 8.5

Bunting decks out the foyer of the Electric Palace Cinema in Bridport, not quite obscuring the late 1930s mural scheme by George Biles, Palmers Brewery pub sign painter. The idyllic sun-kissed scenes run up the terrazzo staircase towards the auditorium, where the Biles murals have been painted out. Note also the original hanging light fitting.

Fig 8.6

A turn-of-the-century postcard view of the Walker Art Gallery (1874–7) in Liverpool, funded by its mayor, brewer and philanthropist Andrew Barclay Walker (1824–93). The gallery, which cost over £50,000, was presented to the (soon-to-become) city in September 1877, and Walker was knighted three months later in recognition of his public service. He was the second son of Peter Walker, who established the eponymous brewing empire.

Fig 8.7
A Halstead Brewery novelty advertising
wagon outside the brewery offices (still
extant) in Trinity Street around 1900.
The shot was taken by Edgar Tarry
Adams (1852–1926), whose family
owned the brewery. As well as being
a keen amateur photographer, Adams
managed the brewery's plant and
machinery, built the brewery chapel and
was deeply involved in local affairs.

extension by architects George & Peto in 1883, Walker went on to buy Osmaston
Manor in Derbyshire the following year for around £250,000. Finally for this brief
survey, two of the most imposing public buildings in Edinburgh were financed from
brewing profits: the McEwan Hall (*see* Fig 8.14) and the Usher Hall, standing within
half a mile of one another in the Old Town. The earlier of the pair was the McEwan
Hall, funded by brewer William McEwan (1827–1913) and donated to the University
of Edinburgh in 1897, after which McEwan was granted the freedom of the city.
The magnificent sandstone building, used for graduation ceremonies and as a public
hall, took almost a decade to complete and cost McEwan £115,000; the spectacular
domed interior features a series of allegorical paintings by William Palin including
figures representing the Arts, Sciences and Literature, as well as an image of
McEwan himself.[12]

The Usher Hall was donated to Edinburgh by Andrew Usher (1826–98) of the
local brewing and whisky distilling family. His gift of £100,000 was made to the city
in 1896, but much argument over a suitable site delayed the start of building until
1910. The hall, designed by Leicester architect James Stockdale Harrison (1874–
1952), was opened on 6 March 1914 by Usher's widow. Since then it has been used
as a concert venue, exactly as Andrew Usher wished; his portrait bust stands in a
niche near one of the main entrances.

Brewers and the church

One of the largest contributions by a brewer to any single cause was the £150,000
spent by Sir Benjamin Lee Guinness (1798–1868) on the complete restoration of
St Patrick's Cathedral in Dublin from 1861 to 1865. A condition of his patronage was
that no professional architect should be involved, so all the work was carried out by
his own builders, the Murphy brothers, to comply with the patron's wishes.
Although the 'vandal restorers', as architects termed them, did destroy a medieval
rood screen, much of the work carried out by the Murphys had been proposed in

earlier restoration schemes.[13] A statue of Sir Benjamin Lee Guinness by the Dublin sculptor John Henry Foley was unveiled outside the cathedral in September 1875.

Bass, Ratcliff & Gretton matched Guinness's generosity to the church. The Bass family in particular were keen church builders, funding the construction of St Paul's Church (1874) in Burton at a cost of £120,000 and providing another £40,000 in endowments. Michael Thomas Bass junior paid for the adjacent St Paul's Institute and Liberal Club (1878), which Michael Arthur Bass gifted to the town in 1892 for use as the town hall; Michael Arthur also paid for the council chamber to be added in 1894. These and other benefactions saved local ratepayers a considerable sum. The pick of the Bass-funded churches was St Chad, with its almost free-standing tower. The church was designed by G F Bodley (1827–1907) in 1903 and completed in 1910 by his partner, Cecil Hare; Herbert Couchman was also involved in its construction. In fact all the late Victorian partners in Bass, Ratcliff & Gretton funded church building or restoration, a remarkable case of 'beer and God in harness' as the *Dictionary of National Biography* described it.[14]

A comprehensive directory of English churches funded by brewing money would almost require a book in itself, but suffice it to say that they ranged from the cathedral-sized down to tiny buildings like the little timber chapel opened in 1883 for employees of the Halstead Brewery in Essex.[15] Known locally as the 'bung chapel', it was rebuilt in 1902 using brick, and still stands, although now in private occupation.

At the other end of the scale is the vast St George's Church (1891–8; Fig 8.8) in Heaviley, a suburb of Stockport. Here the funds came from Sheffield-born George Fearn (1845–1911), whose family had been involved with the local Hempshaw Brook Brewery since it was taken over (via a lottery) by two Yorkshire brewers in 1850. It was one of the largest breweries in the area outside Manchester, and trading as Smith & Bell became a successful venture. George Fearn's father had been brought from Yorkshire to manage the brewery, and George himself joined the firm in 1872, becoming a partner in 1886.[16] He financed building of the church, the nearby schools and the vicarage, choosing as his architects not a national figure but the relatively local practice Austin & Paley of Lancaster; Hubert Austin was actually responsible for the design. Fearn retired from the brewery soon after St George's was complete; even after paying for the church, when he died in 1911 his effects amounted to over £95,000. His splendidly elaborate memorial, in Stockport Cemetery (just across Buxton Road from St George's), takes the form of a 12ft-high scaled replica of the spire and part of the tower of his own church (Fig 8.9).

Fig 8.8
St George's Church, Heaviley, near Stockport, photographed by Bedford Lemere & Co soon after its opening in 1898. One of the largest churches to be built with brewing profits (in this case from the Hempshaw Brook Brewery), the tower and spire combined reached a height of 236ft and a congregation of 1,450 people could be seated inside.

Fig 8.9

The Fearn Memorial in Stockport
Cemetery, now minus two of its
miniature flying buttresses, is a scale
model of part of St George's Church,
seen in the background across the A6.
This unusual memorial, whose sculptor
is unknown, commemorates the brewer
George Fearn who financed the church.

Building in the country

England's stock of country houses was given a substantial boost by Victorian and
later brewing money. The hamlet of Rangemore, three miles west of Burton,
blossomed into an estate village after the Bass family took on and expanded
Rangemore Hall. Michael Thomas Bass initially made his country home on the
Byrkley estate, just over a mile west of Rangemore, in the late 1840s but moved
to Rangemore in 1860. He and his architect Robert William Edis (1839–1927),
a specialist in domestic planning, extended the house dramatically in 1879 and
there were further massive extensions from 1898 to 1901, also by Edis. In the village
Michael Thomas Bass junior and his son, Michael Arthur, paid for All Saints Church
(1866–7) by William Butterfield, with a chancel (1895) by Bodley, a school (1873)
and around 1887 a club, the latter probably designed by Edis (with a 'capital billiard
room' according to Barnard). The hall has now been split up into suites of luxury
private accommodation.

From 1879 Hamar Bass (1842–98), the second son of Michael Thomas Bass,
occupied the Byrkley estate, living at Byrkley Lodge which he rebuilt from 1887 to
1891. His 'large and unlovely' Elizabethan-style pile, again designed by R W Edis,
was eventually demolished in the early 1950s.[17] In a nice continuation of sport's
involvement with beer, the Football Association bought Byrkley Lodge estate in
2001; it is now known as St George's Park, home to the National Football Centre,
which opened in 2012. Another massive mansion was Buckhold House (now
St Andrew's School) near Pangbourne in Berkshire, designed by Alfred Waterhouse

for Dr Herbert Watney of the brewing family between 1884 and 1888 at a cost of £34,000. Running through the house is a frieze of Doulton ceramic tile panels painted by John Eyre, Esther Lewis and John Henry McLennan; one panel includes a view of Watney's Stag Brewery, an unusual image for a domestic setting.[18]

A little later and rather more architecturally fashionable was Blackwell, put up between 1898 and 1900 on the southern fringe of Bowness-on-Windermere for the philanthropist Sir Edward Holt (1849–1928), owner of Manchester's Derby Brewery. Holt chose M H Baillie Scott as his architect, and since Blackwell was to be a holiday home for the Holt family, Baillie Scott was able to be daring and experimental in its design. He produced a delightful essay in the arts and crafts style with beautiful detailing. The house served as a rural retreat for many years and was restored by the Lakeland Arts Trust (1998–2001). Nearby, at Holy Trinity in Winster, is an enamelled bronze plaque designed by Harold Stabler, a memorial to the Holts' son Joseph Holt (1881–1915). Joseph worked at the brewery before being called up to the 6th Manchester Regiment at the outbreak of war; he died at Gallipoli.

Commemoration

Joseph Holt's is one of several church memorials to brewers and their families which do not commemorate the industry as such, but the specific family and its significance in the local community. A prime example is the set of Whitbread memorials at St Mary's Church, Cardington, Bedfordshire. These include funerary monuments to Samuel Whitbread (1720–96), the firm's founder, commissioned by his son from the sculptor John Bacon RA, and to Samuel Whitbread II (1758–1815) by Henry Weekes, a moving depiction of husband and wife kneeling in prayer, carved in 1849.

Other notable brewer memorials include a window at St Ann's Church in Manchester commemorating Henry Boddington (1813–86) of the nearby Strangeways Brewery. It was part of a *c* 1890 scheme designed by the artist Frederic Shields on a theme of the shepherd, and made by Heaton, Butler & Bayne. The Lacon family, owners of the Falcon Brewery in Great Yarmouth, are commemorated at their local parish church in Ormesby St Margaret, notably in the colourful east window of 1939 by Hardman & Co. Its main subject is the Ascension, but the family and brewery symbol – a perched falcon – occupies the bottom right corner. It also appears on their mausoleum in the churchyard.

A unique and totally apt memorial to a brewer is the tower screen at Luxulyan Church in Cornwall, made up of hundreds of clear-glass bottle bottoms, given in 1912 by Walter Hicks (1829–1916) of St Austell Brewery, in memory of his son Walter Hicks junior (1865–1911), who died following a motorcycle accident while on brewery business.

On rare occasions brewer statuary is found away from any religious context, but normally the aim has been to commemorate philanthropic acts rather than the brewing industry, as with the statues of Michael Thomas Bass (1799–1884; Fig 8.10) in Derby and Michael Arthur Bass (Figs 8.11 and 8.12) in Burton, both erected by public subscription. The London brewer Sir Thomas Fowell Buxton (1786–1845), of Truman, Hanbury, Buxton in Spitalfields, was most famous for his anti-slavery campaigning. This is remembered by his statue in the north choir aisle of Westminster Abbey and a delightfully Gothic memorial fountain in

Fig 8.10

The bronze of Michael Thomas Bass (1799–1884), by the sculptor Joseph Boehm, originally stood in Derby's Market Square. It was moved in 1926 to its present location on the Wardwick, outside Derby Museum and Art Gallery, which Bass gave to the city along with its library.

Fig 8.11 (above)

On 13 May 1911 the Lord Lieutenant of Staffordshire unveiled a statue of Michael Arthur Bass (1837–1909), Lord Burton, outside Burton's Town Hall. There was a good crowd, many in a variety of uniforms, and Lord Burton himself was portrayed in the uniform of the Burton Battalion of the Staffordshire Rifle Volunteers (of which he was colonel), cloaked by his baronet's coronation robes.

Fig 8.12 (above right)

The grade II listed 10ft-high bronze of Lord Burton was created by Frederick William Pomeroy (1856–1924), best known as an architectural sculptor, although he produced many public statues. Pomeroy never met Lord Burton, and used photographs and paintings to create the likeness, which was well received.

Victoria Tower Gardens (Fig 8.13). It was designed by the architect Samuel Sanders Teulon in conjunction with Buxton's third son, Charles Buxton (1822–71), politician, philanthropist, a capable amateur architect and partner in the Black Eagle Brewery.

Considering the significance of the industry to the economy, it is perhaps surprising that there are few images of its major historical figures in the public realm. At its greatest, from 1879 to 1880, taxation on liquor amounted to 43.4 per cent of national revenue, while those directly employed in brewing and malting numbered 39,600 according to the 1871 census; the 1907 census of production showed the latter figure rising to 79,680.[19] Although less important as an employer than several other turn-of-the-century industries, the public profile of the brewing industry was high because of its constant battling with temperance organisations. The brewers were seen as a formidable pressure group. Between 1832 and 1914, 90 brewers sat as MPs and the term 'beerage' – which appeared by 1891 – was popularly used to describe brewers as a whole, especially those with peerages. In reality, however, the trade's lobby was normally disorganised, if not absent, and much less effective than their opponents perceived.[20]

As for the brewing workforce, one constant reminder of its value to the country lies in the number of war memorials to be found at industry-related locations. Many of these memorials have been moved, but one of the largest still in its original position is the First World War memorial at the former site of Mitchells & Butlers Cape Hill Brewery in Smethwick. The tall limestone structure, put up around 1920, is rectangular in plan with Classical detailing; the names of the Second World War dead have been added above its base. It now stands at the entrance to a housing development, next to the old brewery fire station.

Fig 8.13

The grade II* listed drinking fountain (1865–6) in Victoria Tower Gardens, beside the Palace of Westminster, is a memorial to the brewer, politician and philanthropist Sir Thomas Fowell Buxton, who played a major role in the passage of the Slavery Abolition Act of 1833. It originally stood in Parliament Square, but was removed in 1949 during preparations for the Festival of Britain, then erected in the Gardens during 1957.

Fig 8.14 (above)

The McEwan Hall (1888–97, architect Robert Rowand Anderson), donated to the University of Edinburgh by the brewer and Edinburgh MP William McEwan. He is remembered not only in the name of the ornate ceremonial hall, but by the inscription on its facade and a millennial plaque erected by the university (bottom right). Above the doorway is a relief of the graduation ceremony by the London firm of architectural carvers Farmer & Brindley.

Fig 8.15 (above right)

The First World War roll of honour at Thomas Daniell & Sons West Bergholt Brewery, where brewing ceased in 1959. The buildings were converted for residential use and the ceramic tile memorial, originally located within the brewery, now suffers from weathering. It records the 68 names of those who served, from the company's West Bergholt and Colchester breweries, with the eight who did not return picked out in red.

Similarly impressive is the Springfield Brewery memorial (1923) from Wolverhampton, which has been relocated to the Black Country Living Museum in Dudley. Topped by a standing bronze figure of a soldier, this is also a First World War memorial altered to include the Second World War roll of honour. Smaller plaques remain in situ at several former brewery sites, including Lichfield Brewery and Morrell's Lion Brewery in Oxford. The First World War plaque from Watney's Stag Brewery in London can now be found at the National Memorial Arboretum in Alrewas, Staffordshire, while the Newcastle Breweries' war memorial was first moved from the Tyne Brewery to the Federation Brewery in Gateshead before finally being installed and rededicated at St Andrew's Church in Newcastle in 2011.

Celebrating the industry

Just as England has only a few statues of its brewers, the industry as a whole has seldom been celebrated through statuary or other imagery. One exception, unsurprisingly, is the town of Burton, which has three modern works on brewing or allied themes. The oldest is *The Burton Cooper* (1977; Fig 8.16), a bronze by James Butler. Burton Civic Society came up with the idea of a sculpture to mark the opening of a new shopping precinct, and the project was supported by the developers and all the major local brewers. The artist took great care to portray the cooper accurately and the piece has always been popular, despite being moved to a cramped spot inside Cooper's Square shopping centre in 1995.[21] Another statue, *The Cooper*, created by local artist Harry Duffey in 1998 with the support of Bass, amongst others, stands at the National Brewery Centre. The most visible (and least liked) of Burton's trio of brewing-themed works is *Malt Shovel* (2001) by Andrew Hazell, a 9m-high stainless-steel shovel commissioned by the local council, which stands upright at the intersection of two busy streets in the town centre.

Fig 8.16 (right)

In amongst the coffee shops at Cooper's
Square shopping centre in Burton is
The Burton Cooper. In order to make the
statue as realistic as possible, the artist
observed Bass's coopers Erdie Lee and
Joe Foster at work during 1977.

Fig 8.16 (right)

In amongst the coffee shops at Cooper's
Square shopping centre in Burton is
The Burton Cooper. In order to make the
statue as realistic as possible, the artist
observed Bass's coopers Erdie Lee and
Joe Foster at work during 1977.

Fig 8.17 (below right)

A detail from one of six relief panels
depicting scenes from local history that
run along the High Street facade of
Wandsworth Municipal Offices.
The Wandsworth panel, including
a figure of a local brewer pouring beer
(centre), was carved in Portland stone
during 1936 by sculptor David Evans
(1893–1959); casks and sheaves of barley
appear in the background.

Fig 8.18 (below)

An elegant relief on one of the six
bronze doors of grade II* listed Norwich
City Hall shows a fermenting vessel
in great detail, representing the
significance of brewing as a local
industry. All the door reliefs were
designed by Nottingham-born sculptor
James Woodford (1893–1976), who was
also responsible for the monumental
bronze doors of the RIBA in London.

Elsewhere, yet another cooper signalled the centenary of Belfast's Ulster Brewery. Ross Wilson's 1997 bronze *The Ulster Brewer* (often called *Barrel Man* as the cooper is seated on his barrel) stands close to the city's Waterfront Hall. It was commissioned by Bass Ireland to mark their 100th anniversary; the brewery itself, in Andersontown, closed in 2005.

Only two English architectural artworks celebrate the industry using a brewing – rather than malting or coopering – image. Both date from between the wars and appear on municipal buildings. A figure of a local brewer pouring out beer forms part of a long historical frieze (1936) on the exterior of Wandsworth Town Hall (Fig 8.17), while the six immense bronze doors of Norwich City Hall (1938; Fig 8.18) bear a series of reliefs designed by James Woodford and depicting local industrial and historical scenes; a finely detailed fermenting tun stands for the brewing industry.

Even the architecture of English breweries is not as visually extravagant as many of those abroad, particularly in Europe and the United States. We have nothing to compare with the four gigantic granite elephants supporting the 1901 gateway of Carlsberg's former brewery in Copenhagen (the sculptor was possibly H P Pedersen-Dan), or the figures of Gambrinus, the spirit of brewing, sported by numerous American breweries from the late 19th century. Internally, English brewhouses generally lack the decoration – often in ceramic tiles or stained glass – of their European peers. After an English brewer visited the Kindl Brewery in Berlin during 1931, he described its remarkable mash tun room with some amazement: 'It was a Cathedral-like structure with stained glass windows, a wonderful floor, and a kind of altar at the end on which there were three magnificent coppers or mash tuns.'[22]

Although we enjoy our home-produced ales at frequent beer festivals, we do not celebrate their history on the same scale as European brewers and drinkers.[23]

Fig 8.19
A 1950s window by P Loffner at the Uerige brewery-cum-pub in Düsseldorf's old town. The Uerige brewery was established in 1862, but wartime bombing forced rebuilding of the premises. The glass harks back to medieval brewing, as three men stir the mash while a boy pours beer for patrons at the table to the rear. The visual celebration of brewing continues throughout the Uerige with wood carving, tiles, paintings and more stained glass.

Fig 8.20 (right)
Hop-related imagery on one of two windows in the Millennium Brewhouse at Shepherd Neame's Brewery in Faversham, designed in 2000 by glass artists Keith and Judy Hill of Staplehurst. The other depicts beer and brewing.

Fig 8.21 (far right top)
A rare British reference to Gambrinus, the spirit of brewing or the King of Beer, on this early 20th-century advertising token for Ye Olde Gambrinus Lager Beer Hall in Soho's Rupert Street. Its proprietor, Austrian-born Charles Manzel (c 1859–1923), is pictured riding a goat in a Gambrinus-like pose. He ran a lager saloon in nearby Glasshouse Street until moving to Rupert Street in 1902. Its huge basement bierkeller, bedecked with German flags and ephemera, was popular with German students until the war brought an abrupt end.

Fig 8.22 (far right bottom)
Reverse of Ye Olde Gambrinus Lager Beer Hall token.

Fig 8.23 (right)

The Drayman (1980), standing in Dortmund Square, just off the busy Headrow in Leeds, was a gift from Dortmund commemorating the tenth year of twinning between the two cities. Its sculptor was Arthur Schulze-Engels (b1910).

Fig 8.23 (right)

The Drayman (1980), standing in Dortmund Square, just off the busy Headrow in Leeds, was a gift from Dortmund commemorating the tenth year of twinning between the two cities. Its sculptor was Arthur Schulze-Engels (b1910).

Fig 8.24 (below)

A Federation Brewery wagon drumming up business in Ashington, Northumberland, around 1920. The Northern Clubs' Federation Brewery was a cooperative brewery established in 1919 and funded by north-east working men's clubs. They first brewed in Newcastle in 1921, moving to the city's Hanover Square Brewery in 1927. Many clubmen invested their life savings in the 'Fed', which strictly controlled its beer prices.

A prime instance is the annual Belgian Beer Weekend. Sampling aside, the highlight is a parade of the Belgian Brewers' Guild (the Knighthood of the Brewers' Mash Staff) through the Grand Place in Brussels, when tributes are paid to Gambrinus and St Arnold of Soissons, the patron saint of Belgian brewers. A curious confirmation of the significance accorded to the brewing industry abroad came in the selection by the people of Dortmund of a sculpture as a gift to their twin city, Leeds, in 1980 (Fig 8.23). The work chosen was the second version of a figure of a drayman – the *Bierkutscher* – carrying a cask of beer; the original bronze was commissioned for the Dortmunder Actien Brauerei (Dortmund Joint Stock Brewery) in 1979 and now stands in the Stadtgarten, a park in central Dortmund. It symbolises the economic importance of the city's brewing tradition, and reflects the prominence of the industry in the view of its citizens.

Perhaps our remaining traditional brewers and the new wave of craft breweries can build on the clear affection for British-style ales and earn the industry the respect it receives abroad. Maintaining the best of brewing's built heritage and even creating innovative new buildings should help cement brewing's place in local communities. There is more to breweries than beer alone.

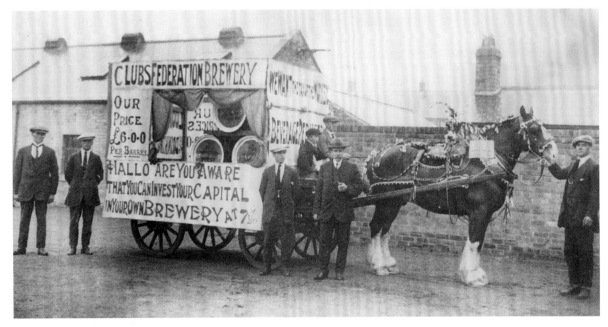

9 The Buildings of the Brewing Industry Today

Fig 9.1

Cheering crowds greet the carriage of King George V and Queen Mary as it passes Charrington's Anchor Brewery on the Mile End Road in 1935, during the course of their Silver Jubilee drive through the East End. The brewery, as befits a significant local employer, looks its decorative best.

Since the heyday of the UK brewing industry, around the end of the 19th century, the number of working breweries has undergone a savage decline. From a total of 3,556 in 1915 the figure decreased to 885 in 1939, and kept on a downward path as the process of company concentration continued. Only 524 remained by 1952, and by 1986 only 117 old-established breweries were still in existence. Today, there are fewer than 40 traditional working breweries in England, plus a handful of plants built from the 1960s onward.[1] However, the picture changes constantly, to give but three recent examples: Highgate Brewery in Walsall went into administration in June 2010 and was up for sale; in late 2012 Hydes Brewery moved from its old Manchester premises to Salford, where the new 40-barrel plant is worked by only five employees; and redevelopment of the Robert Cain Brewery in Liverpool, which closed in May 2013, is probably to include a craft brewery (*see* p 227).

In total, England still retains at least 825 sites where extant buildings were or still are used for industrial-scale beer brewing. Many of these were integrated brewery sites, where all the processes took place, but often only one or two specific buildings now survive, for instance an office, stables or brewer's house. The most significant locations are the 108 (13 per cent) that retain their brewhouse, crucial for the brewing process and for interpretation of the site; there are just under 40 working brewhouses and almost 70 former brewhouses. Particularly to be treasured are the 25 or so breweries that still brew in their original buildings, in whole or part, using at least some traditional equipment. Throughout England, from north to south – Samuel Smith's of Tadcaster to Harveys in Lewes – and east to west – Elgood's in Wisbech to St Austell – these breweries have managed to succeed while respecting their past.

Where change has been necessary to keep abreast of developments in modern brewing, this can be achieved sympathetically without compromising the building. A good example is the installation of a new copper house in 2009 at the grade II listed Wadworth's Northgate Brewery in Devizes. The new plant, seen by visitors on brewery tours, occupies a modified interwar building, while the old copper has been refurbished and is used for occasional seasonal brews (*see* Fig 5.31). Even more spectacular was the insertion of an entire set of German self-cleaning brewing vessels into Robinson's Unicorn Brewery, Stockport in 2012. Visitors now see the new equipment alongside some excellent examples of older brewing kit.

There is already a good deal of legal protection for our national resource of extant brewing industry buildings. Just under half the 825 sites are listed, mostly at grade II. Of the traditional working breweries, 11 are listed grade II (as are 4 pub

Fig 9.2

The redevelopment of Gale's Brewery in Horndean as housing in 2012 and 2013 has left little more than the 1869 tower remaining. This postcard shows the brewhouse (right) with steam rising as brewing takes place, at the centre of an early 20th-century rural community.

brewhouses), although only Harveys of Lewes is listed grade II*. Even in Burton, where a spate of brewery demolitions caused the Victorian Society to report in 1984 that 'the value of the town's industrial heritage does not seem to have been appreciated', there has been progress.[2] At least 61 buildings of the brewing and malting industries survive there, and 42 of these are listed.[3]

These 825 sites form a substantial segment of our built heritage. To complete an overview of the industry's remaining buildings, we should add in at least 66 country house brewhouses, along with the numerous stand-alone maltings unconnected to brewing sites; 658 of these were already listed in 2004, and the number has increased since. After looking at brewery tourism, this chapter goes on to consider how our former brewing industry sites are being utilised; if the conversion of old brewery buildings is carried out intelligently, we can retain the factors that make these places special. Today, our collection of the industry's buildings accommodates many functions, from traditional beer brewing to housing, shopping, entertainment and more.

Visiting working breweries

Brewery tourism has a long and indeed royal pedigree, famously including the visit of King George III to Whitbread's in 1787. Many traditional breweries still engaged in brewing are now opening visitor centres to encourage a broader interest in their work, and to capitalise on the archival material and objects in their own collections. They doubtless also hope to sell more brewery souvenirs, and of course beer. Brewery visiting has become part of the tourism industry, albeit a rather disparate offering. At one end of the range are operations like Shepherd Neame in Faversham, named 2011 Small Visitor Attraction of the Year by Visit England, and Hook Norton, with over 10,000 visitors annually and not only its Brewery Museum but the Hook Norton Village Museum to entice potential customers. At the other end of the scale are, for instance, small craft breweries housed in modern industrial premises where the main draw is the interaction with brewers themselves.

Visitors to country houses may come across brewing equipment in former brewhouses, for instance at Knole, Kent (where the brewhouse is a tearoom) and Charlecote Park (Warwickshire), both National Trust properties. The most complete remaining small 19th-century brewery – Southwick Brewhouse – stands to the rear of the Golden Lion in Southwick (Hampshire). The last regular brewing took place in the mid-1950s; it was restored from 1982 to 1985 and is now a museum combined with a beer shop.

Visitor facilities are becoming more sophisticated. Robinson's Unicorn Brewery of Stockport celebrated their 175th anniversary in 2013 by launching their new visitor centre. Its centrepiece is a splendidly complex domed copper installed in 1929, which has been cut through to expose the glistening pipes of the calandria (*see* Fig 5.52); architects for the venture were the Fairhursts Design Group. Greene King at Bury St Edmunds, for one, has a quite substantial museum, and we should not forget the brewery-related items held in local and national museums, usually part of social history collections. A good example is the Dorset County Museum at Dorchester, with an excellent display of Eldridge Pope material, including a model of the brewery made by the firm's apprentice coppersmiths around 1950. So accurately made were the brewing vessels that it can be used to brew a thimbleful of beer. Of course, the brewing industry has its own dedicated museum, whose story is related below.

The National Brewery Centre

By the 1970s the former joiners' shop of the Bass Middle Brewery in Burton formed the core of the Bass Museum of Brewing. At first the museum concentrated on the firm's own history, based on its substantial holdings of objects and archive material, but over the years its remit grew to include the broader history of beer and brewing, in England and further afield. At one point it appeared to be a highly successful attraction, said to pull in a quarter of a million visitors annually, but by the time Bass's brewing operations were sold to Interbrew in 2000, and then bought by Coors (later Molson Coors) in 2002, the numbers had declined as the museum was not being publicly promoted.

As the Coors Visitor Centre, the museum continued to run until June 2008, when Coors closed it down, citing the expense of funding the site as the main reason. Local and national outcry followed, to the surprise of Coors. There was a protest march through Burton, a petition, and an action group set up determined to oppose closure, including the local MP, Janet Dean, Burton's Civic Society and Chamber of Commerce, local councils, CAMRA and others. Sensing a public relations disaster, eventually Coors agreed to make an initial donation to what would become the National Brewery Centre, and continue its support with an annual contribution.

The new Centre, run by leisure business operator Planning Solutions, reopened to the public in May 2010 and was officially opened four months later by Princess Anne. In late 2010 the Centre's White Shield Brewery was superseded by the William Worthington Brewery (Fig 9.3), set up at considerable cost by Molson Coors within the old joiners' shop. After a sluggish start, visitor numbers have grown considerably and the National Brewery Centre now attracts many tourists from abroad as well as the UK. Greater security for its future came in 2011 when the original museum steering group was officially incorporated as the National Brewery Heritage Trust, allowing it to seek new sources of funding for the Centre and confirming its national status.

Fig 9.3

The William Worthington Brewery, installed during 2010 at the National Brewery Centre, in the former joiners' shop. It replaced the Centre's White Shield Brewery (across the yard, next to the Robey engine shed), although fermentation of the new plant's beer is still carried out there.

So with closure averted, national recognition gained and a safeguarding body in place, the Centre looks set to fulfil its potential as England's national brewing museum. In Europe there are a dozen national or regional brewery museums – six in Germany, three in Belgium and one each in the Czech Republic, the Netherlands and France – as well as several run by operating commercial breweries, like the Guinness Storehouse in Dublin.[4] The comparison is illuminating; our brewing traditions may be different, but they are equally as strong as those of Germany and Belgium. However, we still lack appreciation of the industry's economic and cultural significance.

Housing craft breweries

A handful of modern craft breweries occupy traditional brewing industry buildings, often taking up only a tiny part of the old premises. The Bristol Beer Factory, for instance, brews at the former Ashton Gate Brewery (closed in 1933), while the Shardlow Brewing Company works from the old brewery stables in Cavendish Bridge (Leicestershire), a site associated with brewing since 1819. The Broughs microbrewery has operated from a small corner of the vast Springfield Brewery site in Wolverhampton since 2011. However, a good number of micros are located in modern sheds on industrial estates, convenient but not particularly conducive to brewery visiting.

As yet there is no brewing industry equivalent of the current emphasis placed by wineries worldwide on innovative modern design, making winery architecture as much of an attraction as the wine itself. Wine producers tend to commission architects who will create appealing spaces that celebrate and promote wine culture; the image of the winery is closely linked to brand identity.[5] There are signs

Fig 9.4 (below right)
Between 1996 and 1997 the grade II listed former water pumping station (1854) at Newburn, west of Newcastle upon Tyne, was converted into a home for the Big Lamp Brewery and its brewery tap, the Keelman. With the addition of an internal upper floor, the old beam engine house (right) became the brewery, while reconstruction of the boiler house provided space for the pub. Big Lamp, founded in 1982 and the oldest microbrewery in the North-East, was originally based in Newcastle.

Fig 9.5 (below)
High House Farm Brewery in Matfen, Northumberland, was founded in 2003 and occupies the family farm's grade II listed buildings. On the right are the old engine house, granary, sheds and threshing barn (all 1844), now housing the brewery, bar and shop, while the mid-19th century Dutch barn (left) shelters an outdoor sitting area. The farm grows its own barley for brewing.

of this approach at microbreweries with attached restaurants and bars (or vice versa), where the brewing equipment – preferably a series of glistening vessels – is integrated as a backdrop, and the whole has high design quality.

A notable example is the Meantime Brewing Company's Old Brewery at the Old Royal Naval College in Greenwich. The Old Brewery is housed in a 19th-century building on the site of the 1717 brewhouse that supplied the Royal Hospital for Seamen. The venue is a bar-cum-restaurant with the brewery clearly visible, replete with copper-clad Italian-built vessels on three levels (Fig 9.6). The overall design, by Real Studios, won a *Time Out* design award in 2010, the year it opened. Likewise the Zerodegrees chain of brewpubs utilises the brewing kit as part of their dramatic interiors. The Blackheath Zerodegrees, designed by architects Ratcliffe Stott, opened in 2000; its brewery is mounted on a glazed, two-storey steel frame, drawing attention to the scale of the German-made vessels. Perhaps the success of these experiments will encourage other craft brewers to emulate the architectural ambition of their Victorian forebears.

Fig 9.6

Copper-clad brewing vessels provide a glamorous backdrop to the restaurant in Meantime Brewing Company's Old Brewery at the Old Royal Naval College in Greenwich. Fermenting and maturing vessels occupy the two upper stages. Meantime, founded in 1999, produced its first brew in 2000, and moved its main brewery to a site in north Greenwich during 2010.

Remembering lost breweries

There are over 70 Brewery Streets, Roads, Lanes and Squares in England, and well over 100 variants on the Maltings. Some of these names refer to buildings still wholly or partly extant, like the latest Brewery Lane, named in 2013 and connecting parts of the reconstructed Newcastle University campus close to the former Newcastle Breweries' office. Others provide a reminder of lost breweries or maltings, and may even be more specific, like Worthington Way in Burton (which follows the curving line of the brewery's private railway) and Ruddle Way in Langham (Rutland), where a housing estate now stands on the old Ruddle's Brewery site at the heart of the village.

Former brewery sites are significant in planning terms as they were some of the last remaining locations of industry in the central areas of our major towns and cities. Their demise clearly offered development opportunities, but also problems due to their substantial size. Newcastle's Tyne Brewery, for instance, demolished between 2007 and 2008, left a 9.7ha space immediately west of the city centre, next door to the Newcastle United football ground. The brewery's regional office, an 11-storey 1960s slab block, has already been converted to a luxury hotel, but the Science Central project which is intended to fill the remainder of the site is not expected to be complete until late 2014.

Where brewery buildings really have disappeared completely, occasionally a minor decorative element has been retained in the townscape to remind us of their existence, like the (probably) early 19th-century stone lion from Chester Lion Brewery. When the buildings were cleared in 1969, the trademark beast was rescued and now looks out over the city from his incongruous location on top of a concrete lift shaft at the multi-storey car park built on the site.

It has been suggested that the Chester lion is Coade stone (an artificial ceramic 'stone', in fact a type of stoneware) but judging by its design and appearance, this is unlikely.[6] However, the 1837 lion that stands at the east end of Westminster Bridge is definitely Coade stone (Fig 9.7); he was one of the last products to come from the Coade factory, located just north of the bridge. Sculpted by William Woodington (1806–93), he originally stood on the nearby riverside parapet of Goding's Lion Brewery, demolished in 1949 during site clearance for the Festival of Britain (Fig 9.8).

Fig 9.7 (below)

The Lion Brewery's colossal beast has looked down on tourists from his plinth at the east end of Westminster Bridge for almost half a century. He stands 13ft high and is 12ft from toe to tail; he was made in several separate pieces and cramped together (screwed together with clamps) on an iron frame.

Fig 9.8 (below right)

It is 15 January 1949, and the Coade stone lion topping Goding's Lion Brewery in Lambeth is surrounded by scaffolding, prior to being lowered through the old brewery to the ground the following month. He was made at the nearby Coade works on 24 May 1837; one of his paws bears the date.

Fig 9.9 (above)

One lion that does survive at a traditional working brewery is this grade II listed stone beast, standing in front of the fermenters at Camerons Lion Brewery in Hartlepool. The sculpture is the last remnant of the first Lion Brewery, founded in 1852 by William Waldon. Much of the present brewery was built in 1892.

Fig 9.10 (above right)

Since 1972 a smaller Coade lion rescued from Goding's Lion Brewery has guarded the west or Lion Gate at Twickenham Stadium, home of the British Lions. The gate was erected in 1929 as a memorial to the rugby administrator Sir George Rowland Hill (1855–1928). The golden lion presides over four bronze figures of rugby players by the sculptor Gerald Laing (1936–2011), installed in 1995.

The lion was initially relocated near Waterloo Station before being moved to Westminster Bridge in 1966, where he is now a magnet for tourists. Of two smaller Coade lions at the brewery, one was lost while the other was presented to the Rugby Football Union in 1972 and now tops the Lion Gate at Twickenham Stadium (Fig 9.10).

Finding new uses

Since the 1960s many traditional industrial-scale breweries have been reborn through conversion to new uses. For some, like Hartley's Crown Brewery at West Cowick in East Yorkshire, the change in function has been barely noticeable; the brewery closed in 1957 but still looks much as it did when brewing, and continues as all-purpose industrial and warehouse premises. Other conversions, particularly those involving retail outlets, have been more dramatic, but still prove the point an early proponent of adapting historic buildings put forward, that Victorian builders 'made it possible for a later generation to extend the life span of a redundant industrial building type by a fundamental change of use'.[7]

Several early brewery conversions involved arts-based end uses, for instance in Kendal where almost all the Whitwell, Mark Brewery buildings were retained after brewing ceased in 1968. The Brewery Arts Centre (Fig 9.13) was created by local architect Gordon Stables on the town centre site from 1971 onward, and although several sections have been rebuilt and extended, the venue has kept its slightly higgledy-piggledy industrial look. The brewery's retention and change of function also prevented the loss of its grand terraced garden, now the sole surviving traditional garden left in Highgate; once there would have been many more behind the Georgian houses.

Fig 9.11
Since 1946 the late Victorian buildings of Morse's Crown Brewery in Lowestoft have housed Winsor & Newton's artists' brush-making factory. Externally, the structure appears little changed since its brewing days; the water tank (top right) was made by R Ramsden & Son of London, one of the smaller brewers' engineering firms.

Fig 9.12
Mark Stockman, a 19-year-old rugby league player, carries the Olympic flame past the former Robert Deuchar's Sandyford Stone Brewery in Newcastle upon Tyne during the Olympic Torch Relay on 15 June 2012. The buildings visible date from about 1840, and were reconstructed as a bottling store, offices and warehouse during 1904. Brewing ceased after 1941, and conversion to apartments followed from 1984 to 1986.

Fig 9.13
Kendal's Brewery Arts Centre, formerly the Whitwell, Mark Brewery, seen from its garden, which is accessed via a narrow archway (leading through the original owner's Georgian house) from Highgate, one of the town's main streets.

Other conversions included only a few of the original buildings. Most of Taunton's West Somerset Brewery was demolished during the early 1970s, then the Brewhouse Theatre was erected on part of the site in 1975, with the brewer's Georgian house being used as its restaurant and gallery.[8] Similarly, most structures actually used for brewing at Cirencester Brewery in Gloucestershire had already been demolished before a craft centre and ultimately New Brewery Arts was created on the site from 1977 onward in restored 19th-century buildings previously used for storage.[9]

In Burton, the union rooms of the Bass New Brewery were saved from demolition in 1985, largely due to pressure from Burton Civic Society, and converted from 1989 to 1990 to become the Brewhouse, a mixed-use arts-based community centre. Lighting was improved by the addition of salvaged and refurbished sash windows, supplied by Bass, and an auditorium was inserted. The reconstruction also included provision of office and residential accommodation.[10] This broad mixture of uses has ensured the Brewhouse's continuing success.

These are only a few representative examples of 20th-century brewery conversions, which tended towards the small in scale. The brewhouse was often retained but the lesser buildings, for instance the cooperage and stables, frequently lost. Several more recent and ongoing redevelopment projects involve significantly larger sites and considerable investment.

Redevelopment in the 21st century

Just like breweries themselves, no two brewery conversions are the same. The buildings concerned will differ in age, scale and original function, and the requirements of new users will be hugely variable. It is something of a shock to discover that a building as recent as Ashby House (1989), the former Courage Brewery headquarters office in Staines (Surrey), is to be redeveloped. Its concrete frame is still fit for purpose, but the rest will be dismantled and replaced. More generally, brewery conversions involve structures built during the late 19th and very early 20th centuries, the industry's period of greatest growth. Quite often these will be listed buildings, but even when unprotected buildings are being considered for conversion and adaptive reuse, designers should be encouraged to retain significant structures, detailing and, where possible, plant.

When contemplating adaptation, we need to pick out what exactly is special about the brewery or maltings in question. On larger sites, retention of the specific sense of place – an industrial place with a particular function – is crucial. Overall, of course, the outcome of this conservation-led approach needs to be architecturally and commercially reasonable for the project to be successful. At The Brewery complex in Cheltenham, a mixed-use development opened in 2007, local and historical connections to the new buildings were provided by retention of the malthouse and brewhouse facades from the Cheltenham Original Brewery (later Whitbread's), otherwise mostly demolished in 2004. They form the centrepiece of the development, with a second phase of building still to come. Its brewing associations were further reinforced by the installation of a themed sculpture, the 6m-high steel and copper *Barley* by Sophie Marsham.

The vast fermenting house of Allsopp's New Brewery (1859–60; *see* Fig 7.12) in Burton was converted from 2010 to 2012 by property developers Optima Cambridge to high quality office accommodation for around 1,200 people along with ancillary facilities and space for community activities.[11] Now known as 107 Station Street

Fig 9.14

The smart facade of grade II listed
107 Station Street in Burton, formerly
the fermenting house, or tunnery as it
was known, of Allsopp's New Brewery.
The lower block in the foreground,
originally a single storey and basement,
contained the lavishly fitted out offices.

Fig 9.15

The McMullen's Brewery museum at
Sainsbury's in Hertford, located in the
former copper house of the Old
Brewery, includes the smallest of the
fermentation vessels (left) rescued
from the brewhouse, which itself has
been restored for workspace or
residential use.

(Fig 9.14), the refurbishment included stripping away later alterations to allow original features, like the rows of iron columns, to be seen again, complemented by bold interior design. Just across the railway line to the west is another new conversion, the Travelodge in the former Midland Railway Grain Warehouse No 2 (c 1880s), which opened in September 2012.

A constructive attitude towards the industry's heritage typifies several current large-scale redevelopment schemes, for instance the addition of a Sainsbury's store (opened in June 2012) to the Old Brewery at McMullen's of Hertford. Here, well-executed mural panels in the foyer illustrate the history of the town and brewery, and a small but thorough museum devoted to McMullen's history is accessed through the café (Fig 9.15). The museum, the first at a Sainsbury's store, was a planning requirement for the scheme, which also involved restoration of the brewhouse tower.

One of the largest and most intriguing brewery sites to undergo development recently is the Eldridge Pope Brewery in Dorchester, now known as Brewery Square. The conversion and new-build project involved a tight-knit group of five grade II listed buildings and structures, the biggest being the brewhouse. This was put up between 1880 and 1881 but badly damaged by fire in 1922, resulting in the loss of all brewing equipment. It was rebuilt the following year to the same plan and in similar style by architects Crickmay & Sons of Weymouth, the practice responsible (in part) for the original. The result was an impressively Victorian-looking pile with several datestones and other plaques from the old brewhouse incorporated into the new structure (Fig 9.19). The brewery closed in 2003 and development began in 2009 to a masterplan for the 4.6ha site by architects CZWG, collaborating with Conran and Partners regarding the listed buildings. A cinema and restaurant were the first commercial elements to open, in late 2012.

Fig 9.16
Redevelopment of Warwicks &
Richardsons Northgate Brewery in
Newark as residential and retail
accommodation was completed in 2011,
although the well-preserved 1864
maltings at the rear of the site has yet
to find a new use. The brewery's roof
structure was largely replaced, and
a free-standing addition was erected on
a previously demolished area of the
brewery, maintaining part of its original
footprint.

Fig 9.17
Alnwick's former High Brewery last
brewed in 1963, and although most of its
early 19th-century buildings have been
lost, it is still a substantial site occupying
a prime central position in this rural
market town. Conversion to flats and
offices (The Malthouse development)
began in 2008, but was suspended in
2009 due to poor economic conditions.
It was then put on sale incomplete, and
in early 2014 still awaited a buyer able
to finish the project.

Fig 9.18
The Albion Works (1866–7) of brewers'
coppersmith Henry Pontifex & Sons,
opposite King's Cross station, was
converted to mixed use between 2005
and 2006 as the Brassworks, part of the
Regent Quarter urban regeneration
development; the design was by RHWL
Architects. From the left we see a
corner of the office building (which faces
York Way), part of the three-storey
warehouse, then the long main
workshop range. This was originally
a single-storey structure with a ridge
lantern running the entire length of
its roof.

Great care has been taken to make the most of the site's enjoyably decorative architecture, with new lighting enhancing the polychromatic brickwork of the offices and bonded stores (now retail and the Thomas Hardy Hall) that stretch along the main road. The larger-than-life-size bronze of a dray horse in Dray Horse Yard will be a new addition, signalling a western entrance, while a renovated copper is displayed round the corner in Copper Yard (Fig 9.20). A massive green and white ceramic shield bearing the initials 'EP', originally mounted on the rear of the brewhouse, has been conserved and is now to be found indoors, near the Pizza Express foyer. At the other end of the scale, the brewhouse, now overlooking a new square centred on a broad fountain, will become the luxury Dorchester Brewery Hotel, while the new-build includes a Premier Inn and apartments. The listed maltings was donated to the local Maltings Arts Trust for use as a theatre and arts venue. Initial reaction to the new development has been generally positive; the public spaces retain a definite industrial feel, and the ornate brewery architecture sits comfortably with the new structures.

Fig 9.19
The newly opened fountain in Dorchester's Brewery Square seen in June 2013; in the background is the former Eldridge Pope brewhouse, awaiting conversion to a luxury hotel. Note the chimney's elaborate base, a recurring element in Scamell & Colyer's designs.

Fig 9.20
Development work was still in progress at the former Eldridge Pope Brewery in Dorchester during summer 2013. The restored brewing copper is one of a pair of 1950s vessels which remained in the brewhouse, surviving a 1984 refit. It now stands in Copper Yard, beside the grade II listed former bottling stores and bonded warehouse (left) with its distinctive polychromatic brickwork. The 1880s building, now a restaurant, was one of the first parts of Brewery Square to open, in late 2012.

More questionable, however, were the events at Tetley's Brewery in Leeds, where closure in 2011 was rapidly followed by the demolition of the original brewery building, parts of which dated from 1864 to 1874. Given the immediate availability of an alternative use for this historic structure, the outcome is deeply regrettable and a clear case of a missed opportunity for the city; the site is currently in use as a car park. The art deco offices (1931; Fig 9.21, *see also* Fig 3.53) survived and their transformation into The Tetley, a contemporary arts centre run by Project Space Leeds, was completed in late 2013. The design, by Chetwoods Architects, Leeds working with engineers Arup, included opening up the four-storey central atrium and the preservation and reuse of many original features. The brewery's war memorial was retained and the Tetley archives – the Tetley Collection – are also housed in the refurbished building.[12]

Fig 9.21
Elegant brick detailing on the 1931 art deco office block at the former Tetley's Brewery in Leeds, seen in April 2013 awaiting completion of its conversion to a contemporary arts centre. The massive brewhouse which stood to the rear of the offices was demolished in late 2011.

Three major future projects

Finally we look to the future and briefly consider planned developments at three medium to large brewery sites, each involving an array of listed buildings. These serve to illustrate the possibilities and the design dilemmas inherent in large-scale brewery conversions.

In Liverpool, the 'terracotta palace' of the grade II listed Robert Cain Brewery ceased brewing in May 2013. Plans are already in place to transform the brewery and its surroundings into Brewery Village, seen as a national tourist destination including a mix of apartments and retail along with a cinema and hotel. The restored brewhouse is to contain a top-floor bar and the rejuvenated Cains craft brewery, along with a brewery museum. Once complete, the scheme is projected to attract about 500,000 visitors a year. The plans were exhibited at the brewery during June 2013 in a consultation exercise, and were approved by the local council in November 2013. Partly due to its ornate appearance, the brewery is one of the best-known in England, and its site near the Mersey has huge potential. The intention to continue brewing is to be applauded.

Fig 9.22
The iconic 1902 Ruabon terracotta facade of the Robert Cain Brewery in Liverpool includes several renderings of the Cain's twin-horned gazelle symbol and motto *Pacem amo* (I love peace). The facade was amended to show Daniel Higson's name after he purchased the brewery in 1923, but the gazelles remained.

William Bradford's iconic Tolly Cobbold Brewery (1896 and 1904), on its imposing waterfront site in Ipswich, has not seen industrial-scale brewing since 2003. It is listed grade II, as is the adjoining brewery tap, the mainly 18th-century Cliff House. A 2004 application to convert the substantial brewhouse to flats was rejected and it took another eight years, during which most of the historic brewing equipment was lost (*see* Fig 5.35), before further plans for redevelopment were submitted; these include restoration of the brewhouse to a design by architects Lyall Bills & Young. The intention is to turn the brewhouse into a community attraction, with a restaurant and bar, and a small brewing museum; the fermentation hall will be transformed into a dramatic 300-seat auditorium. The rest of the site is to be mixed-use development with flats and a supermarket arranged around a new piazza. The plans – which specify restoration of Bradford's brewhouse as the first step – were granted outline planning permission in early 2013, and work is set to start in 2014. It will be interesting to see how the designers make the most of the waterside site and integrate the great brewhouse into the whole scheme.

The former Young's Ram Brewery site in Wandsworth is a larger and more complex development, taking in the grade II* listed brewery and three grade II listed structures: an 18th-century brewer's house, the late 19th-century stables and the early 20th-century brewery tap. The Ram Brewery ceased brewing in 2006, but the historic plant, including beam engines and coppers, remains at the site. The initial plans of developers Minerva were rejected in 2010 and a scaled-down version, with one residential tower rather than two, were submitted in late 2012 after much local consultation, including two public exhibitions; outline planning permission was granted by the local council in July 2013. The mixed-use proposals include a 36-storey tower and much commercial space, along with a microbrewery, to be sited in one of the restored listed buildings, and the creation of a brewery museum to display the Young's plant. New public spaces should open up the area, and encourage greater appreciation of its brewery heritage assets, just as the supermarket development in Hertford has revealed the brewery to its residents. We look forward to seeing how this all works out in practice.

Breweries make special places

Although these grand plans are eye-catching, we should remember that smaller scale developments can also have a significant local effect. When Adnams Brewery moved their distribution centre away from the middle of Southwold in 2006, a vacant site was left within the town's conservation area. The company were proud of their award-winning, environmentally friendly new distribution centre and wanted to develop something equally sustainable at the old site on Tibby's Triangle. Architects Ash Sakula won a design competition for the new development with a mixed-use scheme including shops, housing and a brewery museum. The brief later changed, dropping the museum (which opened inside the brewery itself in 2012) and simply comprised houses, flats and a shop, in fact an Adnams Cellar & Kitchen Store with an integral café.

The first phase, the store and café, opened in late 2008, while the residential portion took a few years longer, winning a clutch of design awards in 2012.[13] Beyond the store's street frontage lie new lanes and yards with views of the grade I listed parish church. The site's brewing history is emphasised by the use of two huge copper-lined fermentation vessels, suitably modified, in the café (see Fig 5.54); they break through its envelope and protrude into the public square outside. The redevelopment of Tibby's Triangle has given Southwold a new urban quarter, distinctly contemporary but directly linked with the town's industrial heritage.

As at least 825 historic brewery sites remain in England with extant buildings, you are never far from a beer-related location, whether large or small. Throw in pubs and maltings, and we are something of a beer-themed country; metaphorically, the liquid runs through our veins. Our beer and brewing heritage has been underestimated for too long, and curiously it is the recent redevelopment of large industrial breweries that has brought our brewing culture to the fore, since developers perceive it as a potentially profitable element in their plans. We have seen that the buildings of England's brewing industry range from vast disused sites

Fig 9.23
Harveys Brewery in Lewes provides the backdrop for a Christmas market, and contributes to the festive scene with its nativity mural in the brewhouse window. The mural, by local artist Julian Bell (b1952), has been used every year since 2002; the wise men and other characters are current and former brewery employees.

Fig 9.24
Beers all round – cheers!

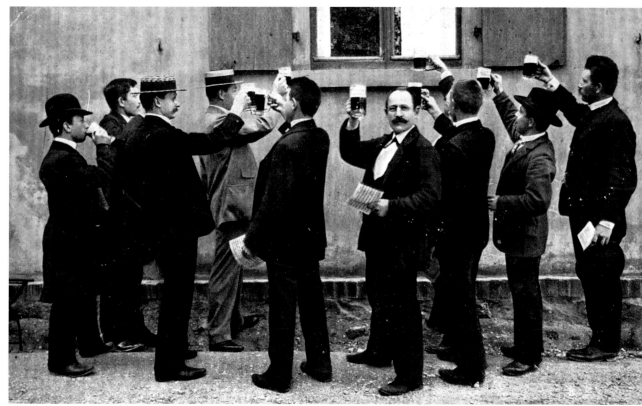

through operating urban and rural breweries to former vaults and stables, and much more besides. Our working traditional breweries are the jewels in the crown, worth visiting and supporting alongside the newer craft breweries.[14] By redeveloping old brewery sites using the principles of constructive conservation, and managing change while recognising historic significance, we continue to emphasise the importance of breweries, brewers and beer in our social and industrial life. As beer once more grows in popularity, the longevity of the industry's buildings, and of the industry itself, ensures that beer and brewing remain at the heart of English culture.

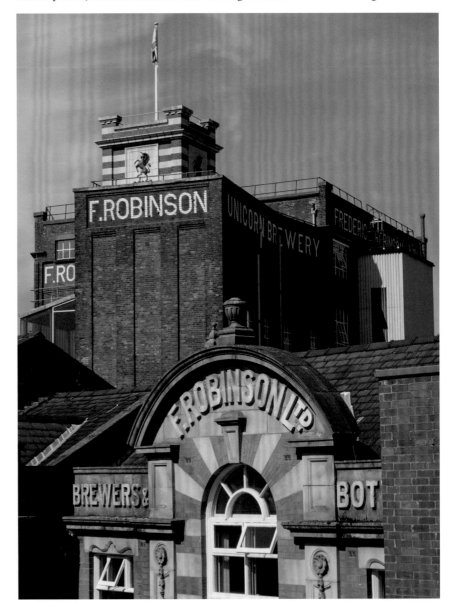

Fig 9.25
Frederic Robinson's Unicorn Brewery is crammed into a tight-knit site in the centre of Stockport, only a few hundred metres from the town's market hall and oldest parish church. The brewery was founded in the mid-19th century but the brewhouse tower, with its glazed terracotta unicorn trademark, dates from the late 1920s.

Notes

Chapter 1

1   Protz 2012, 901–25.
2   The remaining floor maltings are Warminster Maltings (Wiltshire) and Tucker's Maltings, Newton Abbot (Devon), although Crisp's in Great Ryburgh (Norfolk) and Fawcett's in Castleford (West Yorkshire) also operate floor maltings but in conjunction with more modern methods.
3   Dredge 2013, 6–13. The National Hop Collection, held at Queen Court Farm near Faversham, has 780 varieties.

Chapter 2

1   'News item: Burnt mound theory tested to perfection'. *British Archaeology*, **110**, 6, 2010, 6; and Quinn and Moore 2007, 8–11. For a good summary of recent research into ancient brewing techniques, *see* Dineley 2011, 96–108.
2   Topping 2011.
3   Reilly 2012, 42–5.
4   Piggott 1995, 321–7.
5   The Vindolanda Tablets are online at http://vindolanda.csad.ox.ac.uk. *See* Tablet 186 for the purchase of beer in AD 110–111 and Tablet 182 for Atrectus the brewer.
6   Cornell 2003, 25–6.
7   Reynolds and Langley 1979, 27–42.
8   Brandwood, Davison and Slaughter 2011, 2–4.
9   For a full discussion of women and brewing in medieval England *see* Bennett 1996.
10 Brandwood, Davison and Slaughter 2011, 2–4.
11 Unger 2004, 40–1.
12 Wilcox 2002, 15–58.

13 Cornell 2003, 77–8. Although a few Cistercian houses in Wales are known to have sold drink to the secular community; A Davison, pers comm, 27 Aug 2012.
14 Monckton 1966, 77.
15 Corran 1975, 37–8.
16 Mathias 1959, 5.
17 Monckton 1966, 62.
18 Allan 2006, 241–65. The surviving part of Nostell Priory brewhouse has been converted to office space; Wrathmell 2005.
19 For the full story of English country house brewing *see* Sambrook 1996.

Chapter 3

1   Mathias 1959, 5–6.
2   Cornell 2003, 85.
3   Donnachie 1979, 2.
4   Sumner 2008, 289–306.
5   Ball 1977, 11. The Company's minute book contains some of the earliest examples of written English, beginning in 1422.
6   Terry 2011.
7   Corran 1975, 89–90.
8   Mathias 1959, 351–2.
9   Corran 1975, 180–2.
10 Mathias 1959, 350.
11 Pennant 1813, 423.
12 Spiller 1957, 310–22.
13 Watkins 1773, 134–6. An earlier version was published in 1767 as *The Compleat English Brewer*.
14 Combrune 1804, 286. The first edition was published in 1762.
15 Spiller 1957, 311–2.
16 Mathias 1959, 78–85.
17 Sumner 2005, 66–80; and Cornell 2003, 108–9.
18 Spiller 1957, 312.
19 Mathias 1959, 61–2, 551.

20 Brunton 1819, 112–4.
21 Cornell 2003, 129–31.
22 Spiller 1957, 322.
23 'A visit to Messrs. Barclay and Perkins's Brewery'. *Illustrated London News* **10** (249) 6 Feb 1847, 93–5.
24 Pearson 2000a, 8.
25 Page 2012.
26 Mathias 1959, 201–3.
27 Moore 2012, 16–40. For further details on the Royal Victualling Yards *see* Coad 2013, 299–314.
28 Mathias 1959, 543.
29 Brandwood, Davison and Slaughter 2011, 28.
30 Gourvish and Wilson 1994, 19–22.
31 Mathias 1959, 24, 31.
32 Pearson 2000a, 216–7.
33 James 2012, 41–80.
34 Cornell 2003, 133–40.
35 But the American city of Milwaukee was the 19th-century 'Brewing Capital of the World', largely due to its entrepreneurial brewers rather than any special qualities of the local water; Oliver 2012, 590–3.
36 http://zythophile.wordpress.com/2010/11/08/yarmouth-ale-sweet-and-salty/
37 *Liverpool Brewers' and Victuallers' Journal* **1** (1), 1 Mar 1890, 1.
38 Anderson 2012b, 48–51.
39 Gourvish and Wilson 1994, 63.
40 Cornell 2010, 211–16.
41 Glover 1993, 184–5.
42 Sigsworth 1965, 536–50.
43 Gourvish and Wilson 1994, 24–31.
44 Pearson 2000a, 4, 216–7.
45 Barnard 1889–91.
46 Pearson 2000a, 62–6, 224.
47 Barnard 1891, vol 4, 471.
48 Stopes 1870–1902, vol 1, 74.

49 'The Brewers' Exhibition', *Staffordshire Sentinel*, 21 Sept 1880, 2; *Western Mail*, 4 Oct 1880, 2; 'The Brewers' Exhibition', *Sheffield Daily Telegraph*, 18 Oct 1881, 7; 'The Brewers' Exhibition', *The Standard*, 17 Oct 1882, 2. Dale also organised exhibitions for the dairy and printing trades.

50 This competition is now known as the International Brewing Awards.

51 'The National Exhibition and Market', *Brewers' Journal*, 15 Nov 1895, 594; 'Are exhibitions a failure?', *The Mercury* (Hobart, Tasmania), 22 Nov 1895, 4. The latter reported on a London lecture given by maltings expert Henry Stopes, who was against the breakaway.

52 'The National Exhibition and Market', *Brewers' Journal*, 15 Nov 1896, 715.

53 Noszlopy and Waterhouse 2010, 266–8, 295.

54 Humphrey 2006, 5–13.

55 Cordle 2011, 123–4.

56 'Under a cloud', *Liverpool Brewers' and Victuallers' Journal* **1** (1), 1 Mar 1890, 14.

57 Hawkins and Pass 1979, 34.

58 Nicholls 2009, 155–7.

59 Gourvish and Wilson 1994, 326.

60 Ibid, 335.

61 Ibid, 349–50.

62 Sharp 2005, 11.

63 Richards 1957, 5–73.

64 Gourvish and Wilson 1994, 457–8.

65 Millns 1998, 142–59.

66 Anderson 2012a, 3–7.

67 Holmes 2011, 6.

68 Brown with Willmott 2010, 54.

69 Pearson 2012, 6–15.

Chapter 4

1 Patrick 2004, 4–6.

2 Clark, 2004b [http://www.oxforddnb.com/view/article/53563, accessed 25 Nov 2012].

3 Clark 1998, 104–10.

4 Clark 2004c [http://www.oxforddnb.com/view/article/50421, accessed 25 Nov 2012].

5 Patrick 2006, 14–34.

6 Stopes 1870–1902, vol 7, 2.

7 Stopes 1885.

8 Clark 2004a [http://www.oxforddnb.com/view/article/59154, accessed 25 Nov 2012].

9 Stopes 1885, 184.

10 Bradford 1889, 21.

11 Sykes 1897, 428–9.

12 Kilby 2010, 30.

13 Owen 1992, 76.

14 Barnard 1889, vol 1, 91–8.

15 Grant 1976, 28–36.

16 Scamell and Colyer 1880, 105.

17 Gourvish and Wilson 1994, 140–1. From 1853 Ind Coope also had extensive railway sidings at Romford, which connected to the main line via a tunnel and functioned until 1963; Brown 2012b, 18.

18 Barnard 1889, vol 1, 384–7.

19 *Brewers' Journal* **33**, 15 May 1897, 400.

20 Anderson 2005, 2–20.

21 Evans 2011, 78–82.

22 Irving 2009, 2–17.

23 Barnard 1889, vol 1, 105–6.

24 'Brewery Offices, Liverpool', *The Architect* **25**, 5 Mar 1881.

25 Walker 2011, 15–16. The Castle Brewery originated in 1870 as a pub brewhouse belonging to John Caparn. He soon took on Douglas Hankey as a partner, the firm becoming Caparn, Hankey & Co, and the brewery gained its name when the firm registered Newark Castle as its trademark.

26 The maltings (1864) was unusually ornate and contained an early example of a kiln built specifically to dry barley prior to the malting process. Its architect, 'P W' on the building's datestone, is unknown; there are no obvious candidates for 'P W' so could this have been a member of the Warwick family?

27 Wilkins 1871, 10–28.

28 'Obituary, Robert Davison', *Minutes of the Proceedings of the Institution of Civil Engineers* **84**, 1886, 442–4.

29 Barnard 1889, vol 1, 188.

30 'The new stabling', *Civil Engineer and Architect's Journal* **1**, 1837–8, 47–50.

31 Scamell 1871.

32 'Breweries', *The Builder* **29**, 11 Feb 1871, 97–8.

33 Anon 1966, 39.

34 Scamell and Colyer 1880.

35 Barnard 1890, vol 3, 141.

36 Barnard 1890, vol 3, 28.

37 Cooksey 1984, 34.

38 Inscription in author's copy of Scamell and Colyer, *Breweries and Maltings*, previously owned by one of Truman's directors.

39 'On the construction and arrangement of breweries and maltings', *The Builder* **30**, 10 Feb 1872, 99–100.

40 Bradford 1885, 371–3.

41 Bradford 1891, 109–38.

42 Harrap 1895, 48–69.

43 Stovin Bradford 1998, 14–20. Reprinted from a discussion document presented to a meeting of the Midland Counties Section of the Country Brewers' Society, Birmingham, 21 Jan 1932.

44 Much of the detail concerning William Bradford's family was supplied by family historians David Kerr, Georgina Cottee and Jack Kemp, to all of whom I am very grateful.

45 *Brewers' Journal* **18**, 15 Jan 1882, 15.

46 Pearson 2000a, 154–60.

47 Jenner 1990, 18.

48 Barnard 1890, vol 3, 381; Harris 2001, 4–20.

49 Temple 2008, 234–7.

50 Collins 1980, 16–22.

51 *Brewers' Journal* **39**, 15 Mar 1903, 136–7.

52 'Obituary: Mr W Bradford', *The Builder* **116**, 14 Feb 1919, 159; *Brewers' Journal* **55**, 15 Feb 1919, 58.

53 Playne 1914, 159.

54 *Brewers' Journal* **27**, 15 Aug 1891, 409.

55 Hughes 2006, 203–4.

56 Wilson 1983, 197–8, 218.

57 Wilson 1983, 218.

58 Elwall 1983, 37–46.

59 *Home Brewery 1875–1990*, Nottingham, Home Brewery plc, 1990.

60 Scoffham 1992, 42.

61 Images of the three unused designs are available at www.scran.ac.uk/database/results.php?QUICKSEARCH=1&search_term=home+brewery+lion+foundry

62 Part of the Magor Brewery (now owned by AB InBev UK) was used in a 2006 episode of the BBC TV series *Dr Who* as the location of the cyber-conversion factory which produced Cybermen.

63 The Courage Brewery closed in 2010 and was demolished in 2011.

Chapter 5

1 'Obituary, Robert Moreland', *Minutes of the Proceedings of the Institution of Civil Engineers* **104**, 1891, 316–8.

2 Brake 1985, 18, 282–9.

3 Pontifex 1977. Further details of the Pontifex family, particularly their role as manufacturers of artists' copper plates, can be found in the National Portrait Gallery online directory of British Artists' Suppliers, 1650–1950; www.npg.org.uk/research/programmes/directory-of-suppliers/p.php

4 Myers 1996, 49.

5 A Cunningham, pers comm, 23 July 1991.

6 Dodd 1843, 526–48.

7 The National Archives: Public Record Office: PROB 11/1952/362, Will of John Pontifex, Coppersmith, Millwright and Backmaker of Saint Andrews Holborn, City of London, 2 Oct 1841.

8 *International Exhibition 1862: Official Catalogue of the Industrial Department*, London, Her Majesty's Commissioners, 1862, 97.

9 English Heritage Archive, BF095656, Henry Pontifex & Sons copper and brass works, Islington.

10 *Brewers' Journal* **30**, 15 Oct 1894, 554.

11 'Pontifex: Staff told Leeds engineering firm to close', *Yorkshire Evening Post*, 19 April 2010.

12 *Brewers' Journal* **42**, 15 Nov 1906, 666.

13 *Aldenhamiana* 27, 2003, 14–15.

14 Deutsher 2012, 69.

15 Owen 1978, 122–3, 243–4.

16 *Brewers' Journal* **27**, 15 Nov 1891, 578.

17 *Brewers' Journal* **19**, 26 Oct 1883, 361.

18 'Brewing and Breweries No. XIV: Apparatus employed in the process of mashing (continued)', *Engineering* **5**, 26 June 1868, 615–6.

19 Postlethwaite 2009, 18–30.

20 *The Engineer* **50**, 27 Aug 1880, 167.

21 Sykes 1897, 436. Wakefield-born Dr Walter J Sykes (1842–1906) was a public health doctor and chemist. Hchner 1907, 1–2.

22 'Brewing and Breweries No. XVIII: Boiling the wort; coppers and boiling backs', *Engineering* **6**, 31 July 1868, 93–5.

23 *Brewers' Journal* **33**, 15 Oct 1897, 725.

24 'Brewing and Breweries No. XXXIII: Ice-making machines', *Engineering* **6**, 27 Nov 1868, 483–5.

25 Mathias 1959, 58–9.

26 Foskett 1998, 127–34.

27 Sykes 1897, 444.

28 Anderson 2006, 55–83.

29 Bayley 2008, 39–73.

30 Bradford 1889, 50; Scamell and Colyer 1880, 113–17.

31 The plant cost per quarter may be higher for larger breweries, as Scamell & Colyer's estimates suggest. In 1867 the value of fixed plant at Bass & Co in Burton was £140,000. Owen 1992, 91.

32 *Brewers' Journal* **18**, 27 Oct 1882, 302.

33 Jenner 1990, 9.

34 According to the National Archives currency converter, £1 in 1880 would have the same spending worth as £48.31 in 2005; www.nationalarchives.gov.uk/currency/

35 Gourvish and Wilson 1994, 215.

36 Dummett 1981, 205. It remained the world's biggest over two decades later.

37 'Firkin and Fabulous', *Beer*, Winter 2009, 6–13.

Chapter 6

1 Ellis 1736, 28.

2 Roberts 1847, 72.

3 Mathias 1959, 36–9.

4 Moore 2012, 20.

5 Allen 1994, 20. For comparison, the massive water wheel made by William Fairbairn & Sons of Manchester in 1852 for Jameson's distillery in Midleton near Cork is 22ft diameter and 16ft wide. It was used until 1975 to power grain milling.

6 Corran 1975, 124–8.

7 Barnard 1891, vol 4, 337–8.

8 English Heritage Archive, GMW01/02, George Watkins Collection, Steam Engine Record. Anding was an agricultural implement manufacturer and engineer, based at the Albert Iron Works during the early 1850s and probably before.

9 A beam engine from Morrell's Brewery is part of the collection of the Abbey Pumping Station Museum in Leicester.

10 Gourvish 1987, 20.

11 Moore 2012. A semicircular structure (c 1830 onward) which probably housed a horse engine still survives in Worcester, where it drove the water pump for Spreckley Brothers Worcester Brewery.

12 Unger 2004, 168–71. The Brouwershuis stands on Adriaan Brouwersstraat in Antwerp.

13 Mathias 1959, 79–80.

14 Feltham 1806, 39.

15 Fox 2009, 106–8.

16 Mathias 1959, 91–2.

17 Bowie 1978, 168–74.

18 R Greatorex, pers comm, 20 Sept 2012.

19 Mathias 1953, 208–24.

20 Feltham 1806, 40.

21 Dodd 1843, 19–23.

22 Owen 1978, 120–1.

23 Barnard 1891, vol 4, 414.

24 Cooper 1996.

25 Churchward, 2009. *See* www.ipenz.org.nz/heritage/conference/papers/Churchward_M.pdf

26 Barnard 1889, vol 2, 152.

27 Ibid.

28 *Brewers' Journal* **26**, 15 April 1890, 215.

29 *Brewers' Journal* **33**, 15 July 1897, 546.

30 *Brewers' Journal* **40**, May 1904, 312.

31 Bradford 1907, 534–58. There were several early 20th-century articles in the American publication *The Western Brewer* on the subject of electrical power in the brewery.

32 Owen 1992, 152, 158.

Chapter 7

1 James 2006, 21.
2 Worthington's c 1740 townhouse (the firm's offices between1888 and 1975) at 146 High Street still stands, although as the shield and dagger trademark on the porch was only introduced in 1863, it must be a later addition.
3 Owen 1992, 22.
4 Owen 1978, 77–9.
5 Owen 1992, 36.
6 James 2006, 40–1.
7 Cornell 2003, 133–8.
8 Cornell 2010, 109–11.
9 Owen 1978, 80–1.
10 Information on Robert Grace from census and electoral rolls, see also James 2006, 103–5. Barnard's report of his visit to Hardy's Kimberley Brewery is inaccurate in relation to Grace, whose maltings at Kimberley were listed grade II in 2008.
11 James 2006, 291.
12 Owen 1978, 87.
13 Shepherd 1996, 8, 17.
14 Bayley 2010, 2–49.
15 Shepherd 1996, 294–5.
16 Owen 1978, 86–7.
17 A Visit to Bass' Brewery, Burton upon Trent, Bass, Ratcliff & Gretton Limited, 1902, 12–13. The full list of stores as printed was: London, Aberdeen, Belfast, Birmingham, Bristol, Brighton, Cork, Dublin, Edinburgh, Exeter, Glasgow, Hull, Leeds, Leicester, Liverpool, Manchester Newcastle-on-Tyne, North Wales, Nottingham, Plymouth, Sheffield, Southampton, Stockton, Stoke, Wolverhampton, Paris, New York, Boston and Chicago. The North Wales stores were at Blaenau Ffestiniog.
18 The Forth Banks goods station was demolished above platform level in 1972; the open space above the undercroft is now a car park. Redevelopment of the area was under way in 2014.
19 'New London depot for Burton ales', Illustrated London News 23, 16 July 1853, 27–8.
20 Shepherd 1996, 27. The store was located immediately north of what is now Granary Street.
21 Simmons 1968, 31.
22 A Visit to Bass' Brewery, 1902, 23–9.
23 James 2006, 63.
24 Information from the census.
25 Shepherd 1996, 109–12.

Chapter 8

1 Wilson 1983, 81.
2 Crosby 2007, 3–14.
3 Booker and Lycett Green 1973, 77.
4 Dennison and MacDonagh 1998, 132.
5 Cooksey 1984, 38.
6 Pevsner 1974, 89. The Albion's sign, showing Marston's Brewery, is an unusual example of a pub sign depicting a brewery.
7 Yorke 1934.
8 'Brewers' Outings', Brewers' Journal 26, 15 Aug 1890, 513.
9 Pearson 1993.
10 Barnard 1889, vol 1, v.
11 Collins Howard 2009, 101–6.
12 Lloyd Williams 1994, 47–53. The painter William Mainwaring Palin (1862–1947) was born in Stoke-on-Trent and apprenticed to Wedgwood's before attending the Royal College of Art. McEwan specified lavish interior decoration for his hall, and Palin was recommended for the project by the South Kensington Museum.
13 Casey 2005, 604.
14 Welch 2004; online edn, Oct 2009 [http://www.oxforddnb.com/view/article/30634, accessed 15 Mar 2013].
15 Peaty 1989, 21–2.
16 Ogden 1987, 3.
17 Girouard 1979, 400.
18 Atterbury and Irvine 1979, 94.
19 Gourvish and Wilson 1994, 194–7.
20 Gutzke 1990, 78–115.
21 Noszlopy and Waterhouse 2005, 42–3.
22 Stovin Bradford 1998, 20. Reprinted from a discussion document presented to a meeting of the Midland Counties Section of the Country Brewers' Society, Birmingham, 21 Jan 1932.
23 Gilmour 2012, 20–1.

Chapter 9

1 Pearson 2011, 2–3 [http://www.english-heritage.org.uk/publications/brewing-industry/bhs-brewing-ind-shier.pdf, accessed 5 Aug 2013].
2 Cooksey 1984, 42.
3 James 2012, 63.
4 Oliver 2012, 886–8.
5 Stanwick and Fowlow 2010, 9.
6 Morris and Roberts 2012, 77. No evidence is offered for the Coade attribution.
7 Cantacuzino 1975, 169.
8 Taunton's Brewhouse Theatre was placed in administration in February 2013 but re-opened in April 2014.
9 Moss 2009, 13.
10 James 2012, 66.
11 Optima Cambridge Ltd were fined nearly £80,000 in March 2013, resulting from serious violations of regulations relating to asbestos during the renovation of 107 Station Street.
12 Brown 2012a, 10.
13 Catling 2013, 33.
14 Other working traditional breweries not mentioned elsewhere in the text include Thwaites Star Brewery, Blackburn, Lancashire; Fuller's Griffin Brewery, Chiswick W4; Batham's Delph Brewery, Brierley Hill, West Midlands; Holden's Brewery, Dudley, West Midlands; Banks's Park Brewery, Wolverhampton, West Midlands; and Timothy Taylor's Knowle Spring Brewery, Keighley, West Yorkshire. In addition there are four traditional working pub brewhouses that have been in more or less continuous use since they first brewed: Blue Anchor Inn, Helston, Cornwall; Three Tuns Brewery, Bishop's Castle, Shropshire; All Nations Brewhouse, Madeley, Shropshire; and Old Swan, Dudley, West Midlands.

Bibliography

Allan, J 2006 'The Excavation of a Brewhouse at Buckland Abbey in 2005'. *Proceedings of the Devon Archaeological Society* **64**, 241–65

Allen, B 1994 *Morrells of Oxford: The Family and their Brewery 1743–1993*. Stroud: Oxfordshire Books

Anderson, R 2005 'The Trade in 1905'. *Brewery History* 118, 2–20

Anderson, R 2006 'The Sword and the armour: Science and practice in the brewing industry 1837–1914'. *Brewery History* 123, 55–83

Anderson, R 2012a 'The decline and fall of the Big Six UK brewers'. *Brewery History* 146, 3–7

Anderson, R G 2012b *Brewers and Distillers by Profession: A History of the Institute of Brewing & Distilling*. London: Institute of Brewing & Distilling

Anon *c* 1862 *Views of Burton-on-Trent*. London: Rock & Co

Anon 1902 *A Visit to Bass' Brewery, Burton-on-Trent*. Burton upon Trent: Bass, Ratcliff and Gretton, Limited

Anon 1957 'Breweries, maltings and oast-houses'. *Architectural Review* **122**, 62–73

Anon 1966 *Trumans: The Brewers, 1666–1966*. London, Truman Hanbury Buxton & Co Ltd

Arnot, C 2012 *Britain's Lost Breweries and Beers*. London: Aurum Press

Atterbury P and Irvine, L 1979 *The Doulton Story*. Stoke on Trent: Royal Doulton Tableware

Ball, M 1977 *The Worshipful Company of Brewers: A Short History*. London: Hutchinson

Barber, N and Brown, M, Farleigh, R and Smith, K (eds) 2012 *A Century of British Brewers plus plus, 1890–2012*. New Ash Green: Brewery History Society

Barnard, A 1889–91 *Noted Breweries of Great Britain and Ireland*, 4 vols. London: Joseph Causton and Sons

Bayley, P 2008 'An evaluation of the number and distribution of Burton unions'. *Brewery History* 129, 39–73

Bayley, P 2010 'Toothless in Burton: A history of the Crescent Brewery, Burton upon Trent and in particular its association with the Tooth family of Cranbrook, Kent and Sydney, Australia'. *Brewery History* 134, 2–49

Bennett, J M 1996 *Ale, Beer, and Brewsters in England: Women's Work in a Changing World, 1300–1600*. New York and Oxford: Oxford University Press

Booker, C and Lycett Green, C 1973 *Goodbye London: An Illustrated Guide to Threatened Buildings*. London: Fontana

Bowie, G 1978 'Early stationary steam engines in Ireland'. *Industrial Archaeology Review* **2**, 2, 168–74

Bradford, P R 1907 'Notes on the construction and design of breweries and maltings'. *Journal of the Institute of Brewing* **13**, 534–58

Bradford, W 1885 'Brewery construction'. *Brewers' Guardian* **15**, 17 Nov, 371–3

Bradford, W 1889 *Notes on Maltings and Breweries*. London: W Straker

Bradford, W 1891 'Notes on brewery construction'. *Transactions of the Institute of Brewing* **4**, 109–38

Brake, T 1985 *Men of Good Character: A History of the National Union of Sheet Metal Workers, Coppersmiths, Heating and Domestic Engineers*. London: Lawrence and Wishart

Brandwood, G, Davison, A and Slaughter, M 2011 *Licensed to Sell: The History and Heritage of the Public House*, 2 edn. Swindon: English Heritage

Brown, J 2012a 'Drawings are a peek into future'. *Yorkshire Evening Post*, 16 Oct, 10

Brown, J 2012b *London Railway Atlas*, 3 edn. Hersham: Ian Allan Publishing

Brown, M with Willmott, B 2010 *Brewed in Northants: A Directory of Northamptonshire Breweries (including the Soke of Peterborough) 1450–2010*. New Ash Green: Brewery History Society

Brunton, M 1819 *Emmeline with Some Other Pieces*. Edinburgh: Manners and Miller

Cantacuzino, S 1975 *New Uses for Old Buildings*. London: Architectural Press

Casey, C 2005 *Dublin*. New Haven and London: Yale University Press

Catling, C 2013 *Constructive Conservation: Sustainable Growth for Historic Places*. Swindon: English Heritage

Churchward, M S 2009 'Gas engines in Victorian industry, 1870–1950'. Paper given at the 3rd Australasian Engineering Heritage Conference, University of Otago, Dunedin, Nov 2009

Clark, C 1998 *The British Malting Industry since 1830*. London: Hambledon Press

Clark, C 2004a 'Garrett, Newson (1812–1893)', in *Oxford Dictionary of National Biography*. Oxford: Oxford University Press

Clark, C 2004b 'Gilstrap, Sir William, baronet (1816–1896)', in *Oxford Dictionary of National Biography*. Oxford: Oxford University Press

Clark, C 2004c 'Stead, Patrick (1788–1869)', in *Oxford Dictionary of National Biography*. Oxford: Oxford University Press

Coad, J 2013 *Support for the Fleet: Architecture and Engineering of the Royal Navy's Bases 1700–1914*. Swindon: English Heritage

Collins Howard, S 2009 'Elizabeth Whitworth Scott (1898–1972): The architect of the Shakespeare Memorial Theatre'. Unpublished MPhil thesis, University of Bath

Collins, P 1980 'A proposed brewery'. *Old Limerick Journal* **3**, 16–22

Combrune, M 1758 *An Essay on Brewing*. London: printed for R and J Dodsley

Combrune, M 1804 *The Theory and Practice of Brewing*. London: Vernor and Hood

Cooksey, J 1984 *Brewery Buildings in Burton on Trent*. London: Victorian Society

Cooper, J 1996 'New home for Greenall engines'. *International Stationary Steam Engine Society Bulletin* **18**, 2

Cordle, C 2011 *Out of the Hay and Into the Hops: Hop Cultivation in Wealden Kent and Hop Marketing in Southwark, 1744–2000*. Hatfield: University of Hertfordshire Press

Cornell, M 2003 *Beer: The Story of the Pint*. Headline: London

Cornell, M 2010 *Amber, Gold and Black: The History of Britain's Great Beers*. Stroud: History Press

Corran, H S 1975 *A History of Brewing*. Newton Abbot: David & Charles

Crosby, T 2007 'Housing the workforce'. *Brewery History* 124/5, 3–14

Dennison, S R and MacDonagh, O 1998 *Guinness 1886–1939: From Incorporation to the Second World War*. Cork: Cork University Press

Deutsher, K M 2012 *The Breweries of Australia: A History*, 2 edn. Sydney: Beer & Brewer Media

Dineley, M 2011 'Experiment or demonstration? Making fermentable malt sugars from the grain and a discussion of some of the evidence for this activity in the British Neolithic', in Millson, D C E (ed), *Experiment and Interpretation: The Uses of Experimental Archaeology in the Study of the Past*. Oxford: Oxbow Books, 96–108

Dodd, G 1843 *Days at the Factories*. London: Charles Knight

Donnachie, I 1979 *A History of the Brewing Industry in Scotland*. Edinburgh: John Donald

Dredge, M 2013 'Land of hops and glory'. *Beer* 19, 6–13

Dummett, G A 1981 *From Little Acorns: A History of the APV Company Limited*. London: Hutchinson Benham

Ellis, W 1736 *The London and Country Brewer*, 2 edn. London: Messeurs Fox

Elwall, R 1983 *Bricks and Beer: English Pub Architecture, 1839–1939*. London: British Architectural Library

Evans, R 2011 *A Pictorial View of the Last Century at Wethered's Brewery*. Burnley: Hudson & Pearson

Feltham, J 1806 *The Picture of London, for 1806*. London: Richard Phillips

Foskett, R R 1998 *Vatmaking*. London: Science Museum in association with the Cider Museum, Hereford

Fox, C 2009 *The Arts of Industry in the Age of Enlightenment*. New Haven and London: Yale University Press

Gilmour, A 2012 'Beer flows deep down'. *Cheers North East* 25, Nov 2012, 20–1

Girouard, M 1979 *The Victorian Country House*. New Haven and London: Yale University Press

Glover, B 1993 *Prince of Ales: The History of Brewing in Wales*. Stroud: Alan Sutton

Gourvish, T 1987 *Norfolk Beers from English Barley: A History of Steward & Patteson, 1793–1963*. Norwich: Centre of East Anglian Studies

Gourvish, T 1996 'Diffusion of brewing technology since 1900: Change and the consumer.' *History of Technology* **18**, 139–48

Gourvish, T R and Wilson, R G 1994 *The British Brewing Industry 1830–1980*. Cambridge: Cambridge University Press

Grant, A 1976 'The cooper in Liverpool'. *Industrial Archaeology Review* **1**, Autumn 1976

Gutzke, D W 1990 'Rhetoric and reality: The political influence of British brewers, 1832–1914'. *Parliamentary History* **9**, 1, 78–115

Harrap, G T 1895 'Design and construction of breweries and maltings'. *Journal of the Institute of Brewing* **1**, 48–69

Harris, M F 2001 'Gambrinus, the spirit of brewing'. *Brewery History* 105, 4–20

Hawkins, K H, and Pass, C L 1979 *The Brewing Industry: A Study in Industrial Organisation and Public Policy*. London: Heinemann

Hehner, O 1907 'Obituary: Walter John Sykes'. *The Analyst* **32**, Jan 1907, 1–2

Holmes, F and M 2011 *Norwich Pubs and Breweries: Past and Present*. Norwich: Norwich Heritage Projects

Hughes, D 2006 *"A Bottle of Guinness please": The Colourful History of Guinness*. Wokingham: Phimboy

Humphrey, S 2006 'The Hop Trade in Southwark'. *Brewery History* 123, 5–13

Irving, J 2009 'Road, rail and water: The early history of transport at Benskin's brewery'. *Brewery History* 133, 2–17

James, M 2012 'Burton's brewing heritage post-1984: Updating the Victorian Society's report'. *Brewery History* 148, 41–80

James, M C 2006 'Brewery buildings of Burton upon Trent: Reflection and opportunities'. Unpublished dissertation, RICS Postgraduate Diploma in Conservation of the Historic Environment, College of Estate Management, Reading

Jenner, M A 1990 *Harvey & Son, Bridge Wharf Brewery, Lewes: Bicentenary Year*. Lewes: Harvey & Son

Jerrold, B, Doré, G and Ackroyd, P 2005 *London: A Pilgrimage*. London: Anthem Press (originally Jerrold, B and Doré, G 1872 *London: A Pilgrimage*. London: Grant & Co)

Kilby, K 2010 *Coopers and Coopering*. Oxford: Shire Publications

Lloyd Williams, J 1994 'Ale, altruism and art: The benefactions of William McEwan'. *Apollo* **139**, May 1994, 47–53

Mathias, P 1953 'Industrial revolution in brewing'. *Explorations in Entrepreneurial History* **5**, 208–24

Mathias, P 1959 *The Brewing Industry in England 1700–1830*. Cambridge: Cambridge University Press

Millns, T 1998 'The British brewing industry, 1945–95' in Wilson, R G and Gourvish, T R (eds), *The Dynamics of the International Brewing Industry since 1800*. Routledge: London

Monckton, H A 1966 *A History of English Ale and Beer*. London: Bodley Head

Moore, H 2012 'Historic brewery excavations at the former Royal Clarence Naval Victualling Yard in Gosport'. *Brewery History* 148, 16–40

Morris, E and Roberts, E 2012 *Public Sculpture of Cheshire and Merseyside (excluding Liverpool)*. Liverpool: Liverpool University Press

Moss, J 2009 *New Brewery Arts: From the Beginning to the Present Day*. Cirencester: Cotswold Media

Myers, H 1996 *William Henry Pyne and his Microcosm*. Stroud: Sutton Publishing

Nicholls, J 2009 *The Politics of Alcohol: A History of the Drink Question in Britain*. Manchester and New York: Manchester University Press

Noszlopy, G T and Waterhouse, F 2005 *Public Sculpture of Staffordshire and the Black Country*. Liverpool: Liverpool University Press

Noszlopy, G T and Waterhouse, F 2010 *Public Sculpture of Herefordshire, Shropshire and Worcestershire*. Liverpool: Liverpool University Press

Ogden, M 1987 *A History of Stockport Breweries*. Manchester: Neil Richardson

Oliver, G (ed) 2012 *The Oxford Companion to Beer*. New York: Oxford University Press

Owen, C C 1978 *The Development of Industry in Burton upon Trent*. Chichester: Phillimore

Owen, C C 1992 *'The Greatest Brewery in the World': A History of Bass, Ratcliff & Gretton*. Chesterfield: Derbyshire Record Society

Page, K 2012 'Mansion on the Ivel Navigation'. *Biggleswade Chronicle*, 11 May 2012

Pasteur, L 1879 *Studies on Fermentation: The Diseases of Beer, their Causes and the Means of Preventing Them* (originally *Études sur la Bière*, 1876, translated by F Faulkner and D C Robb). London: Macmillan

Patrick, A 2004 *Maltings in England*. Strategy for the Historic Industrial Environment Report No 1. Swindon: English Heritage

Patrick, A 2006 'Victorian maltings in England, 1837 to 1914'. *Brewery History* 123, 14–34

Pearson, L 2000a *British Breweries: An Architectural History*. London: Hambledon Press

Pearson, L 2000b 'Decorative ceramics in the buildings of the British brewing industry'. *Journal of the Tiles and Architectural Ceramics Society* **8**, 26–36

Pearson, L 2011 *Strategy for the Historic Industrial Environment Report: The Brewing Industry*. New Ash Green: Brewery History Society

Pearson, L 2012 'The BHS brewing industry survey: Methodology and analysis'. *Brewery History* 148, 6–15

Pearson, R 1993 *The Bass Railway Trips*. Derby: Breedon Books

Peaty, I 1989 'A brewery chapel'. *Brewery History* 56, 21–2

Peaty, I P 1988 *English Breweries in Old Photographs*. Gloucester: Alan Sutton

Peaty, I P 1997 *You Brew Good Ale*. Stroud: Alan Sutton

Pennant, T 1813 *Some Account of London*, 5 edn. London: J Faulder

Pevsner, N 1974 *Buildings of England: Staffordshire*. London: Penguin Books

Piggott, S 1995 'Wood and the Wheelwright', in Green, M J (ed), *The Celtic World*. London: Routledge, 321–7

Playne, S 1914 *Southern India: Its History, People, Commerce, and Industrial Resources*. London: Foreign & Colonial Compiling & Publishing

Pontifex, C E C 1977 *The Family of Pontifex of West Wycombe, Co Buckingham, 1500–1977*. Hassocks: Pontifex

Postlethwaite, C 2009 'Maitland patent mash tun'. *Brewery History* 132, 18–30

Protz, R (ed) 2013 *CAMRA's Good Beer Guide 2013*. CAMRA Books: St Albans

Putman, R 2004 *Beers and Breweries of Britain*. Princes Risborough: Shire Publications

Quinn, B and Moore, D 2007 'Ale, brewing and fulacht fiadh'. *Archaeology Ireland* **21**, 3 (issue 81), 8–11

Reilly, F 2012 ' 'Barking the yarn' and 'waulking the cloth' '. *Archaeology Ireland* **26**, 2 (issue 100), 42–5

Reynolds, P J and Langley, J K 1979 'Romano-British corn-drying oven: An experiment'. *The Archaeological Journal* **136**, 27–42

Richards, J M (ed) 1957 'The Functional Tradition as shown in early industrial buildings'. *Architectural Review* **122** (726), 5–73

Richmond, L and Turton, A (eds) 1990 *The Brewing Industry: A Guide to Historical Records*. Manchester: Manchester University Press

Roberts, W H 1847 *The Scottish Ale-brewer and Practical Maltster*. Edinburgh: A and C Black

Sambrook, P 1996 *Country House Brewing in England 1500–1900*. London: Hambledon Press

Scamell, G 1871 *Breweries and Maltings: Their Arrangement, Construction and Machinery*. London and Edinburgh: Fullerton

Scamell, G and Colyer, F 1880 *Breweries and Maltings: Their Arrangement, Construction, Machinery, and Plant*, 2 edn. London: E & F N Spon, 1880

Schopper, H 1568 *Panoplia: Omnium illiberalium mechanicarum aut sedentariarum artium genera continens (Book of Trades)*. Frankfurt: Sigmund Feierabend

Scoffham, E 1992 *A Vision of the City: The Architecture of T C Howitt*. Nottingham: Nottinghamshire County Council

Sharp, R 2005 'Brewery heritage denied'. *Architects' Journal* **221**, 9 June 2005, 11

Shepherd, C 1996 *Brewery Railways of Burton on Trent*. Industrial Railway Society: Guisborough

Sigsworth, E M 1965 'Science and the Brewing Industry, 1850–1900'. *Economic History Review* **17** (3), 536–50

Simmons, J 1968 *St Pancras Station*. London: George Allen and Unwin

Spiller, B 1957 'The Georgian brewery.' *Architectural Review* **122**, 310–22

Stanwick , S and Fowlow, L 2010 *Wine by Design*. London: John Wiley

Stopes, H 1870–1902 'A collection of press cuttings, letters and other items mainly concerned with brewing'. British Library Cup.1264.c.17

Stopes, H 1885 *Malt and Malting*. London: F W Lyon

Stovin Bradford, W 1998 'The architecture of breweries'. *Brewery History* 92, 14–20

Stow, J 1971 *Survey of London* (reprinted from the text of 1603, with an introduction by C L Kingsford). Oxford: Clarendon Press

Sumner, J 2005 'Early heat determination in the brewery'. *Brewery History* 121, 66–80

Sumner, J 2008 'Status, scale and secret ingredients: The retrospective invention of London porter'. *History and Technology* **24** (3), 289–306

Sumner, J 2013 *Brewing Science, Technology and Print, 1700–1880*. London: Pickering & Chatto

Sykes, W J 1897 *The Principles and Practice of Brewing*. London: Charles Griffin & Co

Temple, P (ed) 2008, *Survey of London, vol 46, South and East Clerkenwell*. New Haven and London: Yale University Press

Terry, D 2011 'Medieval sport in London'. Paper given at the 29th annual conference of the British Society of Sports History, London Metropolitan University, 2–3 Sept

Topping, P 2011 *Burnt Mounds*. English Heritage: Swindon

Unger, R W 2004 *Beer in the Middle Ages and the Renaissance*. Philadelphia: University of Pennsylvania Press

Wailes, R 1973 'The vanishing small brewery'. *Country Life* **154**, 20 Sept, 815–6

Walker, A 2011 'Bygone breweries: James Hole's Castle Brewery, Newark-on-Trent'. *Donny Drinker* 110, 15–16

Watkins, G 1773 *The Complete English Brewer*. London: J Cooke

Welch, C 2009 'Bass, Michael Arthur, first Baron Burton (1837–1909)' rev. Wilson, R G in *Oxford Dictionary of National Biography*. Oxford: Oxford University Press

Wilcox, R 2002 'Excavation of a Monastic grain-processing complex at Castle Acre Priory, Norfolk, 1977–82'. *Norfolk Archaeology* **44** (1), 15–58

Wilkins, T 1871 'The machinery and utensils of a brewery'. *Transactions of the Society of Engineers*, 10–28

Wilson, R G 1983 *Greene King: A Business and Family History*. London: Bodley Head and Jonathan Cape

Wrathmell, S 2005 'Nostell Priory'. *Archaeology West Yorkshire Joint Services Newsletter*, 21

Yorke, F R S 1934 *The Modern House*. London: Architectural Press

Webography

Barnard's *Noted Breweries*, www.askaboutireland.ie/reading-room/digital-book-collection/digital-books-by-subject/industry-and-trade/barnard-the-noted-breweri/

Brewery History Society, *Historic Breweries*, Swindon, English Heritage, 2011, www.english-heritage.org.uk/professional/research/buildings/historic-breweries/

Cornell, M http://zythophile.wordpress.com/

Grace's Guide to British Industrial History, www.gracesguide.co.uk

Patrick, A *Maltings in England*, Strategy for the Historic Industrial Environment Report No 1, Swindon, English Heritage, 2004, www.english-heritage.org.uk/publications/maltings/

Pattinson, R http://barclayperkins.blogspot.co.uk/

Illustration Credits

Illustrations are reproduced by kind permission as follows:

Image courtesy of The Advertising Archives Fig 4.48

The Bodleian Libraries, The University of Oxford (MS.Gough misc. antiq.2, fol. 20) Fig 3.21

© The British Library Board Fig 3.32 (Evan 4278, 'Lager Beer Brewery'); Fig 3.36 (Maps GOAD.MSS Goad Fire Insurance Plan of London, 1888, sheet 194); and Fig 4.13 (The Pictorial World 04/03/1886 pg 206)

© The Trustees of the British Museum Figs 2.5, 3.3, 3.6, 3.8, 3.11, 4.18 and 5.8

Nick Brown Fig 4.67

Burton Library Fig 7.1

Centre for Buckinghamshire Studies (ph Marlow 273) Fig 3.27

City of London, London Metropolitan Archives Figs 3.7, 3.14 and 5.9

Peter Cracknell Fig 3.56

© Crown copyright.English Heritage Fig 1.5 BB95/05252; Fig 1.11 BB042879; Fig 3.22 BB94/09385; Fig 4.21 BB94/15850; Fig 4.38 BB93/35029; Fig 5.20 BB91/17886; Fig 5.28 BB93/35046; Fig 5.50 BB96/08019; and Fig 6.29 BB024236

Andrew Cunningham Figs 3.44–3.47

© De Agostini/The British Library Board Fig 6.2

© East Dunbartonshire Council. Licensor www.scran.ac.uk Fig 4.61

© English Heritage Fig 1.15 AA030935; Fig 1.16 AA054053; Fig 1.18 AA089667; Fig 3.29 EPW015838; Fig 4.3 EPW025108; Fig 4.50 EPW 023433; Fig 4.57 EPW005635; Fig 5.24 AA024792; Fig 5.30 AA024782; Fig 5.39 AA030956; Fig 6.24 AA030989; Fig 7.13 EAW044096 (AFL03 Aerofilms A44096); Fig 7.17 AA062297; and Fig 7.21 EPW005784

Reproduced by permission of English Heritage Fig 1.7 AA108547; Fig 1.8 AA108548; Fig 1.14 AA108546; Fig 2.7 OS52/F9/88; Fig 3.1 BL19305; Fig 3.18 CC51/00659; Fig 3.20 AA98/05314; Fig 3.23 BHS 01/04/07/025; Fig 3.31 OP05545; Fig 3.35 OP03289; Fig 3.41 BL15157/005; Fig 3.50 CC97/01712; Fig 3.55 MD 96/003267; Fig 3.61 BL 03945; Fig 4.1 JSS01/01/01; Fig 4.7 BB51/01574; Fig 4.10 AA98/05284; Fig 4.11 BL 12762; Fig 4.14 AA98/05294; Fig 4.16 BB71/10958; Fig 4.17 AA108549; Fig 4.26 JSS01/01/08; Fig 4.56 AA108545; Fig 5.1 JSS01/01/02; Fig 5.6 AL2406/019/01; Fig 5.7 AL2406/023/01; Fig 5.11 BB91/27450; Fig 5.33 JSS01/01/03; Fig 5.37 OP03290; Fig 5.44 OP23591; Fig 6.6 CC75/00156; Fig 6.12 JSS01/01/11; Fig 6.22 JSS01/01/07; Fig 6.25 JSS01/01/10; Fig 6.27 SER 1399; and Fig 8.8 BL14811

© English Heritage and courtesy of www.picturethepast.org.uk Fig 4.65

Copyright The Francis Frith Collection Fig 3.38

The grandchildren of Edward (Teddy) Godwin Fig 3.24

James Gray collection/The Regency Society Fig 6.1

R Greatorex Fig 4.35

Hampshire Record Office: HPP35/001: courtesy of Lionel Williams Fig 4.20

Reproduced from the collection of the late Mr William Harrison Fig 8.24

© Erich Lessing/Erich Lessing Culture and Fine Arts Archive, Vienna Fig 2.4

Lincolnshire Archives/Lincolnshire County Council Fig 4.5

© The Lordprice Collection Figs 2.9 and 4.29

Medway Archives and Local Studies Centre Fig 6.18

Sue Miles Fig 8.15

© Museum of London Figs 3.12 and 6.16

The National Archives (WORK 25/195 (1135)) Fig 9.8

Images courtesy of The National Brewery Centre, Burton upon Trent Figs 3.33, 3.57, 4.2, 4.8, 4.59, 5.47–5.49, 7.7, 7.14, 7.20, 7.22–7.27, 7.29–7.31, 8.11 and 9.1

Courtesy of the National Library of Ireland (P_WP_0652) Fig 6.17

© National Museums Scotland. Licensor www.scran.ac.uk Fig 6.13

© National Trust/Rachel Topham Fig 2.13

niemeyer fine arts germany, www.luederhniemeyer.com, e-mail: neimeyer@luederhniemeyer.com Fig 7.19

Courtesy of Nottingham City Council and www.picturethepast.org.uk Figs 4.55, 4.58 and 6.30

Courtesy of Nottinghamshire County Council and www.picturethepast.org.uk Figs 4.39 and 5.21

David O'Connor Figs 2.2 and 2.3

© Lynn Pearson Figs 1.2–1.4, 1.6, 1.9, 2.6, 2.8, 2.12, 3.25, 3.42, 3.43, 3.48, 3.49, 3.51, 3.53, 3.54, 3.59, 3.60, 3.62, 4.30, 4.34, 4.36, 4.40–4.42, 4.46, 4.49, 4.54, 4.62–4.64, 4.66, 5.2–5.4, 5.12–5.15, 5.22, 5.25, 5.26, 5.31, 5.32, 5.40, 5.46, 5.52–5.54, 6.5, 6.14, 6.19–6.21, 6.23, 6.26, 6.28, 7.28, 8.1, 8.2, 8.5, 8.9, 8.10, 8.12–8.14, 8.16–8.20, 8.23, 9.3–9.7, 9.9–9.23 and 9.25

Lynn Pearson Collection Figs 1.1, 1.10, 1.17, 2.1, 2.15, 3.2, 3.5, 3.10, 3.13, 3.16, 3.26, 3.28, 3.58, 4.4, 4.6, 4.9, 4.12, 4.15, 4.19, 4.22–4.25, 4.28, 4.32, 4.33, 4.37, 4.43, 4.45, 4.47, 4.51, 4.52, 4.60, 5.10, 5.17, 5.38, 5.41–5.43, 5.45, 5.51, 6.3, 6.8, 7.2–7.6, 7.8–7.12, 7.15, 8.3, 8.4, 8.6, 8.21, 8.22, 9.2 and 9.24.

Ian P Peaty Collection (photograph by C E Lee) Fig 7.18

Image courtesy of The Potteries Museum & Art Gallery, Stoke-on-Trent Fig 3.17

The Print Collector/Heritage-Images Fig 2.11

Reproduced by kind permission of Rhondda Cynon Taff Library Services Fig 3.39

Copied with permission from an original in Reading Local Studies Library Fig 4.27

© RCAHMS (Aerofilms) Fig 3.30

© Courtesy of RCAHMS. Licensor www.rcahms.gov.uk Fig 3.34

RIBA Library Drawings & Archives Collections Figs 2.10 and 3.19

© The Royal Society Fig 3.9 (RS.8437); Fig 6.9 (RS.10104); and Fig 6.10 (RS.10103)

Reproduced by kind permission of the Trustees of the William Salt Library, Stafford Fig 2.14

Permission of Sandwell Community History & Archives Service Fig 4.31

By permission of Sandwell Museum Service Fig 4.44

Science & Society Picture Library (SSPL) – All rights reserved Fig 1.12 10175984 © NRM/Pictorial Collection/SSPL; Fig 1.13 10315742 © Science Museum/SSPL; Fig 3.15 10624069 © National Media Museum/SSPL; Fig 3.37 10440216 © National Media Museum/SSPL; Fig 3.52 10449849 © Science Museum/SSPL; Fig 5.34 10416378 © Walter Nurnberg/National Media Museum/SSPL; Fig 7.16 10446869 © National Railway Museum/SSPL; Fig 8.7 10440126 © National Media Museum/SSPL; and back cover 10649845 © Past Pix/SSPL

Jeff Sechiari Figs 5.5, 5.18, 5.23, 5.29 and 5.36

Sheffield Libraries, Archive and Information: Sheffield Local Studies Library Fig 6.11

Adam Slater Fig 5.35

By courtesy of the Trustees of Sir John Soane's Museum. Photo: Ardon Bar-Hama Fig 6.7

Reproduced by kind permission of Suffolk Record Office, Ipswich branch Fig 4.53 (HG404/46/5); Fig 5.16 (HG404/46/4); Fig 5.19 (HG404/46/2); Fig 5.27 (HG404/46/2); Fig 6.4 (HG404/46/4); and Fig 6.15 (HG404/46/5)

Wandsworth Heritage Service Fig 3.40

Wellcome Library, London Fig 3.4

Glossary

ABV: alcohol by volume is a standard measure of the quantity of alcohol contained in a drink, expressed as a percentage of the total volume. Typically beer varies between 4 and 6 per cent.

Archimedean screw: machine consisting of a spiral surface, contained within a tube, which is turned about its axis in order to move water or solids through the tube; frequently used for the transport of malt.

Brewery tap: public house attached to a brewery.

Burton union system: fermentation system in which the wort runs into a 'set' of large wooden casks, (often 26 casks in two rows of 13), each of which has a swan neck to discharge yeast into a trough mounted above the casks.

Calandria: tubular heat exchanger used for heating wort, generally sited inside the copper but sometimes external and linked to the copper by piping.

Cask: originally a wooden, stave-built hooped container for beer; since the 1960s normally made of aluminium. Cask sizes were standardised from the end of the 17th century as follows:

Pin	4½ gallons
Firkin	9 gallons
Kilderkin	18 gallons
Barrel	36 gallons
Hogshead	54 gallons
Puncheon	72 gallons
Butt	108 gallons
Tun	216 gallons

Cistern: large, usually open-topped, tank; often used for containing water.

Common brewer: a brewer who could only sell beer away from the brewery, to publicans and other customers, apart from a single permissible outlet at the brewery tap.

Cooperage: area of the brewery where wooden casks were manufactured and repaired by coopers.

Copper: large metal vessel, usually made of copper, stainless steel or a combination of the two, used for heating liquor (water), and for boiling wort with hops.

Dray: horse-drawn or motorised flat-bedded wagon used for the distribution of casks and bottles from the brewery.

Finings: a natural additive, isinglass, produced from the swim bladders of fish, which precipitates yeast when added to beer following fermentation.

Grist: a term applied both to the raw materials (malt and other cereals) that will be milled, and to the ground material.

Jacob's ladder: elevator in the form of an endless chain of buckets or hinged flaps attached to a continuous belt; these open when rising, to take a load, and close when falling.

Kettle: American term for a copper.

Liquor: the water supply used for brewing beer.

Lucam: roofed projection, often from the upper floor of brewhouse tower or stores, sheltering a hoist. Possibly derived from the French *lucarne*, a skylight. The lucam – also known as a lookum towards the end of the 19th century – is a common feature of brewery buildings.

Masher: a masher or mashing machine mixes the grist and hot water before they enter the mash tun.

Mash tun: vessel in which the mixed milled grist and water are held to allow extraction of soluble material to give wort.

Original gravity: an estimate of the amount of dissolved material in the wort before fermentation and hence the potential alcoholic strength of the resulting beer. It is a ratio, a measurement of the wort's density compared to the density of water, which is deemed to be 1.000. In British brewing practice this figure is normally multiplied by 1,000 and expressed as 1000. If the wort density is 1.042, its original gravity is 1042 and it is said to have 42 degrees of excess gravity.

Quarter: the quarter was originally a measure of malt volume. Towards the end of the 19th century this was gradually replaced by a weight equivalent, fixed at 336lb malt. In the late 19th century one quarter of malt was assumed to produce four 36-gallon casks (barrels) of beer at standard original gravity (1055).

Racking plant: area of the brewery where casks are cleaned and filled with beer.

Sparging: spraying spent grains with hot liquor in the mash tun, to wash out remaining wort.

Steeped: barley is soaked, or steeped, in cisterns of water at the maltings until germination begins.

Wort: the sweet liquid (unfermented beer) resulting from mashing malted barley with hot water.

Yorkshire square: fementation vessel originally of stone or slate, but now usually of stainless steel, with upper and lower compartments linked by pipes and a central manhole which facilitates yeast removal.

Measurements Conversion Chart

Imperial measurements are mostly used in this book, as that was the standard system for much of the period of history covered by the book.

1 inch (in) = 25.4 millimetres
1 foot (ft) = 0.30 metres
1 yard (yd) = 0.91 metres
1 mile = 1.609 kilometres
1 acre = 0.4 hectares
1 pound (lb) = 453.59 grams
1 hundredweight (cwt) = 50.80 kilograms
1 ton = 1016.05 kilograms
1 gallon = 4.546 litres
1 pint = 0.568 litres

Brewery Index

Page numbers in **bold** indicate illustrations or a reference within a caption.

* indicates that no brewery buildings are extant. The absence of an asterisk indicates that the whole or part (in some cases a very small part) of the brewery, its maltings, offices or other buildings survives.

References to notes are followed by an 'n'.

Geographical Index

Due to successive administrative reorganisations in England, creating a useful geographical index for towns and cities is problematic, as many unitary authority names are still unfamiliar. The chosen solution, which we hope will enable readers to find brewery locations quickly and easily, is a hybrid combination of historic ceremonial counties such as Cornwall and Yorkshire alongside well known, if rather more recently-named, urban areas like Greater Manchester and Merseyside. Beyond England, for ease of use breweries are listed simply by town or city within each country.

Address details are given in the Brewery Index.

Page numbers in **bold** indicate illustrations or a reference within a caption.

* indicates that no brewery buildings are extant. The absence of an asterisk indicates that the whole or part (in some cases a very small part) of the brewery, its maltings, offices or other buildings survives.

References to notes are followed by an 'n'.

T indicates brewery tours available (at time of writing).

W indicates a working brewery (at time of writing).

General Index

Page numbers in **bold** indicate illustrations or a reference within a caption.

References to notes are followed by an 'n'.

About the Author

Lynn Pearson is an architectural historian, writer and photographer. She has published 20 books, including *British Breweries: An Architectural History* (Hambledon Press, 2000) and *Played in Tyne and Wear* (English Heritage, 2010) a study of the North-East's sporting architecture, part of the groundbreaking Played in Britain series. Her *Tile Gazetteer: A Guide to British Tile and Architectural Ceramics Locations* (Richard Dennis, 2005), written for the Tiles and Architectural Ceramics Society, was runner-up in the 2005 National Reference Book of the Year Awards.

About the Brewery History Society

The Brewery History Society was founded in 1972 to promote research into all aspects of the brewing industry, to encourage the exchange of information about breweries and brewing, and to collect photographic and other archival material relating to brewery history.

The Society publishes a quarterly newsletter and a quarterly journal *Brewery History*, which first appeared in 1972. It also publishes a national directory of historic breweries, now in its 4th edition, and an ongoing series of in-depth county-wide surveys of historic breweries. Amongst other material, its website includes much information on selected breweries and an ever-growing photographic database of defunct brewery liveries.

The Society arranges a programme of events for members including visits to breweries and related sites in the UK and abroad, walks around historic brewing and malting areas led by expert guides, and occasional conferences and seminars.

For more information about the Brewery History Society and to obtain their books on historic breweries, visit their website www.breweryhistory.com

Brewery History Society
Manor Side East
Mill Lane
Byfleet
Surrey KT14 7RS